The Structured Programming Cookbook

The Structured Programming Cookbook

A Productivity Tool for the COBOL Programmer

Paul Noll

Mike Murach & Associates, Inc.
4905 North West Avenue, Suite 102
Fresno, California 93705

Development Team

Originator/author: Paul Noll
Director/writer: Mike Murach
Writer/editor: Judy Taylor
Programmer: Doug Lowe
Art director/designer: Michael Rogondino

Printed in the United States of America.

Library of Congress Catalog Card
Number: 77-088256

Contents

Preface

The Structured Programming Cookbook is designed to increase the productivity of the COBOL programmer. Before using this Cookbook, however, you must master the principles of structured programming as presented in *Structured Programming for the COBOL Programmer* by Paul Noll. In other words, you use Paul's textbook to learn how to increase your productivity by applying the principles of structured programming. You use the Cookbook as a reference to help you develop structured programs after you have mastered the principles.

If you haven't read Paul's textbook but you know the principles of top-down design, HIPO documentation, and structured COBOL, you may find this Cookbook useful by itself. But get Paul's textbook anyway. It presents a coordinated method for designing, documenting, coding, and testing structured programs in COBOL that is unlike any other. In my opinion, any programmer who adopts Paul's method will enjoy a significant increase in productivity . . . even if he or she is already writing "structured" programs.

What this book does

This book has three sections. And each section has a different purpose.

Section 1: Standards and Guidelines This is a reference section that summarizes the important characteristics of Paul's method. It does this for eight different phases of structured programming, including program design, module documentation, and COBOL coding. Under program design, for example, you'll find a summary of the four steps for creating VTOCs (structure charts), a checklist for reviewing and analyzing VTOCs, and a verb list that will help you decide how to describe the function of a module. These summaries will refresh your memory and help you to apply the principles of structured programming in the same way that you learned them.

For each phase in this section, there are two categories: (1) standards and (2) guidelines. The standards summarize those aspects of Paul's method that we think should be rigidly enforced. The guidelines summarize aspects of Paul's method that are useful, but that are either too abstract to enforce or too debatable to be set as a standard for everyone.

Under module documentation, for example, the standards give

rules for naming and numbering the modules, for using indentation in the process box of the HIPO diagram, and for setting off called and calling modules on the HIPO diagram. We feel that all of these standards should be enforced throughout a COBOL shop.

On the other hand, the guidelines for module documentation describe the six steps for preparing HIPO diagrams, the conditions under which it is okay to use two diagrams for one module, and the level of language to be used in the process box of the HIPO diagram. They also summarize when and how to use extended descriptions and give some general reminders for preparing HIPO diagrams. In our opinion, all of these points are either debatable or unenforceable (although they are good as a reference).

I think this section is important for two reasons. First, as a reference, it can improve a programmer's efficiency. Second, it is an instant standards manual for structured programming. If a programming department adopts these standards and guidelines as their own, they will have a standards manual that is more complete and useful than the vast majority of those I've seen.

Section 2: Program Notes If you have read *Structured Programming for the COBOL Programmer*, you know that it centers around four typical business programs. As the book was developed, Paul had many discussions with the members of our staff about these four programs. In fact, we conducted formal walkthroughs for each of the programs and considered several different solutions for each. Although we all agreed that much of this material would be of interest to the COBOL programmer, we omitted it from the *Structured Programming* textbook because it seemed to detract from the book's educational objectives.

In this section, then, we present additional material about each of the four problems and the solutions. For instance, this section will explain why the edit program doesn't use a common module for editing the fields that are in both the sales and the return record. It will present two other VTOCs that will work for the report-printing program and explain why we rejected them. It will explain why code that could have been placed in two or more different modules was placed in the module that it was. In short, I hope this section will raise some questions that weren't raised in the textbook . . . and answer some questions that weren't answered.

Section 3: Model Programs This section presents the specifications for the four business programs followed by the complete program solutions. The solutions include the VTOC, HIPO diagrams for each of the modules in the VTOC, extended descriptions whenever they are needed, and the source listing for the tested COBOL program as run under IBM's OS/VS. In short, this section reads like the program files for four production programs.

The programs in this section are designed to represent the four most common types of business programs. They are (1) a program that *edits* transaction data, (2) a program that *extracts* data from an input file in order to prepare a summary report, (3) a program that *sequentially updates* a master file based on change, addition, and deletion records, and (4) a program that *randomly updates* a master file after *sorting* the transaction records. Although the specifications for these programs are somewhat simplified so the coding won't get unwieldy, the design and logic of these programs can be applied to a wide range of problems.

In my opinion, this is the most valuable section in the book because it can have a major effect on productivity. One point that Paul makes repeatedly in the *Structured Programming* textbook is that a well-designed program should be used as a model for similar programs in the future. That's one of the advantages of structured programming: you don't have to start every program from scratch. If Paul were to develop a sequential-update program, for example, he would use the VTOC, the HIPO diagrams, and even some of the COBOL code from the sequential-update program presented in this Cookbook. In fact, he has used this model solution several times in the past. So if you can use it for the next update program you write, just think of the effect on your productivity.

Who this book is for

As mentioned earlier, this book is designed to increase the productivity of COBOL programmers. As a result, it should also be of interest to programming managers. If a programming manager adopts the standards and guidelines presented in section 1, I think he will have taken a giant step toward the proper implementation of structured programming in his shop.

How to use this book

If this Cookbook is available to you while you are studying *Structured Programming for the COBOL Programmer,* it can aid your studies in four ways. First, by referring to the program specifications, the VTOCs, and the HIPO diagrams in section 3 of this book while you read the other book, you can cut down on page flipping as you move your eye from text to illustration. In other words, the Cookbook can act as the illustration book for most of the major illustrations referred to by the textbook. Second, after you read the chapters on VTOCs, HIPO diagrams, and COBOL coding in the text, you can read the related notes in section 2 of this book for additional insight and perspective. Third, I'm sure you will reach a point in the reading of the text at which you will want to stop and study the complete solution for a problem. Since the complete solutions aren't given in the textbook, the Cookbook gives you the opportunity to do just this. Finally, section 1 of this book can act as a study guide. Since it summarizes the important aspects of each chapter, it provides an efficient apparatus for review.

After you have mastered the principles presented in *Structured Programming for the COBOL Programmer,* the Cookbook becomes your reference for developing structured programs. If you need to refresh your memory on how to develop HIPO diagrams, read the standards and guidelines for that phase of programming in section 1. If you are using one of the model solutions as a guide for a program you are developing and you don't understand some aspect of it, read the program notes in section 2 and you may solve your problem. But most important, use the programs in section 3 as models for your future programs. Borrow portions of VTOCs, complete HIPO diagrams, and segments of code. Borrow anything that relates to the program you're developing. Remember that this is the section that should repay the cost of this book many times over.

If you are a programming manager, your primary interest will undoubtedly be in section 1. And rightfully so. All too often, a company is sold on structured programming. But after the lead group of programmers is trained, nothing happens. Although a few of the programmers may use some of the principles of structured programming in the fashion they think best, there is no standards manual, no enforcement, and no significant effect on productivity.

If I were a programming manager, then, I would first learn Paul's method of structured programming as presented in the text. Next, I would go through section 1 of this book and decide which of the standards and guidelines I think I should enforce in my shop. If my ideas differed significantly from the text, I would modify section 1 as I saw fit, have it retyped, copied, and distributed to my programmers. If my differences were minor, I would simply have a summary of the differences prepared and distribute this along with the Cookbook. In either case, the result is instant standards. Although our list in section 1 may not be perfect, it's a good start; and I don't think you'll go too far wrong by adopting it in its entirety.

Conclusion

I'm excited about this book because I think it can have a major effect on programmer productivity. For a dozen years now, I've heard people talk about standards for developing programs, but I've never seen decent ones. Now, I think section 1 is a step in that direction. And for a dozen years, I've heard people advise others to "stop re-inventing the wheel." But they re-invent it every time they write a new program. Now, I think section 3 is a first step toward ending re-invention.

Because this book tries to do something that hasn't been done before, I'm particularly interested in your reactions to it. So we welcome your comments, criticisms, suggestions, or questions. If you have any, feel free to use the postage-paid comment form near the end of this book. With the help of your feedback, I hope we can create better products for you in the future.

Mike Murach
Fresno, California
August, 1977

Section

1

STANDARDS AND GUIDELINES

This section presents standards for developing structured programs. It starts with standards for overall program development and continues with standards for program design, module documentation, coding, testing, walkthroughs, teams, and development support libraries. Needless to say, these standards are designed to enforce the principles of structured programming as presented in *Structured Programming for the COBOL Programmer.*

After the standards for each aspect of structured programming are presented, related guidelines are given. The guidelines differ from the standards in that they are more general and therefore less enforceable. When taken together, the standards and guidelines represent a good summary of the structured programming textbook.

Program Development

Standards

Sequence of development

Although practical considerations may force a slightly different development sequence upon you, you should try to follow the standard development sequence that is given here. On all programs of 1000 lines or more, you should combine the coding and testing steps (steps 7 and 8) by using top-down testing. You may also want to use top-down testing on programs of less than 1000 lines. The preferred development sequence follows:

1. Get complete specifications.
2. Get related source books and subprograms.
3. Design the program.
4. Code the JCL.
5. Create the test plan.
6. Create the test data.
7. Code the program.
8. Test the program.

Guidelines

Getting the specifications

To make sure you have complete specifications for a program, you need to summarize the specifications you're given. As part of this summary, you should:

1. Create record layouts and print charts for all input and output files.
2. Create decision tables when necessary.
3. List the major functions of the program. To do this, you may want to use a HIPO form as shown in figure 1-1. Here, in the input and output boxes, the programmer has recorded the files that will be input to and output from the program. In the process box, the programmer has listed the major functions of

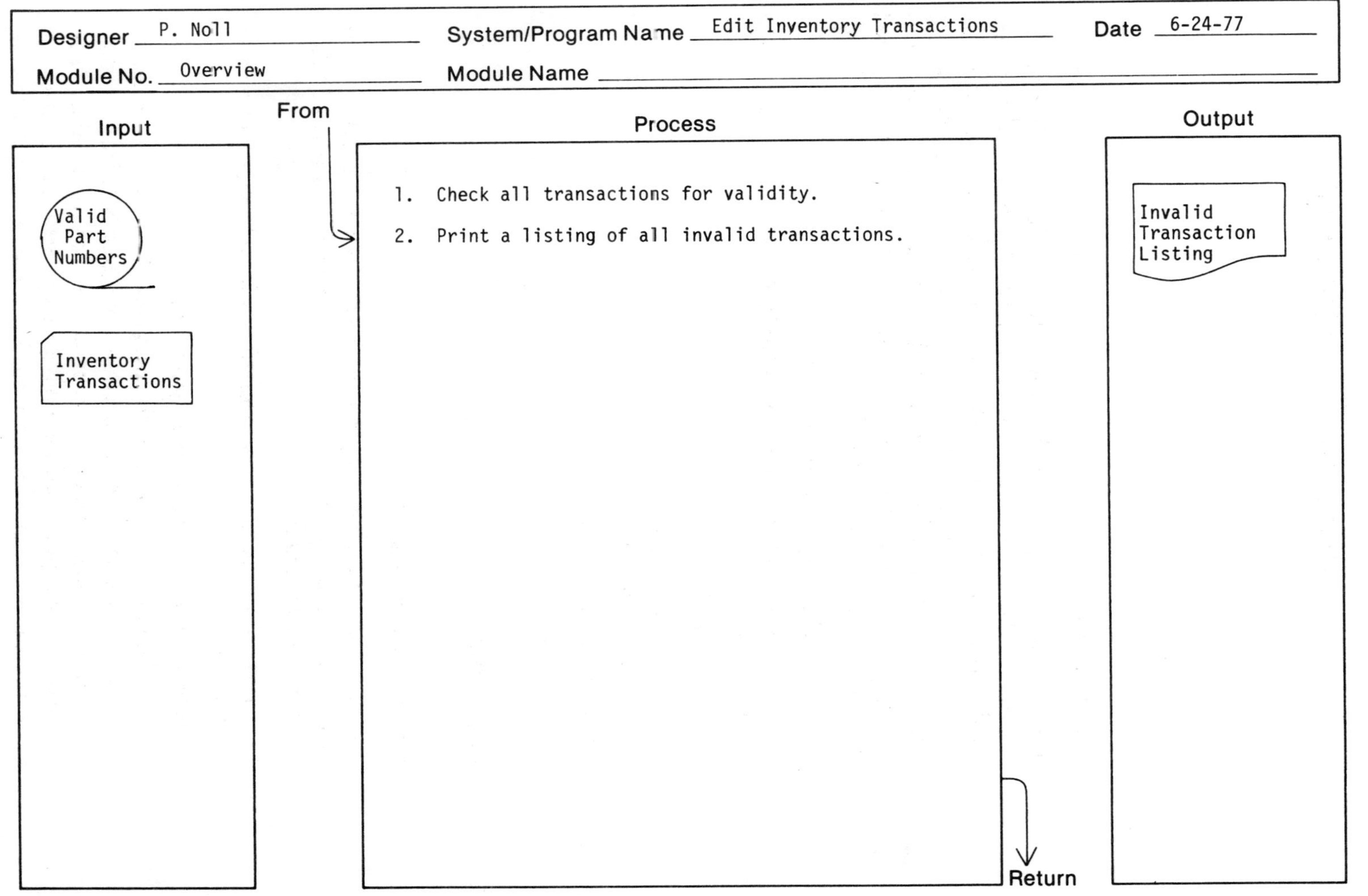

Figure 1-1 Use of the HIPO form for summarizing program requirements

the program. (These are *not* in any way procedural steps.)

4. Look for omissions. Try to look beyond the obvious to decide if you have all the information you need to develop the program.

Using COPY and CALL libraries

1. The COPY library should contain all file and record descriptions. So if you're writing the first program that processes a file, see to it that the file and record descriptions are entered into the library.
2. If a processing module you need for your program is in both the COPY and CALL libraries, use the one in the COPY library.

Coding Sequence

The sequence in which you code the modules is basically up to you. However, you shouldn't code a module until you have coded its calling module.

Program Design

Standards

General

Use top-down design for the development of all programs. As documentation for your design, use the visual table of contents (the VTOC) as shown in figure 1-2. To create the VTOC, you proceed on a level-by-level basis starting with the top level (level 0).

Module names

1. Module names should consist of one verb followed by one or two adjectives followed by one object. It is not acceptable to name a module with only a verb and an object.
2. Because the module number together with the module name will make up the paragraph name for the module in the COBOL program, the module name combined with the module number and separating hyphens must not exceed 30 characters.

Module numbers

1. All module numbers should be written outside of the module box on the VTOC at the upper righthand corner.
2. The top-level module should be given the number 000.
3. The level-1 modules should be given numbers that are multiples of 100 starting with 100. Start with the left module and proceed to the right.
4. From level 2 on down, the modules should be numbered by tens. The most common numbering sequences are level by level from left to right and leg by leg from left to right.
5. When a module is added to a VTOC after numbering, it should be given a number that indicates its most logical place in the VTOC, regardless of its actual placement physically. For instance, a print-cust-detail-line module could be added to the VTOC in figure 1-2 as shown in figure 1-3. Even though this module is physically to the left of level 2, it is given a number that indicates that its logical placement is to the right of module 120.

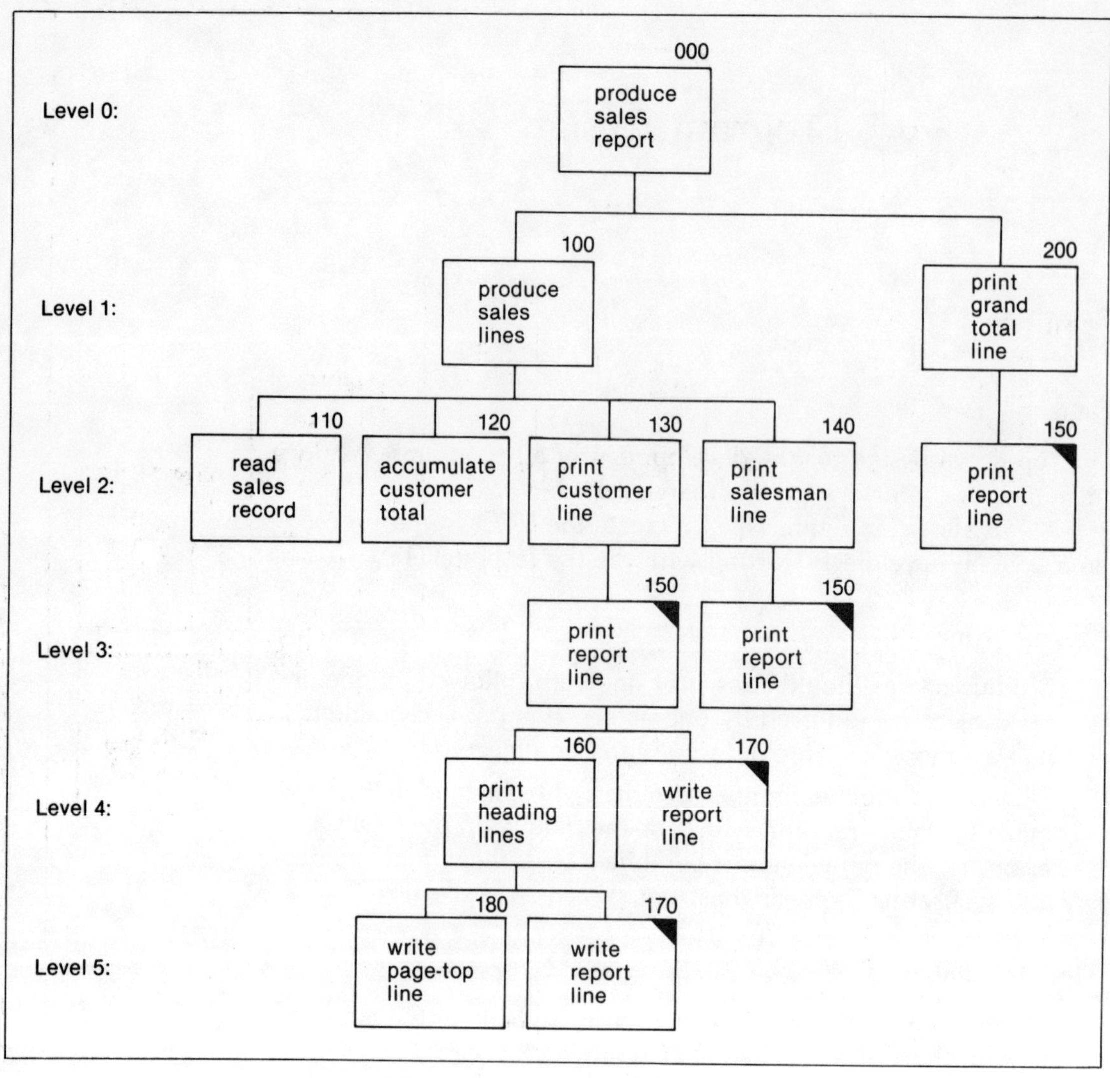

Figure 1-2 The complete VTOC for the extract program

One read or write module per file

The general standard is to have one and only one read or write module per file. This module will contain the READ or WRITE statement for the file. (An I-O file will have both a read and a write module.)

Exception 1: Because a print file generally requires one WRITE statement that will skip to the top of a page before printing and another that will skip as many lines as are indicated by a space-control field, a print file can have two write modules. Furthermore, if a program requires skipping to the channels in a carriage-control tape, there can be one write module for each carriage-control channel that is used.

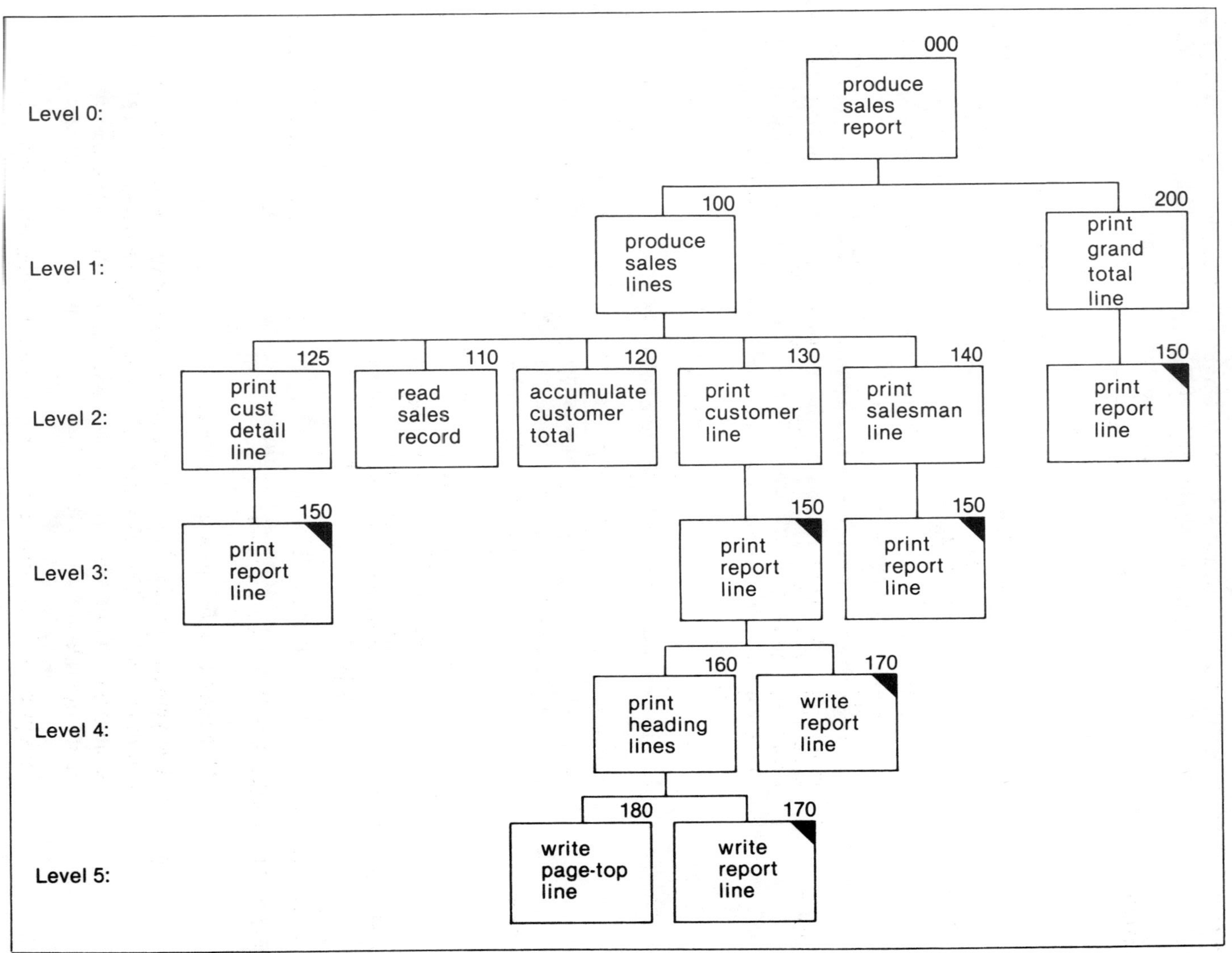

Figure 1-3 VTOC for the extract program with an additional type of output line

Program Design

Exception 2: Because a variable-length file may require one WRITE statement for each record length, a variable-length file can have as many write modules as there are record lengths for the file.

Shade common modules

1. When a module is called by more than one module, it is referred to as a *common module.* Each common module should be shown as subordinate to all modules that call it. And the upper righthand corner of each common module should be shaded as illustrated by modules 150 and 170 in figure 1-2.
2. If a common module has subordinates, the subordinates do not have to be shown each time the common module is drawn. For instance, common module 150 in figure 1-2 has two subordinates which in turn have subordinates. However, these subordinates are shown only once in the VTOC.

Use more than one page for large charts

When a program is large or complex, it may have so many modules that they can't all be drawn on a single VTOC page. In this case, the first VTOC page should only show the top two or three levels of the program. Then, the lowest-level modules on this page should give a page number that will indicate where the VTOC for the completion of the leg can be found. For instance, figure 1-4 illustrates two levels of a VTOC that refers to three subsequent VTOC pages.

Declarative modules

1. The module number of a module that will go in the declaratives section of a program should be preceded by a D.
2. Declarative modules for error processing should be shown on the main VTOC as subordinate to the related read or write modules.
3. If label processing in the declaratives section involves only one module, don't show it on the VTOC. However, if the label processing involves more than one module, create a separate label-processing VTOC.

Guidelines

Four steps for creating VTOCs

1. Create the first draft of the VTOC on a level-by-level basis.
2. Review and analyze the VTOC.

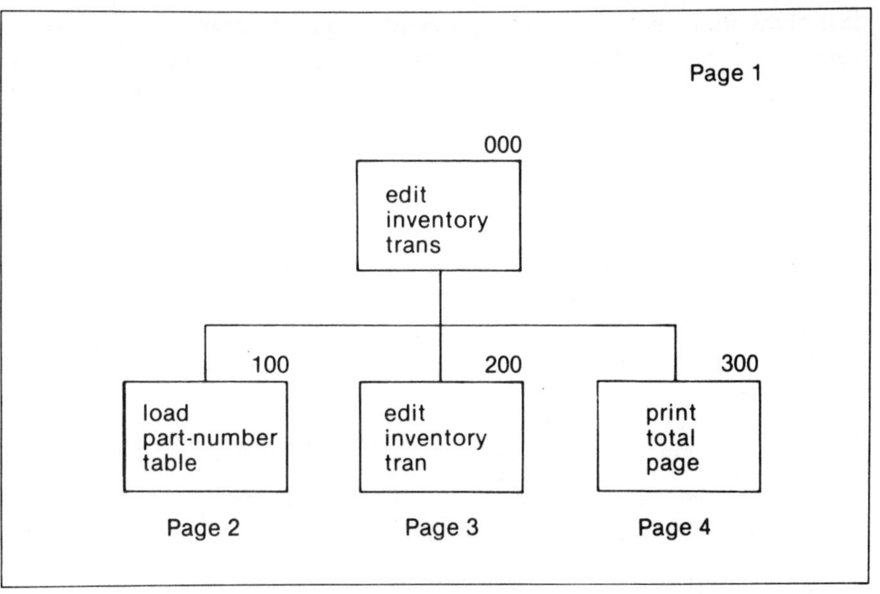

Figure 1-4 The first two levels of a VTOC that has more than one page

3. Number the modules of the VTOC.
4. If necessary, shorten any module names so the resulting paragraph names in the COBOL program will be 30 characters or less.

Level 0

This level should contain one module that represents the entire program. It will repeatedly execute at least one of the modules at level 1.

Level 1

This level should contain at least one primary module that represents the processing for one input record or one set of input records. For instance, module 100 in figure 1-2 represents the processing for one input record. In addition, this level should contain modules that represent *functions* that must be done before or after the primary modules are repeatedly executed.

Level 2 and below

Level 2 should contain the subordinates for each level-1 module. To make sure that all subordinates are shown, you may want to list the functions that you feel make up each level-1 function. Then, make sure that there is one module for each of these functions. This idea is continued for levels 3 and below.

Left-to-right module placement

In general, you place the subordinates at each level from left to right in the sequence in which you think they are likely to be executed. This does not mean, however, that they must be executed in that sequence. And in many cases, they won't be executed in the implied sequence.

Checklist for review and analysis of a VTOC

1. Are all the modules functional? (Can each one be described by one simple imperative statement?)
2. Is the VTOC complete? (Does each module have all of its subfunctions represented by subordinate modules?)
3. Are the verbs consistent? (Do the same verbs always imply the same subfunctions?)
4. Are the modules independent? (Are control codes only passed to the calling module?)
5. Is proper subordination shown? (Do the subordinates actually represent the subfunctions of the calling module?)
6. Are the control spans reasonable? (General guideline: From two to nine subordinate modules make for a reasonable control span.)
7. Are the modules too large? (General guideline: 50 lines or less of source code per module.)

The principle of parsimony

1. Put off the details of the problem until it's absolutely necessary to confront them. Implication: Don't solve more than the problem at hand.
2. Resist the temptation to code when you are designing the program.
3. The simplest solution is usually the best solution.

Input verbs	Suggested meaning
Get	Read and edit records; dispose of invalid records; can be used for one record or a set of records.
Read	Physically read records; count them if required.
Return	Sort language—verb used to make a record available in an output procedure; count records if required.

Output verbs	Suggested meaning
Print	Do everything associated with printing a line. This includes: (1) formatting the output line, (2) moving a proper spacing value into a space-control field, (3) calling a module to physically write the line, (4) increasing the line-count field, (5) resetting total fields to zero in preparation for the next group of records, and (6) setting up control or data fields in preparation for the next group of records.
Punch	Punch output cards; count records if required.
Put	(1) Format output record and call a module to physically write it on the output file. (2) Store an entry in a table; count entries if required.
Release	Sort language—verb used to make a record available in an input procedure; count records if required.
Rewrite	Physically write an output record in the same location on a direct-access device from which the last record was read; count records if required.
Write	Physically place an output record on the output device; count records if required.

Figure 1-5 List of possible module verbs and their suggested meanings (part 1 of 2)

Verb list

Figure 1-5 is a list of module verbs broken down by function (input, output, or processing). We have suggested meanings for all of them; these meanings conform to the way the verbs are used in the four programs presented in this book. You may want to use these verbs in different ways, or you may prefer entirely different verbs. But be consistent in the meaning you assign to any verb. In other words, don't use a verb to mean one thing in level 1 of your first VTOC and another thing in level 2 or in your second VTOC.

Processing verbs	Suggested meaning
Accumulate	Develop totals by successive addition of intermediate totals.
Add	Add a record to a file.
Analyze	Examine or evaluate the fields within a data record; may include arithmetic computation.
Calculate	Develop results by using any combination of arithmetic operations.
Change	Modify a record in a file.
Compare	Compare two fields or records.
Convert	Change something from one form to another.
Create	Develop a record, table, or file.
Delete	Remove a record from a file.
Determine	Find out; may include arithmetic computation.
Edit	Check data fields for validity.
Format	Prepare output to be written.
Load	Read and store entries in a table; sort them if necessary.
Match	Compare the control fields of two different records.
Post	Update a master record based on the data in a transaction; this verb emphasizes the transaction's role in the processing—use it when the transactions determine which masters must be processed.
Prepare	General verb; read records, accumulate or calculate new data fields, prepare output for writing; use *only* in control modules.
Process	General verb; operate upon the input fields to do whatever needs to be done; use this verb *only* in control modules, but avoid it whenever possible.
Produce	General verb; read records, accumulate or calculate new data fields, prepare output for writing; use *only* in control modules.
Search	Look for in a table or a file.
Sort	Arrange records in order desired.
Store	Place entries in table or fields in storage.
Update	Add records to, change records in, or delete records from a master file based on the data in a transaction; this verb emphasizes the master record's role in the processing—use it when all masters have to be processed whether they're updated or not.
Validate	Check data fields for validity.
Verify	Check data fields for validity.

Figure 1-5 List of possible module verbs and their suggested meanings (part 2 of 2)

Module Documentation

Standards

General

1. Document modules using the HIPO diagrams (also known as IPO diagrams or simply IPOs) from IBM's HIPO (Hierarchy plus Input-Process-Output) system of documentation. Figure 1-6 is an IPO for a level-0 module.
2. Create one IPO for each module in the VTOC.

Module numbers and names

1. The module number on the HIPO form is the same as the one used on the VTOC.
2. The module name on the HIPO form is made up by hyphenating the module description that is used in the module box on the VTOC.

Indentation

Use indentation in the process box to make your documentation clear and easy to follow. In particular, do the following:

1. When a statement is too long for one line in the process box, break it up at a sensible place and indent the second and subsequent lines. For example, step 3 in figure 1-6 is too long for one line. So the programmer broke it up at the varying and UNTIL clauses and indented these clauses on the next two lines.
2. Indent phrases starting with words that indicate some condition must be met: UNTIL, AT END, invalid key, etc.
3. Indent statements that tell what to do when a condition is met. For example, in figure 1-7, the statement that tells what to do when the AT END condition is met is indented from AT END.
4. In an IF statement, indent the statements that are to be done if the condition is met. If the IF statement has an ELSE clause, line up the IF and ELSE and indent the statements in the ELSE clause. This is shown in figure 1-8.
5. Be consistent in your indentation. You will use the same state-

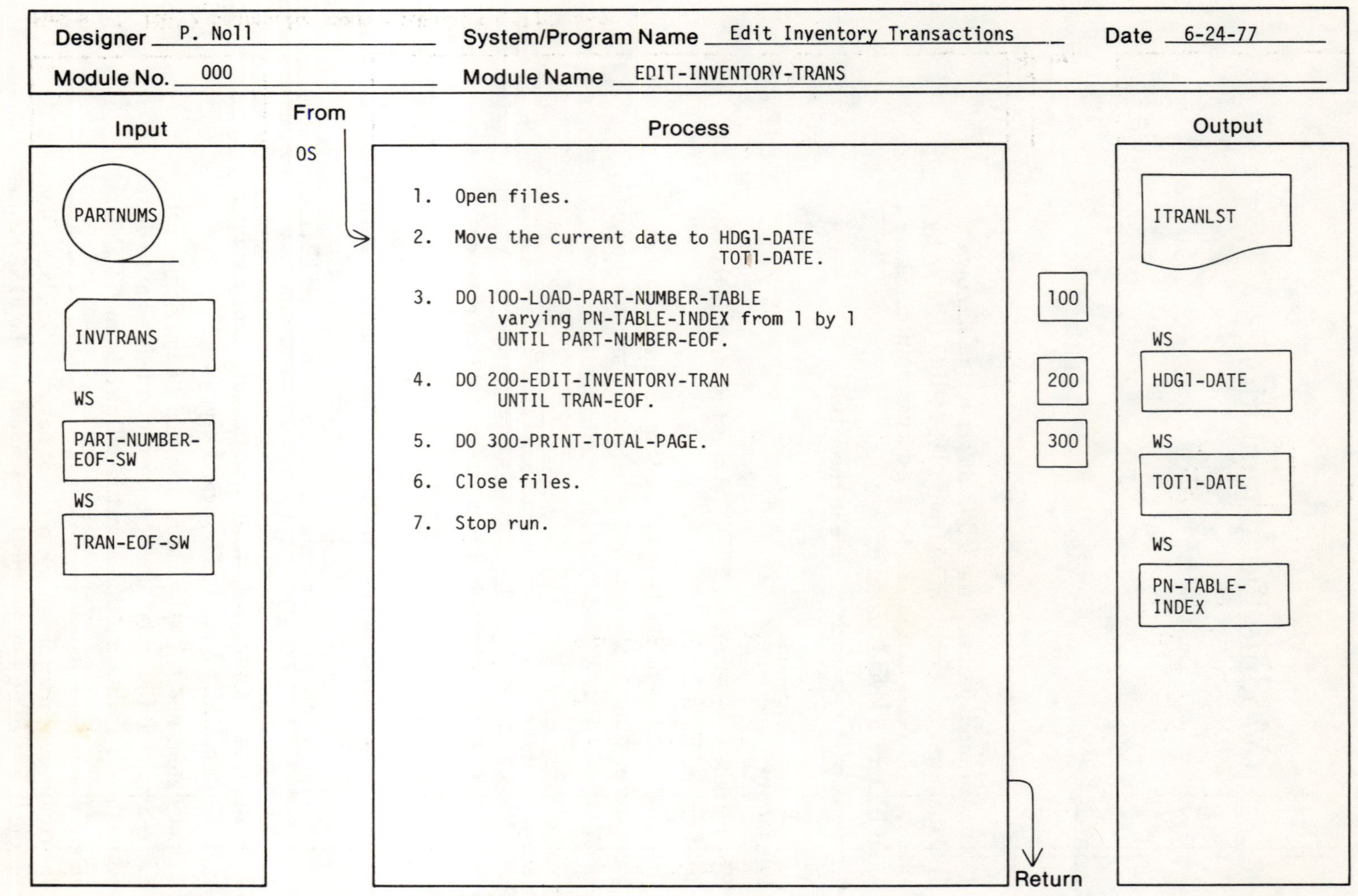

Figure 1-6 HIPO diagram for module 000 of the edit program

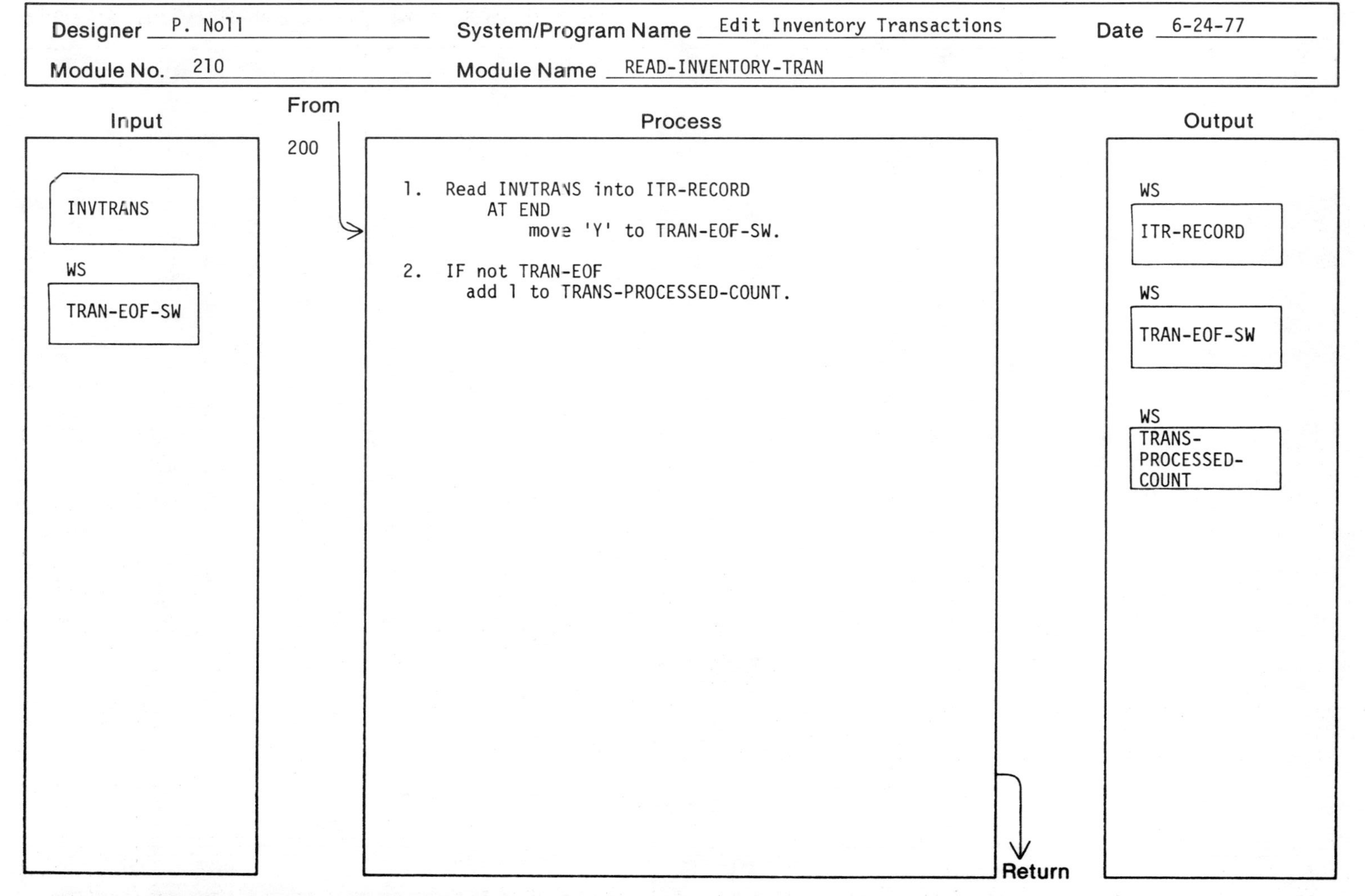

Figure 1-7 HIPO diagram for module 210 of the edit program

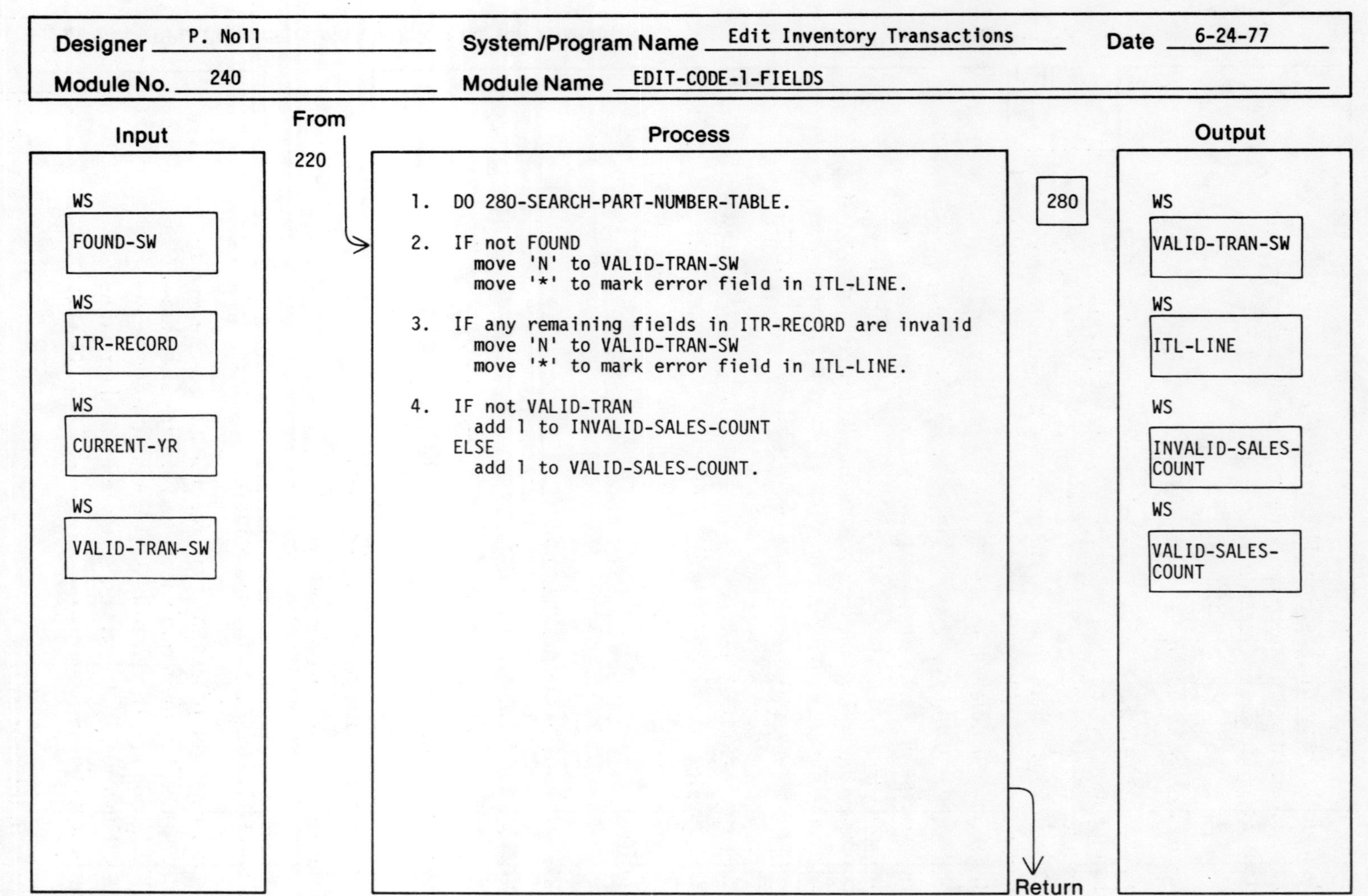

Figure 1-8 HIPO diagram for module 240 of the edit program

ments again and again, so indent them the same way every time.

6. Be logical in your indentation. Use indentation as a tool to make your documentation understandable to yourself and to anyone else who might have to read it.

Called and calling modules

1. Indicate what modules will be called by the module you're documenting. To do this, write the numbers of all called modules in the space between the process and output boxes to the right of the steps that call the modules. In figure 1-6, for example, module 000 calls module 100 in step 3, module 200 in step 4, and module 300 in step 5.
2. Indicate the calling modules for the module you are documenting. To do this, write the numbers of all calling modules near the upper lefthand corner of the process box. For example, you can see in figure 1-8 that module 240 is called by module 220. If module 240 were a common module, the numbers of its other calling modules would be written underneath 220. In figure 1-6, the calling module given is OS. This means that control is passed to the module from the operating system, since module 000 is the top-level module of the program.

Guidelines

Six steps for preparing HIPO diagrams

1. Complete the heading.
2. Record the input, output, and processing requirements.
3. Set off the numbers of the called modules.
4. List the calling modules.
5. Use extended description when necessary.
6. Adjust the VTOC when necessary.

Using two HIPO diagrams for one module

In general, when the processing steps for a single module require more than one IPO, the module itself will require more than 50 lines of COBOL code and should be broken down into two or more modules. However, if after analysis you feel that the module size will be acceptable, use a second IPO to finish the processing steps.

Language in the process box

1. Use a combination of pseudocode and COBOL when recording the processing steps. Use COBOL for all file, record, and data

names that you will need to code in the program. Use structure words like DO, UNTIL, IF, and ELSE to specify the structures you need. Use everyday English to clearly explain whatever else will happen in the processing steps. (This is illustrated in figures 1-6 through 1-8.)

2. If a module consists of *only* one or two statements, it's okay to code it in COBOL itself.
3. Don't code the program twice! Don't use so much COBOL in the process box that the documentation turns out to be a coded module on an IPO form.

Using extended description

1. When the processing in a module is complicated and you need to go into some detail to clarify one or more of the steps, use an extended description form. For example, figure 1-9 is an extended description for the module in figure 1-8. It gives the rules for determining the validity of each input field. When using an extended description form, the HIPO diagram should indicate the overall logic of the module; the extended description form should document the details.
2. Use the reference column on the form to relate each entry in the extended description to a step or steps in the HIPO diagram. For example, in figure 1-9 there is a 3 in the reference column opposite ITR-UPDATE-CODE, since checking the validity of ITR-UPDATE-CODE is part of step 3 in the HIPO diagram.
3. Because the extended description form consists of an area for notes and a column for references, you can use it to record or refer to any documentation that will clarify the requirements of a module. In other words, you can use it to summarize processing requirements (as in figure 1-9), to record a specification table, to refer to a table that is found somewhere else, and so on.

Some reminders

1. Keep the modules independent. When you're documenting one module, it's okay to check other IPOs for trivial points: proper data names, whether a switch has been set, whether a field has been moved, and so on. But if you continually need to refer to the processing steps in one IPO in order to create a later IPO in the same program, something's wrong. Go back to your design and make your modules independent or break them down into more clearly defined functions.
2. Move subfunctions down the line. Some subfunctions, like counting records or resetting total fields, are trivial enough that they don't require separate modules, yet they're hard to place in

Designer: P. Noll — System/Program Name: Edit Inventory Transactions — Date: 6-24-77

Module No.: 240 — Module Name: EDIT-CODE-1-FIELDS

Notes		Ref.
Validity is:		
ITR-UPDATE-CODE	Must be 'C'	3
ITR-CUST-ORDER-NO	Any data	3

ITR-ORDER-DATE
  ITR-ORDER-DAY
  ITR-ORDER-MONTH
  ITR-ORDER-YEAR
	Numeric with
	  day less than 32
	  month less than 13
	  year = current year or
	  current year - 1
		3

ITR-BRANCH-NO	Numeric and less than 25	3
ITR-SALESMAN-NO	Numeric	3
ITR-CUST-NO	Numeric	3
ITR-QUANTITY	Numeric	3
ITR-PART-NUMBER	Numeric with match in the valid-part-number file	1
NOTES:		
All numeric fields must be greater than zero.		

Notes	Ref.

Figure 1-9 Extended description for module 240 of the edit program

the existing modules. In such cases, move the subfunctions down the line in the VTOC and make them part of some low-level module. For example, we suggest that you count records in read or write modules and that you reset totals in print modules. Avoid putting trivial subfunctions in control modules because they tend to obscure the control logic.

3. Document only the function specified by the module name. In some cases, you and the other members of your programming group will agree that certain verbs will have conventional meanings in your shop; that is, the verbs will include certain subfunctions not normally implied by their definitions. In the absence of such conventions, however, document only the function named by the module. It's better to create a separate module for a function that doesn't conform to any convention than to put it in a module where it will be difficult to find later on. (Our suggested verb meanings are given in the verb list in figure 1-5.)
4. Check to make sure your program won't abort (1) by attempting to operate on input data if there are no records in the input file (an empty file) or (2) by trying to read a record after the end-of-file condition has been reached.

COBOL Coding

Standards

Modules

1. Each module in the VTOC is coded in a single paragraph in the COBOL program. Exception: An input or output procedure in a SORT statement must be a section that ends with an EXIT paragraph.
2. The paragraph name for each module consists of the module's number and name taken from the IPO diagram. The number and name are separated by hyphens with the number first.
3. The modules (paragraphs) are placed in the program in the order specified by their module numbers.

Blank comment cards

Use blank comment cards (an asterisk in column 7 and blanks in the rest of the card) to vertically format the program listing. To do this, place blank comment cards before and after division headers, declarative headers, section headers, and paragraph headers as shown in figure 1-10. In addition, use them to highlight the logical groupings in the Data Division by putting them before and after FD statements and 01-level items as shown in figure 1-11.

Data Division

Data names Use hyphens to separate the parts of data names so the names are clear and easy to read. Also, use a two- or three-letter prefix in the names of all the fields in a single input or output record to show that the fields are related. For example, in figure 1-11 all the fields in the transaction record start with the prefix TR.

Grouping data items Do not use any 77-level items. Instead, group items under general 01-level headings. For example, you can group all total fields under an 01 item called TOTAL-FIELDS as shown in figure 1-11. If all the items in a group have the same USAGE or are synchronized, specify this at the group level as shown for SUBSCRIPT-FIELDS in figure 1-11.

```
 IDENTIFICATION DIVISION.
*
       .
       .
*
 DATA DIVISION.
*
       .
       .
*
 PROCEDURE DIVISION.
*
 DECLARATIVES.
*
       .
       .
*
 MAIN SECTION.
*
 000-UPDATE-INVENTORY-MASTERS.
*
       .
       .
*
 100-UPDATE-INVENTORY-MASTER.
*
       .
       .
       .
```

Figure 1-10 Using blank comment cards to space the source listing

COBOL Coding

Switches When condition names are used for a field that has only two possible conditions, the field is called a *switch.* Here are the basic rules that apply to switches:

a. All switch names end in SW.
b. The condition represented by the switch should be self-explanatory if you drop the SW from the switch name. Thus, VALID-TRAN-SW would be the switch name for the condition named VALID-TRAN, which would indicate a valid transaction.
c. The switch is on if it has a value of Y (for yes) and off if it has a value of N (for no).
d. If a switch must have a starting value, initialize it by giving it a VALUE in working storage.

Flags When condition names are used for a field that has more than two possible conditions, the field is called a *flag.* The condition names for a flag may be closely related to the flag name, like GROUP-1, GROUP-2, and GROUP-3 for a flag named GROUP-

```
 DATA DIVISION.
*
 FILE SECTION.
*
 FD  TRANSACTION-FILE
     LABEL RECORDS ARE STANDARD
     RECORDING MODE IS F
     RECORD CONTAINS 28 CHARACTERS
     BLOCK CONTAINS 140 RECORDS.
*
 01  TR-INPUT-AREA              PIC X(28).
*
 FD  PRINTER-FILE
     LABEL RECORDS ARE STANDARD
     RECORDING MODE IS F
     RECORD CONTAINS 133 CHARACTERS.
*
 01  PRINT-AREA                 PIC X(133).
*
 WORKING-STORAGE SECTION.
*
 01  SWITCHES.
*
     05  TRAN-EOF-SW            PIC X           VALUE 'N'.
         88  TRAN-EOF                           VALUE 'Y'.
     05  VALID-TRAN-SW          PIC X.
         88  VALID-TRAN                         VALUE 'Y'.
*
 01  PRINT-FIELDS               COMP            SYNC.
*
     05  LINE-COUNT             PIC S999        VALUE +57.
     05  LINES-ON-PAGE          PIC S999        VALUE +56.
     05  SPACE-CONTROL          PIC S9.
*
 01  COUNT-FIELDS               COMP-3.
*
     05  VALID-RECORD-COUNT     PIC S9(5)       VALUE ZERO.
     05  INVALID-RECORD-COUNT   PIC S9(5)       VALUE ZERO.
*
 01  TOTAL-FIELDS               COMP-3.
*
     05  CUSTOMER-TOTAL         PIC S9(7)V99    VALUE ZERO.
     05  SALESMAN-TOTAL         PIC S9(7)V99    VALUE ZERO.
     05  GRAND-TOTAL            PIC S9(9)V99    VALUE ZERO.
*
 01  SUBSCRIPT-FIELDS           COMP            SYNC.
*
     05  COMMISSION-LEVEL-SUB   PIC S99.
     05  YEARS-SERVICE-SUB      PIC S99.
*
 01  TR-RECORD.
*
     05  TR-TRAN-CODE           PIC X.
         88 TR-DELETE                           VALUE 'D'.
         88 TR-ADD                              VALUE 'A'.
         88 TR-CHANGE                           VALUE 'C'.
     05  TR-BRANCH-NO           PIC XX.
     05  TR-SALESMAN-NO         PIC XXX.
     05  TR-CUSTOMER-NO         PIC X(5).
     05  TR-TRAN-DATE.
         10 TR-TRAN-MONTH       PIC 99.
         10 TR-TRAN-DAY         PIC 99.
         10 TR-TRAN-YEAR        PIC 99.
     05  TR-QUANTITY            PIC 9(5).
     05  TR-ITEM-NO             PIC X(6).
```

Figure 1-11 A structured Data Division

COBOL Coding

FLAG; or they can be unrelated, like TRAINEE, SALESMAN, and ASSOCIATE for a flag named STATUS-FLAG.

Indentation Indent the entries in the Data Division as follows:

a. Leave two spaces between the level number and the data name.
b. Indent each successive level four spaces from the previous level.
c. Align PIC, VALUE, SYNC, and USAGE clauses.

These indentation standards are illustrated in figure 1-11.

Procedure Division

One STOP or GOBACK statement A program may have only one ending statement. It can be either a STOP RUN statement or a GOBACK statement.

Section names Do not divide your program into sections except when you are required to do so; that is, when you are using the sort feature or declaratives. Even when section names are required, they should *not* be used in PERFORM statements.

Indentation Figure 1-12 shows the proper use of indentation in the Procedure Division:

a. If a statement is longer than one line, break it up at the start of a clause or phrase (*never* in the middle of a word) and indent the succeeding lines by four spaces. (See how example 4 in figure 1-12 is broken at INTO, example 5 at AFTER ADVANCING, example 7 at GIVING, and example 8 at VARYING.)
b. In statements like the OPEN, CLOSE, and MOVE, align similar elements such as file or data names. (See examples 1, 2, 3, and 4.)
c. Indent conditional clauses, such as AT END, INVALID KEY, and ON SIZE ERROR, by four spaces. (See examples 4, 6, 7, 8, and 9.)
d. Imperative statements that are executed when a condition is met are indented four spaces from their related conditional clauses. (See examples 4, 6, 7, 9, 10, and 11.)
e. In general, indent the IFs in nested IF statements four spaces from the previous level. (See example 10 in figure 1-12.) If there are several levels of nested IF statements, however, each subsequent level may be indented only two more spaces instead of the usual four. Then, you won't run out of coding space by the time you reach the fourth or fifth level.
f. The ELSE that goes with a previous IF is aligned directly under

Example 1:

```
OPEN INPUT   TRANSACTION-FILE
             OLD-MASTER-FILE
     OUTPUT NEW-MASTER-FILE
             REPORT-FILE
             ERROR-FILE.
```

Example 2:

```
CLOSE TRANSACTION-FILE
      OLD-MASTER-FILE
      NEW-MASTER-FILE
      REPORT-FILE
      ERROR-FILE.
```

Example 3:

```
MOVE SPACE          TO PR-RECORD.
MOVE TP-ITEM-NO     TO PR-ITEM-NO.
MOVE TP-ITEM-DESC TO PR-ITEM-DESC.
```

Example 4:

```
READ TRANSACTION-FILE
    INTO TR-INPUT-AREA
    AT END
        MOVE 'Y'        TO TRAN-EOF-SW
        MOVE HIGH-VALUE TO TR-ITEM-NO.
```

Example 5:

```
WRITE PR-OUTPUT-AREA
    AFTER ADVANCING SPACE-CONTROL LINES.
```

Example 6:

```
WRITE NM-OUTPUT-AREA
    INVALID KEY
        PERFORM 420-PRINT-ERROR-MESSAGE.
```

Figure 1-12 Proper use of indentation in the Procedure Division (part 1 of 2)

the IF. Be careful, though. The compiler will pair an ELSE with the first previous IF that doesn't have an ELSE, regardless of your indentation. So check to make sure all IFs and ELSEs are properly paired. (See example 10.)

g. In linear nesting, the ELSE and IF clauses aren't indented. Instead, each ELSE clause is aligned under the first IF clause, and the IF contained in the ELSE follows on the same line. The imperative statements that are to be executed if the condition is met are still indented four spaces. (See example 11 in figure 1-12.)

COBOL Coding

Example 7:

```
MULTIPLY TR-QUANTITY BY TB-UNIT-PRICE
    GIVING IL-SALES-AMOUNT
    ON SIZE ERROR
        PERFORM 360-PROCESS-INVALID-TRAN.
```

Example 8:

```
PERFORM 110-READ-ITEM-CODE-TABLE
    VARYING TABLE-SUB FROM 1 BY 1
    UNTIL TABLE-EOF.
```

Example 9:

```
SEARCH ITEM-CODE-TABLE-ENTRY
    AT END
        PERFORM 320-PRINT-ERROR-MESSAGE
    WHEN IT-ITEM-NO (IT-INDEX) EQUAL TO TR-ITEM-NO
        MOVE IT-UNIT-PRICE (IT-INDEX) TO TP-UNIT-PRICE.
```

Example 10:

```
IF CR-CUST-CODE EQUAL TO 1
    MOVE .020 TO DISCOUNT-PERCENT
ELSE
    IF CR-CUST-CODE EQUAL TO 2
        MOVE .050 TO DISCOUNT-PERCENT
    ELSE
        MOVE .000 TO DISCOUNT-PERCENT.
```

Example 11:

```
IF CR-CUST-CODE EQUAL TO 1
    MOVE .020 TO DISCOUNT-PERCENT
ELSE IF CR-CUST-CODE EQUAL TO 2
    MOVE .050 TO DISCOUNT-PERCENT
ELSE
    MOVE .000 TO DISCOUNT-PERCENT.
```

Figure 1-12 Proper use of indentation in the Procedure Division (part 2 of 2)

Compound conditions When using compound conditions, align the parts as shown in figure 1-13. In addition, whenever NOT, AND, and OR are mixed in a compound condition, use parentheses to dictate which part of the condition should be evaluated first. (The compiler starts with the innermost set of parentheses and works outward.)

Relational operators Write out the words GREATER THAN and LESS THAN. Don't use the symbols since they aren't available on all print chains. For consistency, you may also use EQUAL TO instead of the equals sign, although the equals sign is available on all print

Example 1:

```
PERFORM procedure-name
    UNTIL condition-1
      AND condition-2
       OR condition-3
      AND condition-4.
```

Example 2:

```
IF          condition-1
         OR condition-2
        AND condition-3
    statement-group-1
ELSE
    statement-group-2.
```

Figure 1-13 Proper indentation when using compound conditions

chains I have used. If you prefer to use shorter forms, you can simply use EQUAL, GREATER, and LESS.

Forbidden usages Do *not* use the following in the Procedure Division, except as noted:

a. ALTER
b. EXIT (*except* when using the sort feature)
c. GO TO (*except* when using the sort feature)
d. GO TO DEPENDING (use linear IFs for implementing the case structure)
e. PERFORM THRU
f. Sections (*except* when using the sort feature or declaratives)

Guidelines

Comments

Comments should only be used to tell what's going on in a segment of coding, not to tell how it's being accomplished. The main reasons for using comments are (1) to clarify what is happening when the pseudocode from the HIPO diagram doesn't translate into COBOL, (2) to relate a block of code to other documentation (such as a decision table), and (3) to explain an abstruse segment of code that can't be coded in a straightforward manner because of language restrictions. *Never* use comments to explain something the code should make clear by itself.

Sequence of code

The paragraphs in the Procedure Division are placed in the sequence given by the module numbers that are the first characters of the paragraph names. If declaratives are used, these paragraphs are placed in sequence by module number within the declaratives section. As a result, all paragraphs within the Procedure Division should be easy to locate.

We also recommend that all of the programmers in a shop use standard coding sequences in the Environment and Data Divisions. For instance, we recommend that SELECT statements be coded in this sequence: (1) input files, (2) I-O files, (3) output files with print files last, and (4) sort files. Then, the FD statements in the file section of the Data Division should be coded in the same sequence used for the SELECT statements. Finally, the record descriptions in the working-storage section should be coded in a regular pattern. We recommend this sequence:

1. switches like TRAN-EOF-SW and VALID-TRAN-SW
2. flags like STATUS-FLAG and COMMISSION-FLAG
3. control fields (holding fields for comparing the control field of a new record with the control field of a previous record)
4. print fields like LINE-COUNT and LINES-ON-PAGE
5. counters like TRAN-COUNT and DUPLICATE-COUNT
6. total fields like CUSTOMER-TOTAL and GRAND-TOTAL
7. subscripts like RATE-TABLE-SUB
8. indexes like RATE-TABLE-INDEX
9. tables
10. record descriptions (in the same order as the related files are listed in the SELECT statements)

In addition, we recommend you code line descriptions for print files in this order: (1) heading lines, (2) body lines, (3) total lines. If you use regular coding sequences like these, it will be easier for you to locate code as you go from one program to another.

Data Division

Meaningful names Give meaningful names to all data items and 88-level items. A COBOL name can be up to 30 characters long, so don't skimp. Use as many of the 30 characters as you need to make the names in your program easy to understand—not only easy for yourself, but for others as well.

Condition names Use condition names frequently. In particular, condition names should be used for switches, for flags, and for codes that are likely to change during the life of the program.

```
*
 01  HDG-LINE-2.
*
     05  HDG2-CC                 PIC X.
     05  FILLER                  PIC X(20)   VALUE '                    '.
     05  FILLER                  PIC X(20)   VALUE '    SLSMN. NO.    CUST'.
     05  FILLER                  PIC X(20)   VALUE '. NO.    SALES AMOUNT'.
     05  FILLER                  PIC X(20)   VALUE '                    '.
     05  FILLER                  PIC X(20)   VALUE '                    '.
     05  FILLER                  PIC X(20)   VALUE '                    '.
     05  FILLER                  PIC X(12)   VALUE '            '.
```

Figure 1-14 Defining a constant line of printer output

PIC and VALUE clauses Whenever possible, start PIC clauses in column 32 and VALUE clauses in column 44.

Defining a constant print line To define a print line in working storage that consists primarily of constants, divide the line into a carriage-control field, FILLER fields of 20 characters each, and a final FILLER field of as many characters as are needed to complete the line. Then place the literals wherever you want them to print in the line. This technique is illustrated in figure 1-14. If you start the VALUE clauses in column 44, the periods for the 20-character literal lines will fall in column 72, the last legal coding position.

Procedure Division

NEXT SENTENCE Whenever possible, avoid using NEXT SENTENCE in IF statements.

Linear nesting If an IF statement tests one field repeatedly for a series of values, linear nesting can be used. An example of linear nesting is shown in figure 1-15. Do not use a linear nest within a larger IF nest.

Levels of nesting When you have to go beyond five levels of nesting in nested IF statements, check your program design. Maybe you can simplify the problem by revising the VTOC.

Compound conditions Use compound conditions whenever they closely approximate the decisions that have to be made by the program. In other words, if two or more different conditions have to be evaluated before any action can be taken, it may make more sense to combine them in a single conditional statement than to check for each condition separately.

```
 PROCEDURE DIVISION.
*
        .
        .
        .
        IF TR-ACTIVITY-CODE EQUAL TO 1
            PERFORM CODE-1-FUNCTION
        ELSE IF TR-ACTIVITY-CODE EQUAL TO 2
            PERFORM CODE-2-FUNCTION
        ELSE IF TR-ACTIVITY-CODE EQUAL TO 3
            PERFORM CODE-3-FUNCTION
        ELSE IF TR-ACTIVITY-CODE EQUAL TO 4
            PERFORM CODE-4-FUNCTION
        ELSE IF TR-ACTIVITY-CODE EQUAL TO 5
            PERFORM CODE-5-FUNCTION
        ELSE IF TR-ACTIVITY-CODE EQUAL TO 6
            PERFORM CODE-6-FUNCTION
        ELSE IF TR-ACTIVITY-CODE EQUAL TO 7
            PERFORM CODE-7-FUNCTION
        ELSE IF TR-ACTIVITY-CODE EQUAL TO 8
            PERFORM CODE-8-FUNCTION
        ELSE IF TR-ACTIVITY-CODE EQUAL TO 9
            PERFORM CODE-9-FUNCTION
        ELSE
            PERFORM DEFAULT-FUNCTION.
```

Figure 1-15 Nested IF statements in linear form (the recommended alternative to the case structure)

Implied subjects and relational operators You may use implied subjects and relational operators as long as the conditional statements are easy to understand. Once it becomes unclear what the implied subject or operator refers to, though, you should state the complete condition.

The case structure The case structure should be implemented by using linear IF statements. For example, figure 1-15 is equivalent to a case structure with nine cases.

The sort feature When you use the sort feature with an input or output procedure, you will have to use section names, a GO TO statement, and an EXIT paragraph consisting only of the EXIT statement. This is one case in which all three are acceptable.

Declaratives When you use declaratives, you must use sections. Your program will consist of (1) the declaratives section and (2) a section that contains the rest of the program.

Paragraph length In general, you should try to keep the length of your COBOL paragraphs at around 50 lines or less. If a paragraph is over 50 lines, you should check it for readability. If the paragraph is easy to read and understand, no changes are necessary. If not, you should consider revising the VTOC for the program so the paragraph can be divided into two or more modules, thus increasing readability.

Testing

Standards

General

1. A test plan such as the one in figure 1-16 must be prepared for each program before any test data is developed. This plan will indicate (1) the sequence in which the modules will be tested if top-down testing is used, (2) the sequence in which the batches of test data will be supplied to the program, and (3) the source of each batch of test data.
2. Top-down coding and testing must be used for every program of more than 1000 lines of source code.

Guidelines

Creating a test plan

1. Review the IPOs for the program and make a list of all the conditions that need to be tested.
2. If top-down testing is used, decide the sequence in which the modules will be tested.
3. Decide the sequence in which the conditions that you listed in step 1 should be tested. The guiding rule here is to test in a sequence that will point up major errors first. A general sequence that can be used is this: (1) valid conditions only, (2) independent error conditions, (3) contingencies (error conditions that result when two or more conditions are combined), and (4) volume conditions like page overflow or exceeding the maximum size of a table.
4. Decide where the test data will come from: Will you create it yourself, will "live data" be available, or what?

Creating the test data

1. For the early test runs, be sure to keep the volume of data low. Otherwise, it will be difficult to locate bugs and the cause of the bugs.

Test phase	Data	Data source
1. Modules 000, 100 and 200	None	Not applicable
2. Add modules 110 and 120	Three part-number records	Self
3. Add modules 210, 220, 240, 250 and 280	Two valid transactions, one for each transaction code, and one with the first part number in the table, one with the last part number	Self
4. Add modules 230, 260, 270, 290, and 300	Invalid transactions that will test all possible causes of invalid fields	Self
5. Contingencies	Mixed data from steps 3 and 4; any new records that might cause contingent errors	Self
6. Page overflow and maximum table size	As many part-number records as the program is supposed to provide for; 150 transactions, with enough invalid transactions to cause page overflow	Test data generator

Figure 1-16 A test plan for the edit program using top-down coding and testing

2. Always determine in advance what the output for each batch of test data should be.

Using debugging statements

1. Before testing, you should insert debugging statements such as DISPLAY, TRACE, and EXHIBIT into the modules. These will help show what is happening as the program executes.
2. To indicate what modules have been executed during the test run, you can use a DISPLAY statement at the start of each paragraph. For instance,

```
DISPLAY '100-LOAD-PART-NUMBER-TABLE'
```

could be the first statement in module 100 of an edit program.

Coding program stubs

1. A program stub should contain a few statements that simulate the processing that the module will do when it is coded completely.
2. Do not develop elaborate program stubs. At some point, it

becomes easier to code the module itself than to simulate it.

3. The first statement in each stub should be a debugging statement that indicates the number or name of the module (see step 2 in "Using Debugging Statements"). These statements will help you determine whether the stubs were called properly.

The sequence of top-down testing

When top-down testing is used, you normally can test the modules of your program in many different sequences. When planning the sequence, you should keep these points in mind:

1. Try to find the major errors first. So if you have any doubts about some portion of your design or its implementation, test that portion first.
2. Outside pressures may influence your testing sequence. For instance, a user or operations group may be concerned about some phase of the program. If so, test that phase first.
3. When there are no other considerations, you should test the major control modules of your program first. After that, it is logical to test the program one leg at a time.

Walkthroughs

Standards

Formal walkthroughs should be conducted at least three times during the development of a program:

1. after the program specifications have been developed
2. after the program is designed (VTOC only or VTOC and IPOs)
3. after the test plan and test data have been developed

In addition, informal reviews should be held for coding and user guide preparation. This can simply mean that one programmer reviews your coding and user guides, and you do the same for him.

Guidelines

Types of walkthroughs

1. Specifications
2. Design (VTOC alone or VTOC and IPOs)
3. Test plan and test data
4. Coding
5. User guide

Walkthrough format

1. A walkthrough is initiated by a programmer when he's ready for a public review of some phase of his work.
2. The programmer invites from two to six colleagues to participate in the walkthrough.
3. At least 48 hours before the meeting, the programmer gives an agenda like the one in figure 1-17 to the participants. Besides giving general information about when and where the meeting will be held, the agenda specifies the program name, the type of walkthrough that will be held, the material that will be reviewed, and the walkthrough objectives (that is, what the materials are to be reviewed for).
4. Along with the agenda, the programmer hands out copies of the

Notice date: May 26, 1978

Originator: Paul Noll

Meeting date and time: Wednesday

May 31

1:30 P.M.

Location: Room 578

Program: Produce sales report

Type of Walkthrough: Design

Materials:

1 Specifications

2 VTOC

3 IPOs

4

5

Objectives:

Please review for

1 completeness and logic

2 meaningful names

3 naming consistency

4

5

6

Team:

	Name	Present	Resolution Initials	Resolution Date
Moderator	Mike Murach	Yes		
Secretary	Judy Taylor	Yes		
Member 1	Doug Lowe	Yes		
Member 2				
Member 3				
Member 4				

Date of resolution June 2, 1978 Originator's signature

Figure 1-17 A walkthrough form that serves as an agenda and as a record of followup

materials listed on the agenda to each participant. The participants then have at least 48 hours to review the materials so they will be prepared for the actual walkthrough.

5. No managers are allowed at a walkthrough—this is a time for finding errors, not for evaluating programmers.
6. At the walkthrough, an action list is made of all the questions, errors, and possible trouble spots raised during the meeting. However, no attempt is made at this time to correct anything. The purpose of the walkthrough meeting is error detection, not correction.
7. The programmer follows up the meeting in two ways. First, within an hour of the meeting, he makes and distributes copies of the action list to each of the walkthrough participants. Second, within two days of the meeting, he lets each of the participants know in writing what he did to resolve each of the items on the action list.

The meeting

1. Select one participant to be moderator and one to be secretary. The moderator's job is to keep the meeting on track; it's up to him or her to make sure the comments don't become too trivial or too personal. The secretary is in charge of writing down items on the action list.
2. The main part of the walkthrough consists of detecting errors. Sometimes, however, the meeting begins with the programmer giving an overview of his program. Since the materials given to the participants are usually self-explanatory, a walkthrough should *not* begin with an overview unless there is a solid reason for having one.
3. When a question is raised, the programmer should be given a chance to explain his work. If it's agreed that the point is or could be a problem, it goes on the action list.
4. Avoid pointing up trivial errors (such as syntax errors, missing punctuation, or inconsistent names) at the walkthrough. Instead, a participant should mark these errors in red on his own materials and hand them to the programmer at the end of the meeting.
5. All of the walkthrough members should participate actively in the meeting. To do this, they have to prepare ahead of time by going through the walkthrough materials the programmer gave them and listing any problem areas and potential errors they find. Then at the meeting, they'll be able to raise their own questions, as well as intelligently discuss the points raised by the other participants.

Followup

1. The easiest way for a programmer to tell the other walkthrough members what he did about the items on an action list is to simply write his resolutions on the action list itself. (This is shown in figure 1-18.) Then he can make copies and distribute them. Notice that the explanations aren't long, but they say enough so the other participants know what action was taken on each point.
2. If a major error is found in a walkthrough, the best resolution may be for the programmer to redo the material and hold another walkthrough.
3. Anytime a formal walkthrough is held, a report should be made to management. The easiest way to do this is to use an agenda form like the one in figure 1-17. After the participants are satisfied with the programmer's resolution of the points on the action list, they initial the form; then the originator signs it and turns it in. Notice that the form simply gives the agenda and states that all the problems were solved. It doesn't give any indication of who found how many errors, how many errors there were in all, how crucial or trivial the errors were, etc.

Action List

Originator: Paul Noll
Program: Produce sales report
Type of walkthrough: Design

Questions:	Resolution:
1. Is there an unnecessary level in the VTOC? Can modules 130, 140, and 150 be moved from level 3 to level 2?	Changed. The modules have been moved to level 2. See attached VTOC.
2. Will module 120 process the first record in the file?	Changed. It didn't work. See attached IPO.
3. Should control field changes be made in module 120 (the major control module) rather than in the print modules?	Changed. I moved the control field changes from the print modules to module 120. See attached IPO.
4. Is the module name for module 120 meaningful?	Changed. From "process sales record" to "produce sales line."
5. Inconsistency in use of TR and TRAN in several IPOs (marked in red and returned).	Changed. All references are now TRAN.

Figure 1-18 Action list for a design walkthrough including resolution of the questions raised

Checklist for effective walkthroughs

1. No manager present
2. Error detection only
3. Two hour time limit
4. The right participants
5. Vested interests
6. Show results
7. No counting
8. No sandbagging

Chief-Programmer Teams

Standards

Since the history of chief-programmer teams is brief and limited in scope, I think it's too early to set standards for their use. One fact that is apparent already, though, is that chief-programmer teams are relatively difficult to create and staff. So of all the structured programming techniques that you may want to implement, I would recommend that this be your last priority. Nevertheless, I think the use of teams can make significant contributions to programmer morale and productivity, so you may want to start experimenting with them as soon as you have implemented the standards for structured design, module documentation, coding, and testing.

Guidelines

The essential team members

On any chief-programmer team, there are at least three members:

1. *The chief programmer* is in charge of the project and the team. He should have personnel ability so he can deal effectively with the other team members and with management. And he should be technically proficient so that he can plan the program or programs done by the team (he will often code the most difficult parts of these programs). His duties will generally include all of the following:
   a. designing programs
   b. staffing the team
   c. controlling and reviewing the team's work
   d. acting as moderator at walkthroughs
2. *The backup programmer* has to be able to take over if anything should happen to the chief programmer. Ideally, then, he has the same skills as the chief programmer. In actual practice, however, he is usually an up-and-coming programmer who doesn't have the chief's experience but does show chief-programmer potential.
3. Although the duties will vary from company to company, the *controller* (or librarian) is generally in charge of all the paperwork and machine procedures for the team. He must have

enough technical experience to interface with the computer and with the team's programmers. He must also be a well-organized person in order to keep track of all current program listings, test runs, documentation files, source code changes, and so forth. He usually serves as walkthrough secretary.

Other team members

Other positions may be added to a chief-programmer team either for a short period of time or for the duration of a project. Some common extra positions follow:

1. The *administrator* is in charge of the team's administrative duties. His job is to worry about things like budget and the proper utilization of staff. He can thus free the chief from administrative detail.
2. *Programmers, junior programmers* and *trainees* are responsible for carrying out the programming tasks assigned by the chief.
3. *Technical specialists* may be assigned to a team for a short period of time if the team is working on some project that requires specialized knowledge.
4. A *technical writer* may be assigned to a team for a short period of time if the team's project has unusual requirements in terms of documentation or user guides.
5. A *secretary* does the clerical tasks of a team such as typing, filing, drawing charts, and running errands. In some cases, a secretary will divide his or her time between several teams, since a single team may not have enough clerical work to keep a secretary busy fulltime.

Development Support Libraries

Standards

Because development support libraries are still in the experimental stage, it is too early to recommend standards for their use. Nevertheless, every installation should plan on implementing these libraries as soon as practical. Their use can relieve programmers of many tedious details and thus add a large measure of professionalism to the average programming department.

Guidelines

Internal library

1. The internal library is a machine library (usually on a direct-access device) that contains all current program data in machine-readable form. The internal library includes files of job-control language, source code, object code, load modules, and test material.
2. In order to use an internal library, you will have to develop or buy software and procedures that can:
   a. create and update library files
   b. retrieve modules or programs for compilation
   c. initiate test runs
   d. back up and restore libraries
   e. produce status listings for libraries

External library

The external library contains current listings of everything stored in the internal library plus related information like operating procedures, maintenance data, and status information. The procedures for the external library tell the programmer how to request a compilation or test run, how to submit source code for keypunching, etc. They also tell how the external files should be maintained and what they should contain.

Controller (Librarian)

1. The controller is in charge of seeing that the development support libraries are kept up-to-date and that programmers follow the procedures established for the libraries. He has to be able to perform at three levels: (1) clerical, to take care of the paperwork involved; (2) programming, to handle the interface with the computer and with the programmers; and (3) management, to enforce the procedures and to interpret the large amount of management information he has access to.
2. Although it's difficult to decide just how much prestige and what degree of skill should be assigned to the position of controller, we recommend that the job be a growth step towards a management position.

Section

2

PROGRAM NOTES

This section presents notes for each of the four programs presented in section 3. It is intended to give additional perspective about each of the problems, the VTOCs, the IPOs, and the COBOL listings. The programs in sequence are the edit, the report extract, the sequential update, and the random update with sorting.

The Edit Program

An edit program checks the fields within a transaction record to make sure they contain valid data. If the edit program detects an invalid field within a record, the record is not released for further processing. In addition, the error record is usually listed on an error listing so the errors can be corrected and the data can be resubmitted for processing. In some installations, you will find an edit program referred to as a *validation*, or *verification*, *program*.

One common type of checking that is done within an edit program is making sure numeric fields contain numeric data. This type of checking will catch one of the most common types of keypunching errors—that is, skipping a required field so that it contains blanks. Since attempting to perform an arithmetic operation on a blank field will often cause an abnormal program termination, numeric checking can save many reruns.

Beyond numeric checking, an edit program may do many other types of checks such as code checking, limit checking, and logical checking. Code checking refers to a test that makes sure a code is valid. For instance, 2, 3, 5, P, and T may be valid transaction codes, while L, 2, 3, 4, and 5 are valid customer-classification codes. Limit checking refers to a test that makes sure that the data in a field is within acceptable limits. For instance, the month in a date field shouldn't be over 12, and the day shouldn't be over 31. And logical checking refers to a test for conditions that logically should never occur. For example, it is illogical that an hourly employee will work over 120 hours in one week or that an appliance store will sell more than one (or at most two) stoves to one customer.

To make it easier for operations people to correct invalid records, the error fields are usually highlighted on the error listing. This can be done by printing a message to the right of the error line indicating the fields in error. Or it can be done by printing an error code next to the fields that are in error. In some cases, it may be impossible to indicate all errors within a record, so the error listing only indicates the first error that is detected within any one record.

An edit program may check only one type of record, but it can also check several different types. If it does, the error listing may require a different output format for each type of error record.

As you will see in the random-update program, an editing routine can be combined with another major function like updating.

In such a case, invalid records will not be used to update the master file, though valid records will. The edit program that follows is useful because it is a good model for edit routines, whether they are separate programs or parts of other programs.

Program specifications

The edit program in this book edits two types of records: sales and return records. However, the record formats are so similar that one output line format can be used to list both types of invalid transactions. The error fields are highlighted on the error listing by printing an asterisk (*) to the left of each error field. Although the program specifications don't give the rules for editing each of the fields in the transaction records, the rules are given in the extended descriptions for modules 240 and 250. In general, all numeric fields are checked to make sure that they contain valid numeric data that is greater than zero. In addition, the date fields are limit-checked, and the part-number field must contain a number that can be found in the table of valid part numbers.

In actual practice, an edit program like this would probably write the valid transactions on an output tape to be used for subsequent processing. Also, the first heading line on the invalid transaction listing is likely to be dropped after the first page of the report has been printed, so only the column headings would print after page 1. These are minor changes, however, that don't affect the basic design of this program.

VTOC

Since this program is limited in complexity, there aren't too many different ways that the VTOC can be structured. Obviously, the part-number table has to be read and loaded before starting to edit the transaction records. And the total page must be printed after the records are edited. Moreover, all three of these level-1 functions break down into clearly defined subfunctions. In my opinion, then, there isn't much that can be debated in the first three levels of the VTOC shown in section 3.

If there is room for debate, it concerns the edit leg of the VTOC as shown in figure 2-1. For instance, the first question my students usually raise is, why are levels 3 and 4 needed at all? Since only three fields in the sales record differ from those in the return record, why shouldn't one module do the editing for both records?

My answer here is that one of the goals of structured programming is to provide for future changes (maintenance). And though it may be true that only three fields differ today, what about five years from now? That's why I have designed my VTOC to accommodate any changes in either the sales or the return record.

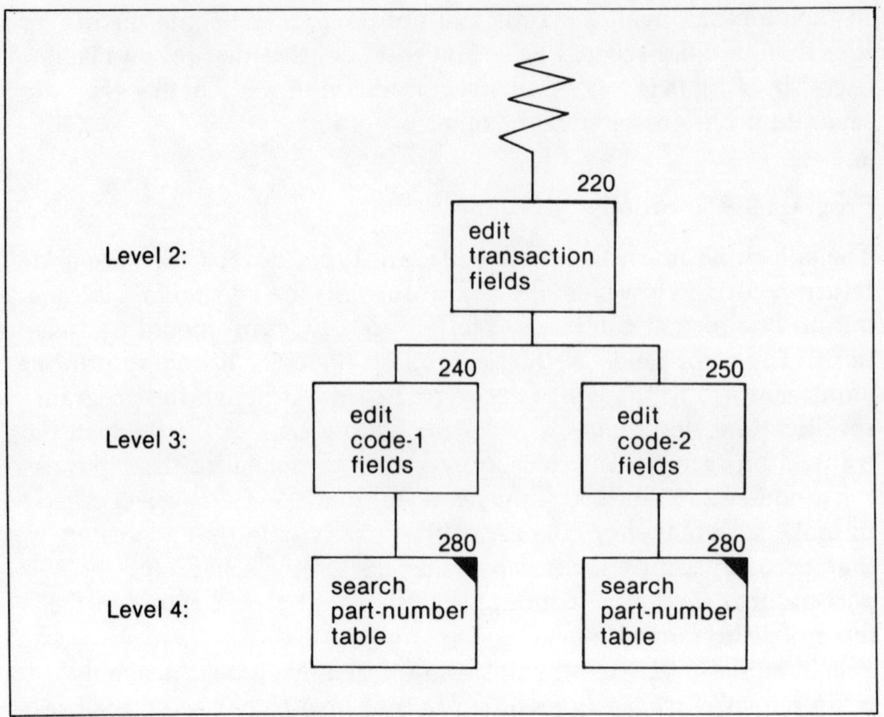

Figure 2-1 The edit leg of the VTOC for the edit program

Of course, there is a point at which it doesn't pay to provide for future changes. If, for example, the only difference between the two records was the return-authorization-code field, I would agree: forget the code-1 and code-2 modules and do all of the editing in module 220. Then, if a change is required later on, it's still a small matter to modify the program.

Where is the break-even point? If I were to set a guideline, it would be this: If more than 20 percent of the fields differ from one type of record to another, use a different edit module for each type of record. Since there are a total of ten different fields in the sales and return records in this edit program and three vary from one record to the next, I recommend separate edit modules.

The next question that usually comes up is, why not add an edit-common-fields module to level 3 as shown in figure 2-2? My objection to this structure is that it would increase the complexity of module 220 considerably since a count must be kept of valid and invalid transactions by transaction type. (To check me out on this point, you may want to review the IPOs for modules 220, 240, and

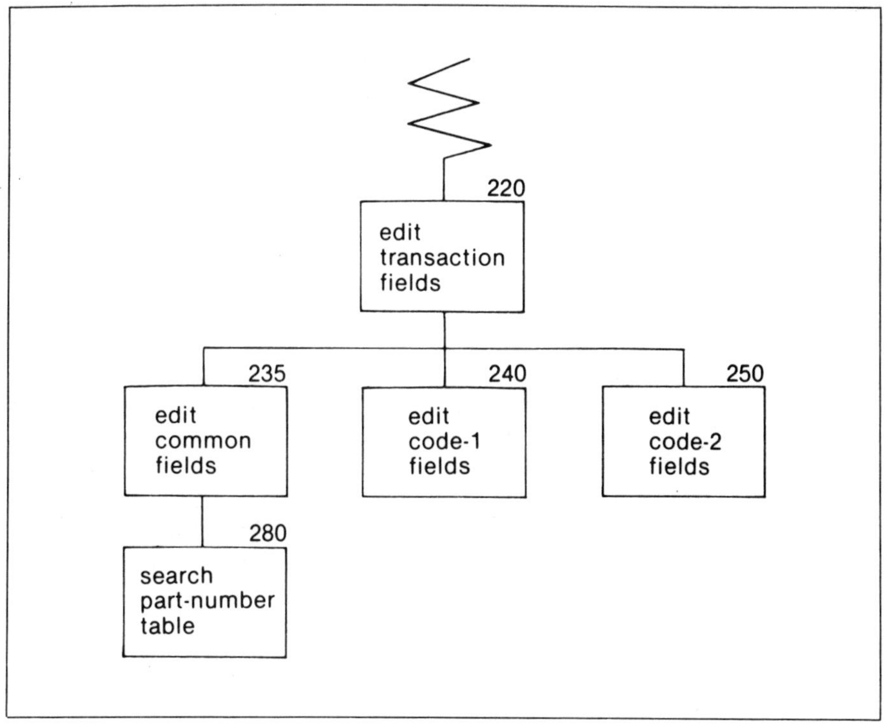

Figure 2-2 An unacceptable structure for using a module that edits the fields that are common to both record types

250.) What's worse, however, the structure shown in figure 2-2 doesn't logically represent the program specifications. So if you want to use a common editing module, I recommend a structure like the one shown in figure 2-3.

The question now becomes, when should you use a common module for editing the fields that are found in both types of records and when should you simply duplicate the code? To me this depends on the amount of code that has to be duplicated. If the records have 20 fields in common, by all means use a common module. If only 3, why not duplicate the coding. In my opinion, this edit program with its 6 duplicate fields is on the borderline.

In summary, I want to remind you that a search function should always be treated as a separate module. Although it will often consist of only a single statement (the SEARCH statement), the code it generates isn't trivial. And in a complex program, a search module is likely to be called by more than one module. In short, treat a search function as you would treat a read or write function: isolate it in its own module.

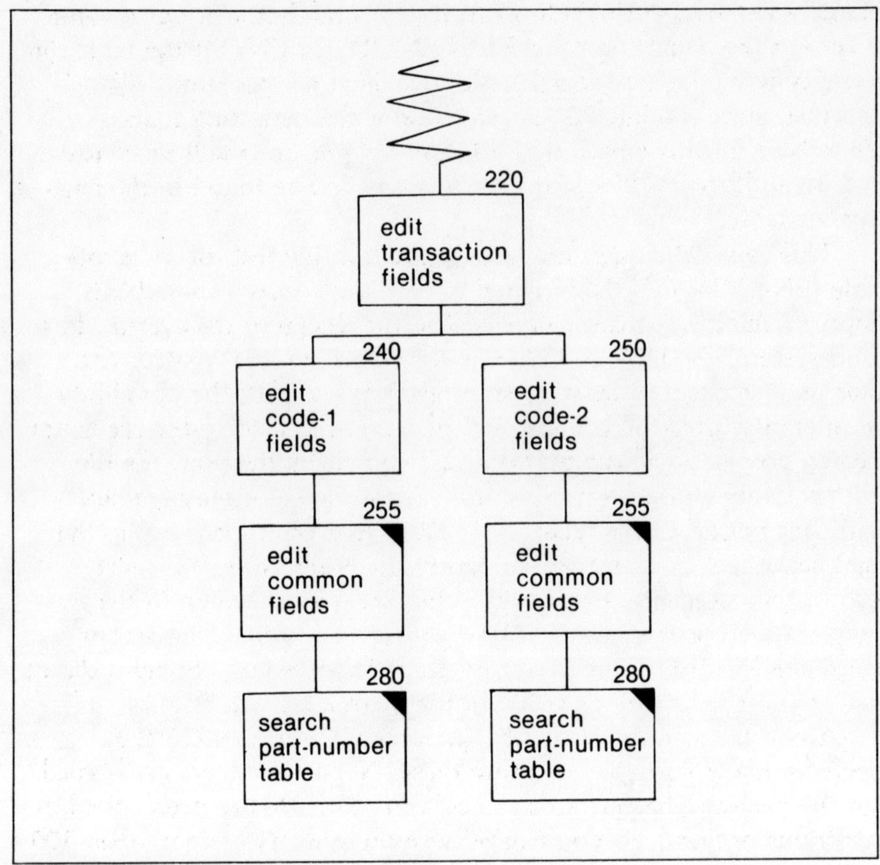

Figure 2-3 An acceptable structure for using a module that edits the fields that are common to both record types

IPOs

000-EDIT-INVENTORY-TRANS Notice that this top-level module contains the code that would traditionally be placed in an initialization or housekeeping module. I'm referring to steps 1 and 2. Furthermore, this module also contains the code that would traditionally be placed in an end-of-job or termination module (steps 6 and 7). This means that subordinates of the top-level module are only created for *functions* that must be done before or after the main processing functions; there should never be an initialization or end-of-job module at any level that contains code that is only related because it's done before or after the main functions of the program.

100-LOAD-PART-NUMBER-TABLE This module will put a value of zero in the entry-count field (PN-ENTRY-COUNT) if the table file is empty (contains no records). Nevertheless, the program will continue, since module 000 doesn't stop if the table isn't loaded properly. And this means that all input transactions will be considered invalid because the part numbers will not be found in the part-number table.

This raises the question, should module 000 test for an empty table (PN-ENTRY-COUNT equal to zero) and stop if the table is empty? I think the answer depends on the design of the system. In a good system, the table file is printed at the time it is created, and later on it is checked by user personnel. As a result, the possibility of an empty table file is very low. In fact, even if the table file is not created properly and the mistake isn't caught by the user, the file will probably contain some records. For instance, it may contain some but not all of the records, or all of the records but not in the right sequence. So a test for an empty file really doesn't protect against the possibility of a faulty table file. Nevertheless, in the interest of eliminating one possible source of trouble, I do recommend checking for an empty table file in module 000, though I didn't want to complicate module 000 in the textbook itself.

Along the same lines, neither module 000 nor module 100 checks to make sure that no more than 100 part numbers are loaded into the part-number table. If the part-number file has been edited in a previous program so you can be sure there won't be more than 100 part-number records, this is no problem. Nevertheless, it can't hurt to check. As a result, I recommend changing step 3 in module 000 so the PERFORM statement will stop executing module 100 (1) when the part-number file reaches EOF or (2) when PN-TABLE-INDEX is greater than 100. (Here again, I didn't include this code because I didn't want to complicate module 000 in the textbook.)

120-PUT-TABLE-ENTRY As I mentioned in the textbook, when you realize that module 120 contains only one statement, you may want to move it up into module 100. This will, of course, change your VTOC.

200-EDIT-INVENTORY-TRAN You might notice that this module does nothing if module 210 detects the end-of-file condition for the transaction file. As a result, the program will not abort if the transaction file is empty.

210-READ-INVENTORY-TRAN The number of transaction records is counted in this read module. This follows the principle of moving code to the lowest-level module whenever there is a choice of where to place it.

220-EDIT-TRANSACTION-FIELDS Linear nesting is used in this module to perform a different edit module for each valid transaction code. If the transaction code isn't valid, the linear nest executes the default code, which (1) highlights the transaction-code field as invalid, (2) moves N to the valid-transaction switch, and (3) adds one to the invalid-transaction-code count. This same type of linear nest can be used for as many different transaction codes as are valid.

230-PRINT-INVALID-LINE Notice that a data name (LINES-ON-PAGE) is used to indicate the number of lines that should be printed on each page, not counting the first heading line. Because this number may have to be changed due to operational changes, you should never use a literal for this purpose. And because page overflow takes place when LINE-COUNT is *greater* than LINES-ON-PAGE, LINES-ON-PAGE should have a value that is one less than the number of lines to be printed on each page, not counting the first heading line.

240-EDIT-CODE-1-FIELDS This module illustrates why the design shown in figure 2-2 shouldn't be used. If the editing for code-1 records is divided over two modules at the same level, it becomes more difficult to keep the count of valid and invalid sales transactions, as is done in step 4.

260-PRINT-REPORT-HEADING Step 10 of this module moves 2 to the SPACE-CONTROL field so a line will be skipped before printing the first invalid record on each page of the listing. Some of my students have suggested that this code really pertains to printing an invalid line (not a heading line) so it should be placed in module 230 (print-invalid-line). I agree with this logic and would find no fault if it were placed after the DO statement in step 2 of module 230. On the other hand, I have followed my principle of moving code down the line when its placement is debatable.

270-WRITE-REPORT-LINE This module writes all the lines on the invalid-transaction listing except the first line on each page (the PAGE-TOP line). After each line is printed, the SPACE-CONTROL value is added to LINE-COUNT (step 2). Thus, LINE-COUNT contains a value equal to the total number of lines printed on a page, not counting the first line. Then, in module 230, LINE-COUNT is compared to LINES-ON-PAGE to determine when page overflow should take place. (Remember that the value of LINES-ON-PAGE doesn't count the first line on the page, either.) Since SPACE-CONTROL can be used in all WRITE statements for a print file except when skipping to the top of a page, this technique for counting the lines per page and testing for page overflow can work for all print files.

280-SEARCH-PART-NUMBER-TABLE As I mentioned earlier, a search routine should always be placed in a separate module since (1) the code it generates isn't trivial and (2) it is likely to be called from several parts of the program.

290-WRITE-PAGE-TOP-LINE Notice that LINE-COUNT is returned to zero in this module (step 2). Although this could also be done in module 260, it is logical here and it follows the down-the-line principle.

300-PRINT-TOTAL-PAGE In a straightforward module like this, I don't think it's necessary to show everything on the IPO. That's why I summarized some of the processing in steps 5 and 6. These steps mean to (1) move the proper data for each total line into each total-line area, (2) move the proper spacing value into the SPACE-CONTROL field, and (3) print the line by calling module 270.

COBOL listing

Because the coding follows the IPOs in a straightforward manner, I don't want to dwell on the coding. However, I do want you to note how the use of the standards and guidelines in this book has led to an extremely readable program. By grouping switches, count fields, and print fields, the programmer has made it easy to find things in the working-storage section of the Data Division. Because the Procedure Division is structured and because indentation and blank comment cards are used within it, it is easy to read and understand from the top down.

Only three modules in the COBOL listing deviate much from the pseudocode used in the IPOs. In module 000, the programmer realized that he needed another date field to compare with the transaction date fields to check their validity. As a result, three COBOL statements are inserted between steps 1 and 2 of the IPO for this module. These statements create constant fields that contain the value of the current year (CURRENT-YEAR) and the preceding year (CURRENT-YEAR-MINUS-1). In a case like this, it would be wise to change the IPO to reflect this coding.

In modules 240 and 250, step 3 of the IPOs is expanded considerably. For instance, step 3 of module 240 becomes seven IF statements. In addition, the programmer has decided to set the VALID-TRAN-SW to N at the end of the module rather than each time an invalid field is detected. He does this by testing to see whether any asterisks (*) were moved into ITL-LINE, thus indicating that one or more invalid fields were detected. If so, he sets the VALID-TRAN-SW to N. Here again, it would be good to change the IPOs to reflect these logic changes. For example, steps 3 and 4 in the

IPO for module 240 should be changed to:

```
3.  IF any remaining fields in ITR-RECORD are invalid
      move '*' to mark error field in ITL-LINE.

4.  IF ITL-LINE not equal to spaces
      move 'N' to VALID-TRAN-SW
      add 1 to INVALID-SALES-COUNT
    ELSE
      add 1 to VALID-SALES-COUNT.
```

Thus, modules 000, 240, and 250 all illustrate the need for IPO changes based on considerations that become apparent as the program is actually coded.

The Extract Program

An extract program reads one or more input files and extracts from them the data needed to prepare an output report. This report may be a simple *listing* in which one line is printed for each input record. It may be a simple *summary report* in which one summary line is printed for each group of input records; for instance, a sales-by-salesman report in which one line is printed for each salesman. Or it may be a *multilevel summary report* in which summary lines are printed for more than one type of group; for instance, a sales-by-customer-within-salesman report in which one line is printed for each customer followed by a summary line for each salesman which is an accumulation of all customer totals. In addition, a report may combine a listing of all records with interspersed summary lines.

An extract program may operate upon the records in a transaction or a master file. It may operate upon the records in two or more files so the program must merge the data from the files. And the report extraction may be done in combination with some other major function like editing or updating.

When a summary report is prepared, the input file must be in sequence based on the data in a *control field.* For instance, item number is the control field if a sales-by-item report is to be prepared, so the transaction file must be in item-number sequence before the extract program is run. Similarly, a file must be in sequence by a control field within a control field if a two-level summary report is to be extracted.

In order to prepare a summary report, the control field from one record must be compared with the control field from the previous record. If the new control field is greater than the old control field, it indicates that a summary line should be printed. If the control fields are equal, it means that the data from the new record should be applied to the group being processed, so no line should be printed. And if the new control field is less than the old control field, it indicates that the input file is not in sequence (an error condition). Needless to say, if a multilevel summary report is to be prepared, the problem is complicated because comparisons must be done based on more than one control field (like customer and salesman number).

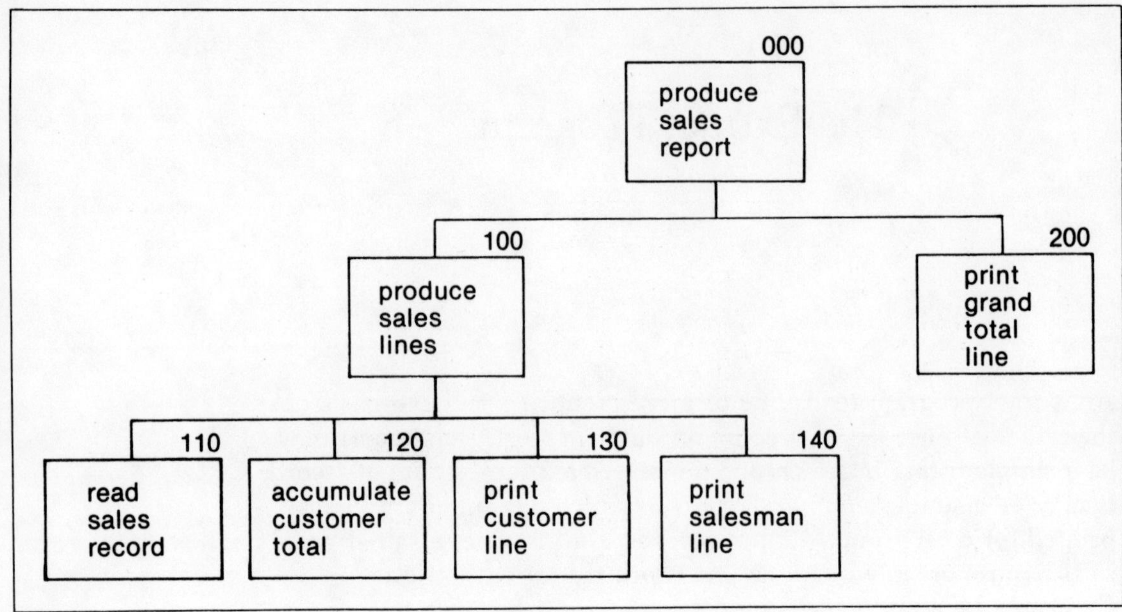

Figure 2-4 The basic structure of the extract program

Program Specifications

The extract program in this book prepares a two-level report from a transaction file of sales records. The input file is in sequence first by customer number, then by salesman number. The report summarizes sales by customer and salesman.

The specifications for this program are unrealistic in several ways. For instance, only three columns of data are required on the sales report when an actual report would probably give more information. Similarly, the input record layout indicates only eight fields when an actual record might contain many more. Finally, a report like this is likely to require salesman and customer names, and this data is likely to be in other files, in which case more than one input file would be required.

Regardless of the simplifications, however, this program is a good model for developing other extract programs. As you will see, it demonstrates the essential procedures required by an extract program. In particular, it shows how two holding fields—one for customer number and one for salesman number—are used so the control fields for one record (the new record) can be compared with the control fields for the previous record (the old record).

VTOC

If you look at the VTOC in section 3, you will see that its basic structure is quite simple, as shown in figure 2-4. The other blocks in the structure chart (150 through 180) represent a general print

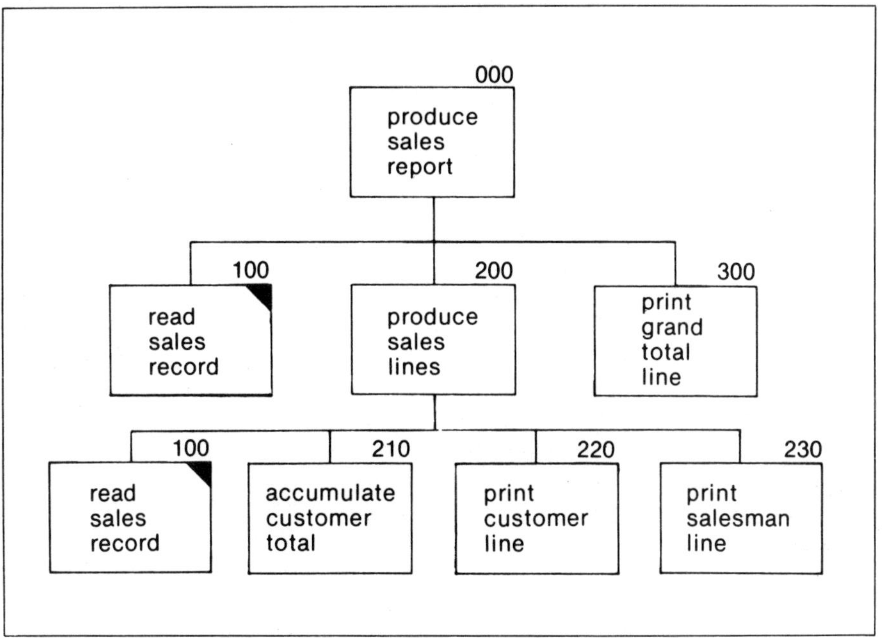

Figure 2-5 A structure for the extract program that shouldn't be implemented because modules 000 and 200 aren't independent of each other

routine that will test for page overflow and print page headings when needed. Because you may be tempted to change the basic structure in figure 2-4, let's talk about two alternatives.

First, if you have written programs like this using traditional methods, you know that the first record read by the program has to be treated differently than the records that follow. As a result, the traditional program normally read and processed the first record in an initialization module. Using this thinking, you may want to use a structure chart like the one shown in figure 2-5. Here, using a common read module, you can read and process the first record in module 000, then process subsequent records via module 200. In fact, other systems of structured programming recommend just this approach.

To me, however, this approach is illogical. And it is a throwback to traditional thinking. When you use the structure shown in figure 2-5, module 200 depends upon the processing done in module 000. As a result, these modules aren't properly independent; they must be closely coordinated. Furthermore, why should this program require a read module as a subordinate to the top-level module when other programs don't? This is procedural, not functional, thinking. In my opinion, then, the structure shown in figure 2-5 will lead you into trouble.

Second, if you proceed on a level-by-level basis (as you should), you may arrive at the basic structure shown in figure 2-6. Although

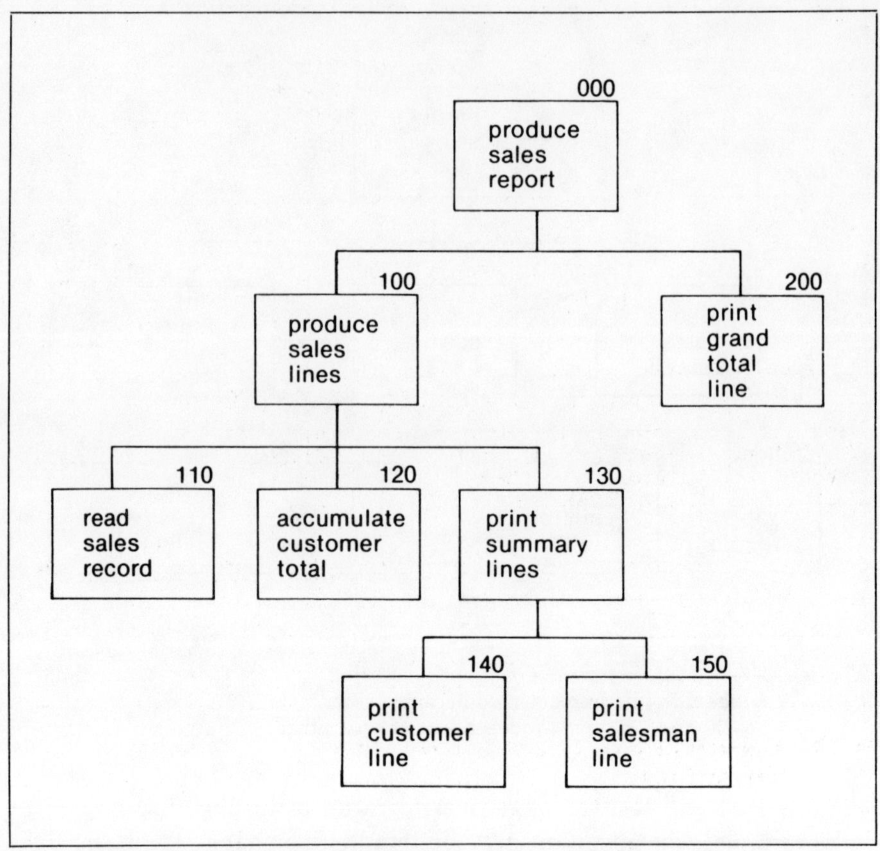

Figure 2-6 An acceptable structure for the extract program

this is perfectly acceptable, it introduces another level of control. Since the control span for module 100 in figure 2-4 is only four, I see no reason for this extra level.

On the other hand, the basic idea presented in figure 2-6 can be useful as you develop reports with more than two types of body lines. If, for example, you are developing a summary report that lists all records and has three levels of totals, you can use this idea to create a VTOC like the one in figure 2-7. This will reduce the control span of the primary control module of level 1, so the IPO diagram and the resultant coding will be simplified.

One final thought about the complete VTOC for this extract program concerns the general print routine (modules 150 through 180). The use of this routine to print all lines in the program assumes that it is okay to skip to the next page at any point in the printing of the report. In some programs, however, you may not

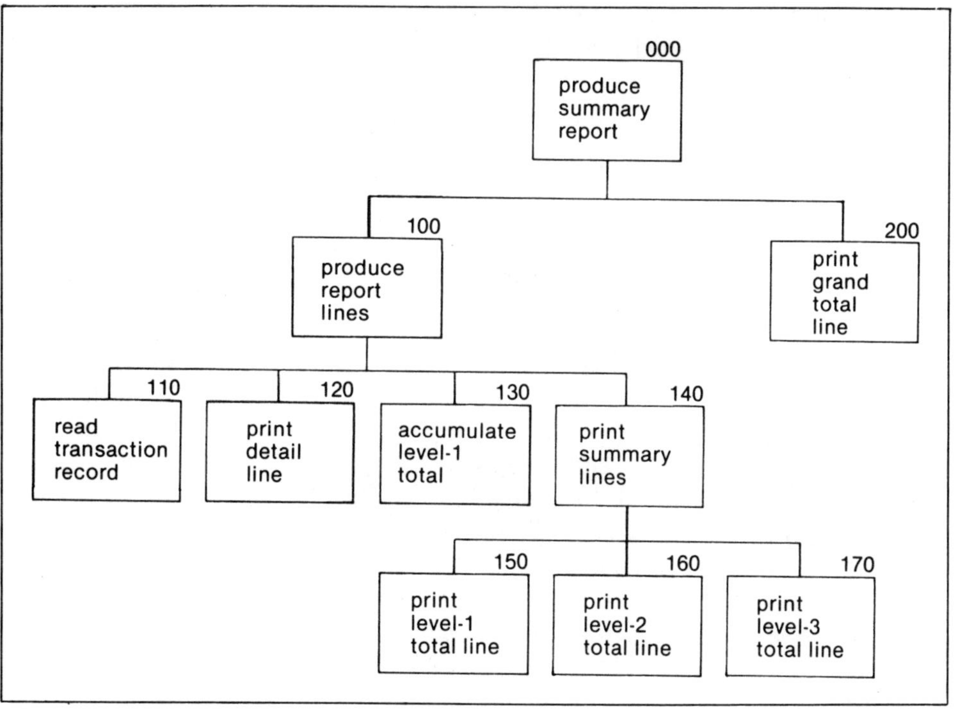

Figure 2-7 A general structure for printing a three-level summary report

want to skip between the printing of related total lines. In this program, for example, you may not want to skip between the printing of a customer total line and a salesman total line. In other words, you may not want the last customer line for a salesman on one page and the salesman total on the next. To make this adjustment, however, would mean only a minor change to the VTOC and to the IPO for module 140. Quite simply, module 170 (the write-report-line module) would be substituted for module 150 as the subordinate module for module 140. This again illustrates how easy it is to modify a well-structured program.

IPOs

100-PRODUCE-SALES-LINES This module illustrates the use of a first-record switch so the first record in a file can be processed differently from the subsequent records. As I mentioned in the VTOC discussion, I think this is a better way of handling the first record than reading and processing it in the top-level module as would be done using the structure in figure 2-5. As you can see, if the transaction file is empty, the first-record processing will be done, but that's all. Since this processing only involves moving one literal and two working-storage fields, the program will not abort, control will return to the top-level module, and the program will end normally.

I want you to notice how easy it is to follow step 2 even though three levels of nesting are used. Also, I want you to notice that all control-field changes are coded within this step, even though some could be moved down-the-line into modules 130 and 140. As a result, the subordinate modules are completely independent, and this module contains all of the control code for the entire program. So if you discover a bug during testing, it should be easy to find its cause. A three-level program will add only one level of nesting, so this code should remain manageable no matter how complex the report is.

You may have noticed that the code in step 2 doesn't provide for an out-of-sequence condition. However, this could easily be added to this module. By moving Y into TRAN-EOF-SW when an out-of-sequence record is read as shown in the IPO in figure 2-8, control is passed back to the top-level module and the program ends. If the system sorts the records just before this extract program is executed, however, I don't feel that this out-of-sequence testing is necessary.

110-READ-SALES-RECORD This module reads one record and, when the end-of-file condition is reached, moves Y to the end-of-file switch and HIGH-VALUES to the salesman-number control field. Then, because TR-SALESMAN-NO will be greater than OLD-SALESMAN-NO, module 100 will print the last customer and salesman total lines before returning control to the top-level module. When coding a program like this, I always define the control fields as alphanumeric (PIC X). And I always use HIGH-VALUES rather than a literal value of all nines to force a control change because you can never be sure that all nines isn't a valid control-field number.

120-ACCUMULATE-CUSTOMER-TOTAL My only caution here is to resist the temptation to put a short module like this in line—that is, within the code of the calling module. As long as it represents a legitimate function (as this module does), it should remain independent. Remember, there is always the possibility that the report or the computations will be expanded, so keeping this module separate provides for easy maintenance.

130-PRINT-CUSTOMER-LINE This module illustrates the extended meaning I allow for the verb *print.* Besides printing the customer line, this module adds the customer total to the salesman total and resets the customer total to zero.

140-PRINT-SALESMAN-LINE This module also illustrates the

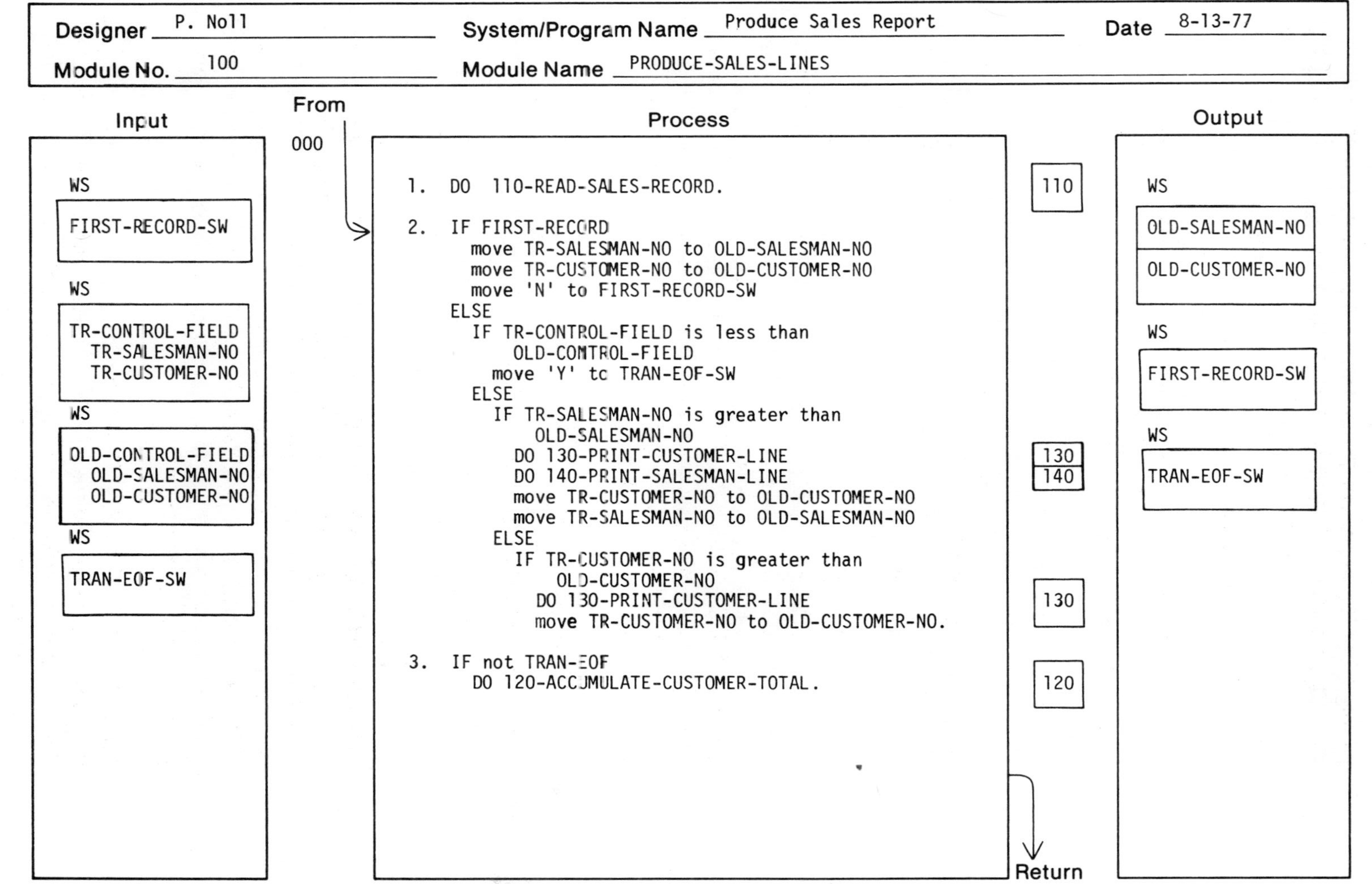

Figure 2-8 HIPO diagram for module 100 of the extract program with a test for an out-of-sequence file

extended meaning of the verb *print*. Here, the print module adds the salesman total to the grand total and resets the salesman total to zero.

150-PRINT-REPORT-LINE This module is the top module in the general print routine. In step 1, it tests to see whether or not page overflow should take place, and, if it should, it calls module 160. After page overflow takes place and the page heading is printed, the next report line is moved into the output area for the print file and the line is printed via module 170. This should explain why modules 130 and 140 move the lines to be printed into a work area called NEXT-REPORT-LINE rather than the output area for the print file. At the time that module 150 is called, you don't know whether heading lines will be printed next or whether summary lines will be printed.

COBOL listing

The one thing I want to point out in the COBOL listing is the coding for module 100. Note how readable it is even though three levels of nesting are used and all control code changes are embedded within this nest.

The Sequential-Update Program

The sequential-update program is the workhorse program in most data processing installations. It is used to keep a wide variety of files up-to-date. In many cases, an edit program is used to validate transaction files before they are processed by an update program. And extract programs are often used to prepare reports from data stored in the up-to-date master files.

The term *update* is a general term that includes adding records to a file, deleting records from a file, and changing records within a file. When records are changed, it can mean simple maintenance such as changing the address of a customer record in a customer file. Or it can mean increasing or decreasing the values in fields based on transaction activity such as sales or receipts into inventory. In some cases, more than one transaction file is used to update a master file in a single update program. For instance, three transaction files—one for receipts, one for returns, and one for sales—can be used to update an inventory master file.

The general procedure that is used in a sequential-update program is to read one record from each transaction file and one from the master file and to compare the control fields of these records. If the control field of a transaction and the control field of a master are equal, it means that the transaction should be either a deletion or a change record, and processing continues accordingly. If the control field of the transaction is greater than that of the master, it means there are no more transactions for the master (or perhaps there were none at all) and the master should remain as it is. If the control field of the transaction is less than that of the master, it means that the transaction didn't have a matching master record, so the transaction should represent an addition record which should be added to the master file. Needless to say, the transaction files have to be in the same control-number sequence as the master file; for instance, a transaction file has to be in item-number sequence before it can be used to update an inventory file.

Since a sequential file can be stored on tape or on a direct-access device, the processing within a sequential-update program may vary depending on the device used. When tape files are used, for example, the original master file (the old master) must be read in its entirety and the updated master file (the new master) must be written on a different tape. The new master tape will include changed and added records as well as unaffected records, but it won't include deleted records.

Although a sequential file on disk can be updated in the same way, it's not always necessary to rewrite the entire master file. If, for example, only deletions and changes are to be processed, the changed records can be rewritten in their original locations on the disk file. To indicate that master records are deleted, a delete code can be moved into the first byte of a master record and the master record can be rewritten in its original disk location. To add records to the file, however, does require that the entire file be rewritten in a new disk location. Regardless of these procedural variations, all sequential-update programs have the same general structural requirements.

Program specifications

The sequential-update program in this book updates an inventory master file stored on tape based on three types of transaction records: addition records, change records, and deletion records. As a result, it provides for all possible combinations in an update program. If a change or deletion record is unmatched in the master file, it indicates a transaction error. And if an addition record is matched, it indicates a transaction error. Such records are to be written on a file of error transactions.

Although this program is realistic in that it provides for all update possibilities, the record layouts themselves are unrealistic. In actual practice, an inventory master record has many more fields than are shown in the record layout. Similarly, the change and addition records would normally contain more fields. In designing this problem, however, I wanted to focus on the logic requirements of the program, not on the input and output.

The model solution assumes that the transaction records have been sorted and edited before the update run. As a result, it doesn't sequence-check the transaction records, and it doesn't check for error conditions that should have been caught in the editing run. In particular, the model program assumes that the edit program will check to make sure that there aren't two or more addition records with the same item number.

VTOC

Although this program has limited complexity because the transaction and master record layouts have been simplified, the VTOC in figure 2-9 is a good model for most update programs. I have used it for several different update programs and have found it easy to adapt from one program to another. In fact, I use the same IPOs and most of the same code for modules 000, 100, 110, 120, 130, 140,

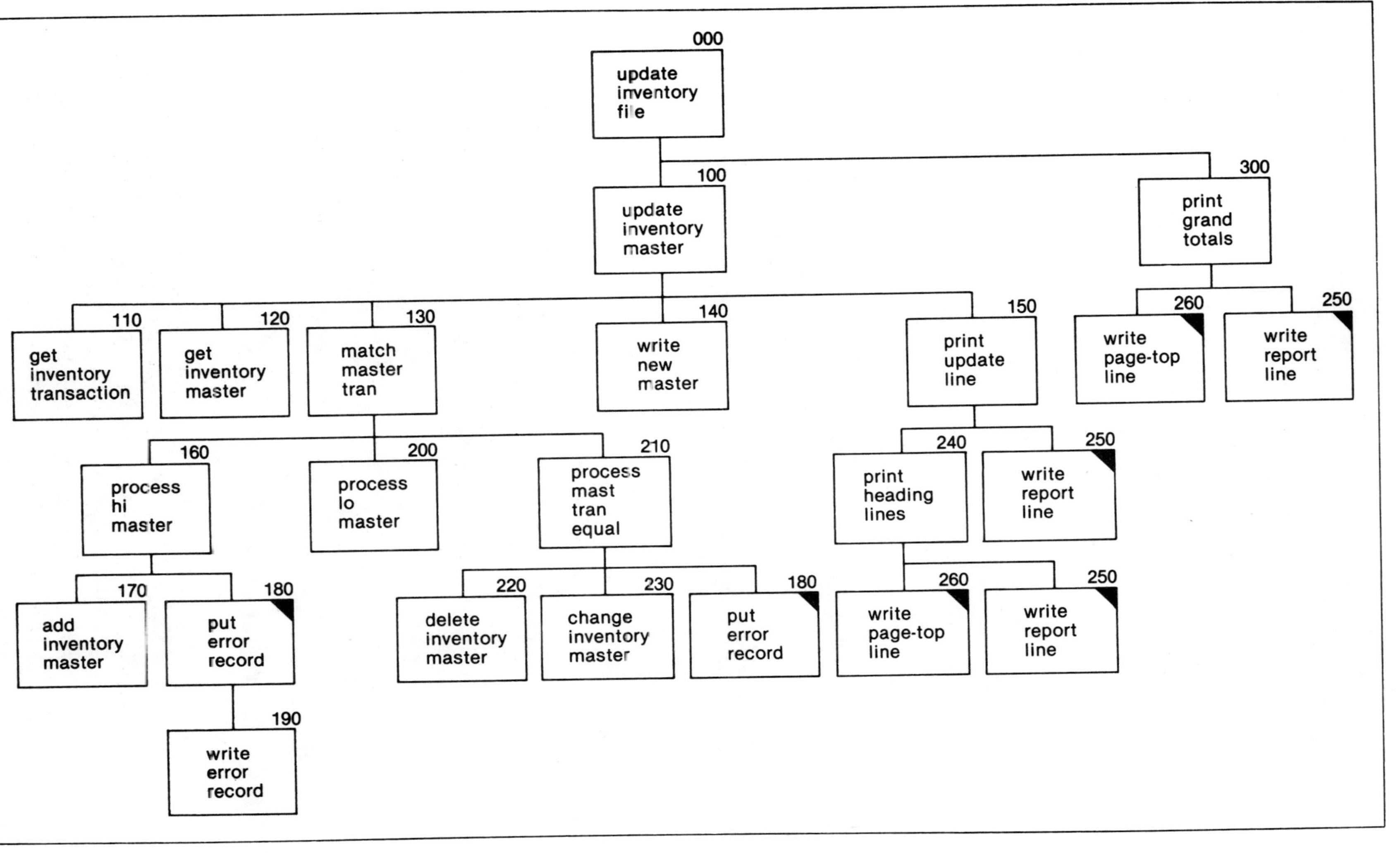

Figure 2-9 The complete VTOC for the sequential-update program

160, 200, and 210 each time I write a new update program. The primary changes, then, are in the work modules, not the control modules. Specifically, the add, delete, and change modules reflect major changes as you go from one update program to another. Furthermore, if your update program only processes changes, you won't have an addition or deletion module at all; and so forth.

Although an update program can be designed in many different ways, the idea is to find a structure that is simple, settle on it, and use it as a model for all of the update programs that you write. I've settled on the one in figure 2-9, so it's hard for me to accept VTOCs that differ significantly from it.

Some of my students, however, criticize my solution. They say that my "match" module (130) and my "process" modules (160, 200, and 210) don't represent functions; they say these modules are procedural. As a result, they prefer a solution like the one in figure 2-10. Here, they use the same work modules as I do (170, 220, 230, and 180), but they've consolidated the logic from my match and process modules into a single module (130). I see their point, and I have no argument with this solution (though I still prefer mine).

IPOs

000-UPDATE-INVENTORY-FILE Note that step 3 performs module 100 until a condition named ALL-RECORDS-PROCESSED is met. This condition means that all of the records in both the transaction and the master file have been read and processed. This switch is turned on in module 210 when the control fields for both master and transaction are equal to HIGH-VALUES.

100-UPDATE-INVENTORY-MASTER This module relies on four switches: one that indicates that another transaction should be read, one that indicates that another master should be read, one that indicates that a master record should be written, and one that indicates that a line should be printed on the update listing. When one or more of these switches are on, the corresponding module is performed and then the switch is turned off. Note that the switch could be turned off in a lower-level module, but doing it here keeps the logic obvious.

110-GET-INVENTORY-TRANSACTION Unlike the previous programs, this program doesn't turn an end-of-file switch on when the end-of-file condition for the transaction file is detected. Instead, it moves HIGH-VALUES into the transaction control field, which forces a greater-than comparison when the transaction control field is compared to the master control field in module 130. As I said in the discussion of the extract program, I believe you should define all control fields as alphanumeric (PIC X). Then you should move

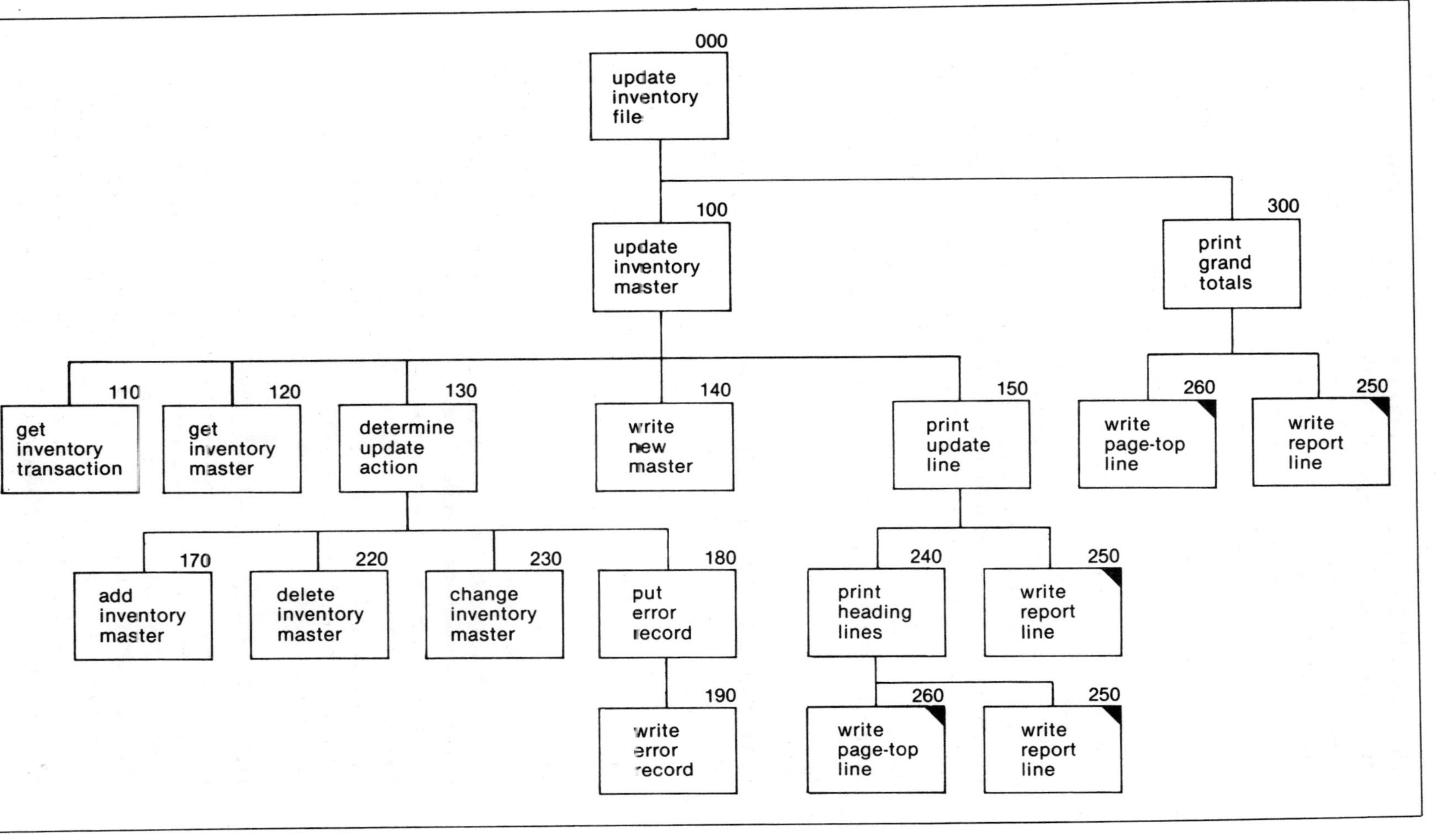

Figure 2-10 An acceptable alternate VTOC for the sequential-update program

HIGH-VALUES (not nines) into the master control field when the end of the file is reached and you want to force a greater-than comparison.

120-GET-INVENTORY-MASTER As in module 110, this read module doesn't use an end-of-file switch. Instead, it moves HIGH-VALUES into the master control field to force a greater-than comparison.

130-MATCH-MASTER-TRAN This module consists of only one step that covers the three conditions that are possible when the master and the transaction control fields are compared. Because HIGH-VALUES is moved into the control fields when there are no more records in the transaction or master files, this code will work if the transaction file is empty and it will process all records in both files.

160-PROCESS-HI-MASTER When the control field in the master record is greater than the one in the transaction record, it indicates that the transaction is unmatched. That means no master record has the same control-field number as the transaction. As a result, the transaction should be an addition. If it isn't, it's an error. The code for these conditions is embodied in a single IF-ELSE statement in this module.

170-ADD-INVENTORY-MASTER This module prepares for writing a new master record and printing a line on the update listing. It also turns three switches on: the write-master switch, the print-update switch, and the need-transaction switch. After these functions are performed, module 100 turns off the switches.

180-PUT-ERROR-RECORD If a transaction is invalid (a matched addition or an unmatched change or deletion), this module writes the transaction on an error file. It also turns the need-transaction switch on so another transaction will be read.

200-PROCESS-LO-MASTER If the master control field is lower than the transaction control field, it means (1) that there are no more transactions to be processed for this master record or (2) that there were no transactions at all for this master record. In either case, the master record should be written on the new master file. As a result, this module prepares for writing the new master and turns on the write-master and need-master switches. Once again, these switches are turned off by module 100 after the required functions are performed.

210-PROCESS-MAST-TRAN-EQUAL If the master control field is equal to the transaction control field, it means the transaction should be a change or deletion record. If not, the transaction is invalid. On the other hand, if the master control field is equal to HIGH-VALUES, it means that both files have reached the end-of-file condition (since the master and transaction are equal, both control fields must contain HIGH-VALUES). In this case, the all-records-processed switch should be turned on. This code is embodied in an IF-statement nest in this module.

220-DELETE-INVENTORY-MASTER This module prepares for printing a line on the update listing. Then, because no master record should be written on the new master file for this control field (it is deleted), the need-master switch is turned on. In addition, the print-update and need-transaction switches are turned on.

230-CHANGE-INVENTORY-MASTER This module changes the old master record in working storage and prepares for printing a line on the update listing (steps 1, 2, and 3). In addition, it turns the print-update and need-transaction switches on. Note that the write-master switch isn't turned on yet because this program provides for more than one change record for a single master record. As a result, the write-master switch is only turned on in module 200, the process-lo-master module.

COBOL listing

Because the COBOL code closely corresponds to the pseudocode used in the IPOs, the COBOL listing for this program should be easy for you to understand. Note that all of the paragraphs in the Procedure Division are short and manageable. However, if a more realistic layout is used for the master and change records, module 230 could easily exceed a page of code and still be perfectly understandable.

When coding this program, the programmer decided to use condition names for each type of transaction. He thought this would improve the program's readability. In TR-RECORD, then, you can find the condition names CHANGE, DELETION, and ADDITION assigned to the acceptable values for TR-ACTION-CODE. This in turn means that the code for modules 160 and 210 differs slightly from the pseudocode in the IPOs. For instance, the IPO for module 160 says

```
IF TR-ACTION-CODE is A
```

and the COBOL code says

```
IF ADDITION
```

Because this is a trivial difference, I wouldn't insist on changing the IPO in a case like this, although you certainly wouldn't be wrong in doing so.

The Random-Update Program

Although most files are updated on a sequential basis, it is sometimes more practical to update them on a random basis. If, for example, a file must be available to some teleprocessing program on a random basis, it may be efficient to update it randomly. The alternative in such a case is to sort the file, update it on a sequential basis, and reload the file for random access. Similarly, if the transaction activity of a file is very low, it may be more efficient to update on a random basis, rather than to sort, update, and reload.

In actual practice, most files that can be accessed on a random basis are stored in some sort of indexed file organization. In this case, the records can be accessed sequentially as well as randomly. As a result, these files are likely to be updated sequentially. However, if the activity for the file is very low, it may be more efficient to update an indexed file on a random basis.

When updating on a random basis, records can be changed, deleted from, or added to the file. The general procedure is to get a valid transaction and to randomly access and read the master record with the same control-field number (or *key*). If the transaction is an addition record and a matching master record *can* be found, it indicates an error condition (a duplicate). If the transaction is a change or a deletion record and a matching master record *can't* be found, it also indicates an error condition.

In many types of file organization, a deleted record isn't actually removed from the file; instead, a deletion code is moved into its first storage position indicating that the record is no longer active. For instance, HIGH-VALUES is moved into the first byte of an ISAM record to indicate that it is deleted when running under IBM's OS/VS. Then, all programs that process the file must ignore any records with the deletion code.

Depending on the file organization and device used, it may pay to sort the transactions before the update run. Since an ISAM file is loaded in sequence, for example, sorting the input transactions before using them to randomly update the file will reduce the access-mechanism time required for the update run. As a result, you will often find COBOL sorts within random-update programs. Sorting will also group the transactions so you won't have to read a master record more than once if more than one transaction record applies to it.

Because transaction data should always be edited before it is used to update a master file, an edit program is commonly run before a random-update run. In some cases, however, the edit routines will be contained within the update program itself. Then, only valid transactions will be used to update the master file, while the invalid transactions are listed so they can be corrected and resubmitted for processing.

Program specifications

The random-update program in this book updates an inventory master file based on only one type of transaction: receipts to inventory. Since a random update only operates on the master records affected by the transactions, this is acceptable in terms of efficiency. In fact, it's not uncommon for a random-update program to process only one type of transaction, one of low volume, while a sequential-update program for the same file processes the high-volume types of transactions. Since a sequential-update program operates on all of the records in a master file, processing receipt records alone would not be practical for sequential files.

As before, the record layouts for this program are unrealistic. In actual practice, an inventory master record would contain many more fields, and a receipt record would contain more fields and would be used to update more than one field in the master record. As before, however, I want you to concentrate on the logic of the program, not the input and output requirements. Rest assured that the logic and structure shown in the solution will work for a random-update program no matter how many fields the transaction and master records contain.

Because the input transaction file is in random order and the valid-transaction output file must be in item-number sequence, a sort is required within this program. Since sorted transactions can improve the efficiency of a random update on an indexed sequential file, this sort should be done before the update portion of the program.

Although the specifications don't give the detailed editing rules for the receipt records, you can find them in the extended description for module 470. The invalid-transaction listing illustrates how invalid fields can be highlighted by placing a message in the error-code column of the listing.

VTOC

My VTOC for this program is given in figure 2-11. Note that the edit leg of the VTOC disposes of invalid transactions so only valid transactions are passed back to module 400. Note also that the use of the COBOL SORT statement forces me to use the structure

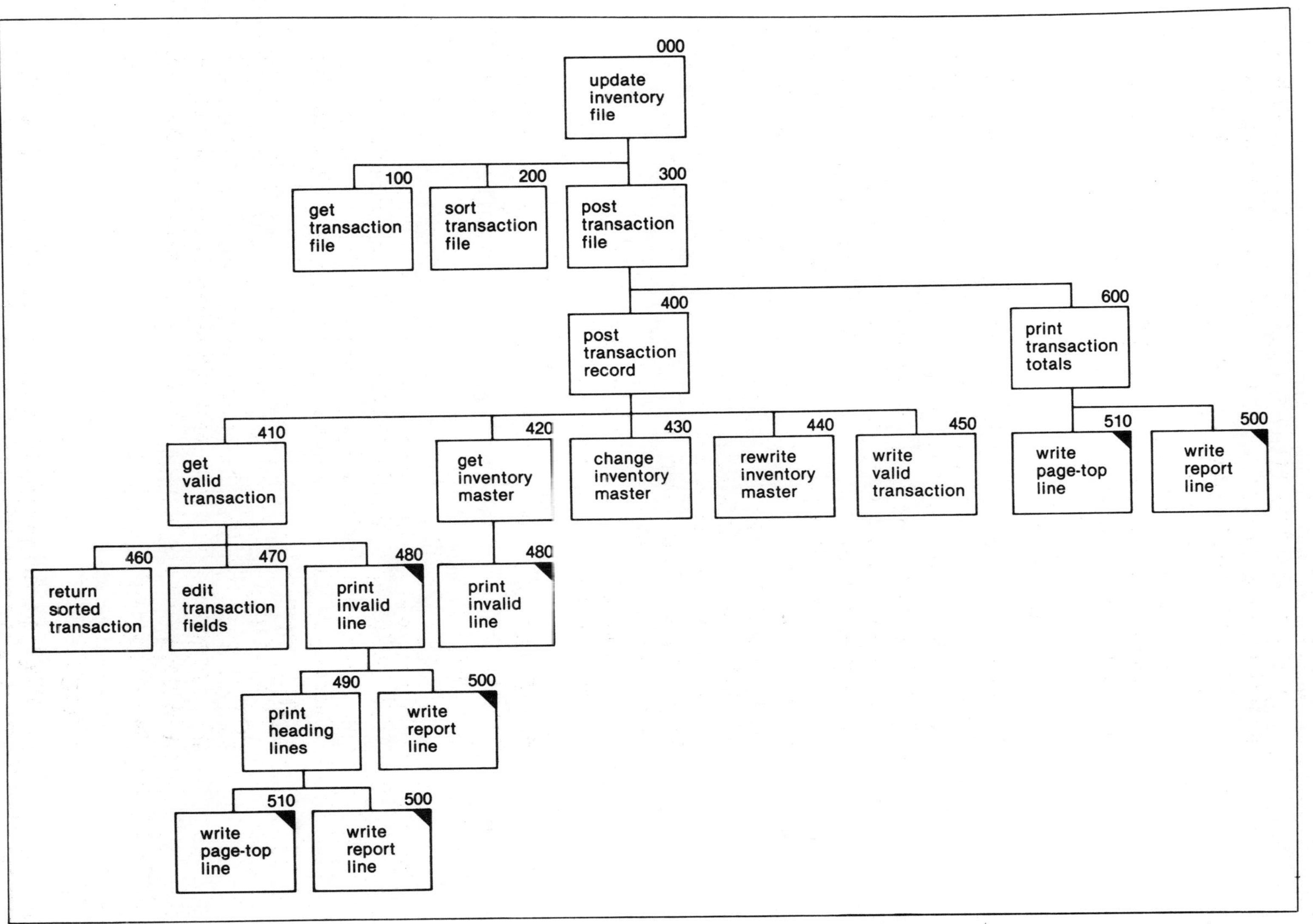

Figure 2-11 The complete VTOC for the random-update program

shown in the top three levels of the chart. Module 300 is actually the output procedure for the SORT statement, so it becomes in effect a top-level module for the processing done by the program after the sorting is done. This is explained in detail in the text, so I won't dwell on it here.

Although there are many ways that a program like this can be structured, figure 2-11 gives a structure that is adaptable to a wide range of problems. A minor variation of this chart is given in figure 2-12, which is explained in more detail in the text. Briefly, though, the edit leg in this VTOC doesn't dispose of the invalid transactions, so it must pass an invalid-transaction code back to module 400 to tell it to print a line on the invalid-transaction listing. Similarly, module 420, the get-inventory-master module, must pass an invalid-transaction code to module 400 when the master record can't be found so the invalid transaction will be listed.

Both of these VTOCs are good models for random updates that you might write in the future. Although the problem specifies ISAM file organization, the basic structure can be used no matter what file organization you're dealing with. And if additions and deletions are combined with changes, it is a small matter to incorporate them into the basic structure. For instance, figure 2-13 gives a VTOC for updating a master file based on change, deletion, and addition transactions. It is a variation of the basic structure shown in figure 2-11. Here, the change and deletion modules will have to pass an invalid-transaction code to module 400 if the master record can't be found so a line will be printed on the invalid-transaction listing. Similarly, the addition module will have to pass an invalid-transaction code if an active master record with the same key can be found (a duplicate). If no duplicate is found, module 450 calls module 510 to write the inventory master. If a duplicate is found but the delete switch is on, module 450 calls module 500 to rewrite the added master in the deleted master's space.

IPOs

000-UPDATE-INVENTORY-FILE This top-level module contains the SORT statement because the transaction file is to be sorted before the master file is updated. If the sort fails at any time during the execution of the SORT statement, the program will continue with step 4. This step will display a message indicating that the sort failed if the SORT-RETURN code is anything but zero. After the sort is completed, all of the processing is done in the output procedure of the SORT statement, so the top-level module of the update portion of the program is module 300.

300-POST-TRANSACTION-FILE This module, which is the start of the output procedure for the SORT statement, performs module

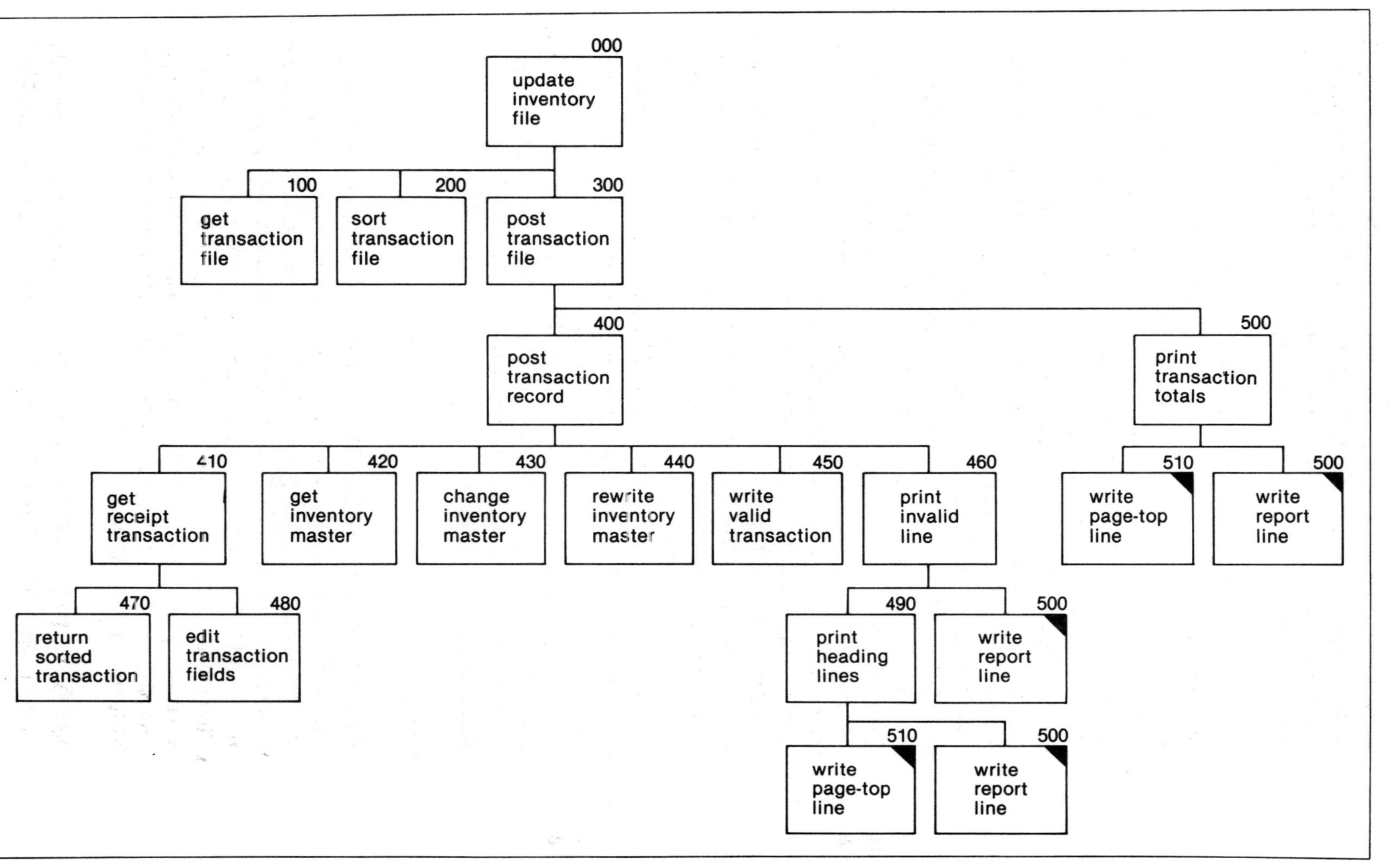

Figure 2-12 An acceptable alternate VTOC for the random-update program

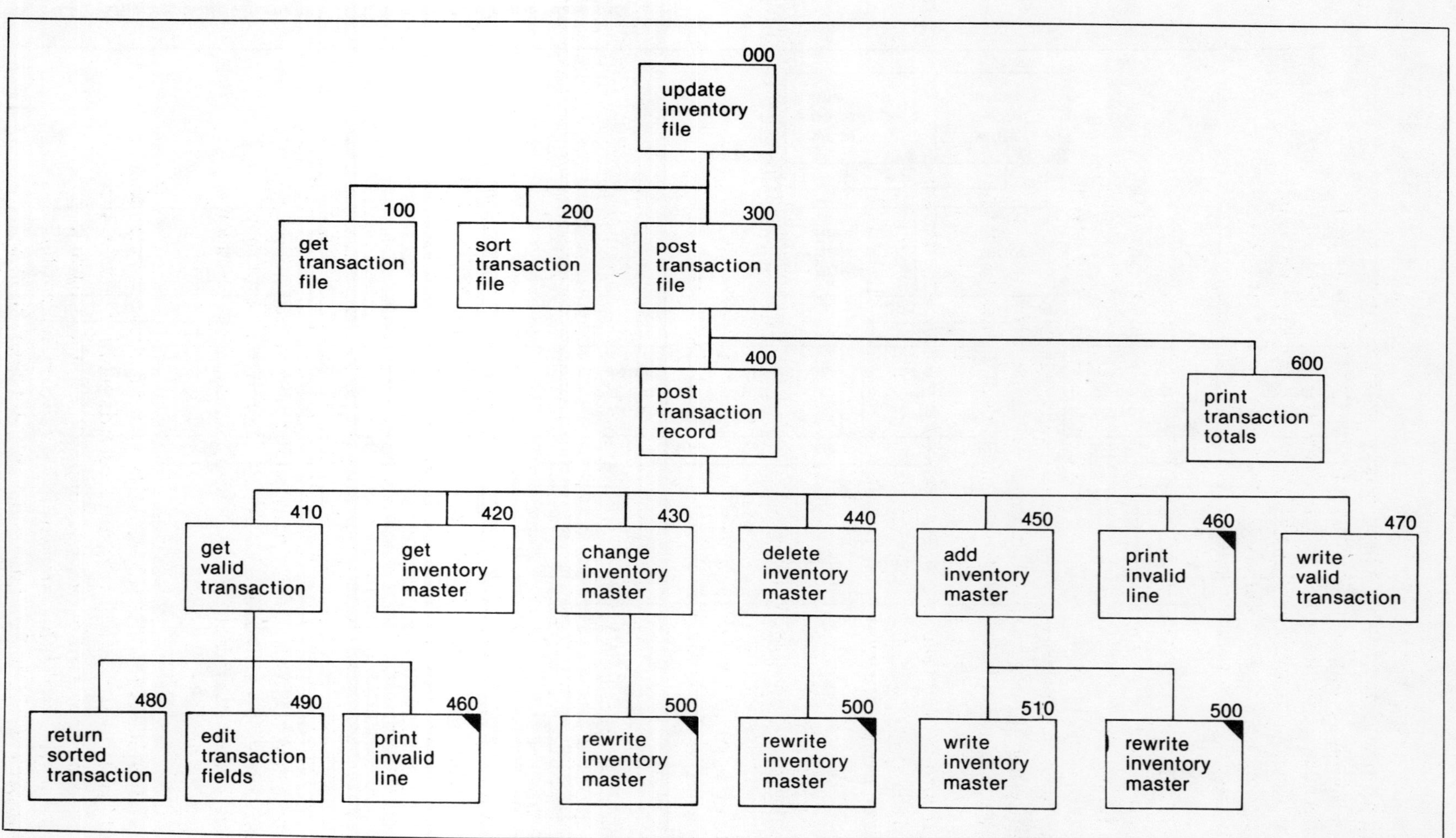

Figure 2-13 The basic structure for a random-update program that processes change, deletion, and addition records (based on the VTOC in figure 2-11)

400 until all transaction records have been processed. Then, it performs module 600 to print the totals on the invalid-transaction listing. Because all of the remaining modules in this program are part of the output procedure of the SORT statement, the third step in this module branches to 300-EXIT, which will be the last paragraph in the output-procedure section.

400-POST-TRANSACTION-RECORD This module uses a compound condition in step 1 so only valid transactions are used to update the master file. Then, in step 2, if the master record is found, this module does the updating by performing the change and rewrite modules. This is the simplest way of handling the update process, but if more than one transaction applies to a single master record, the master will be read and written more than once, which is not an efficient process. As a result, this module could be changed so the master record is only read and written once, regardless of how many transactions apply to it. If only one receipt record is possible for any one master record, however, there is no point in coding the module any differently.

After a valid transaction is processed, step 3 turns VALID-TRAN-SW off. Otherwise, step 1 would never perform module 410 again since the condition VALID-TRAN would already be met. Although this switch could be turned off in lower-level modules, turning it off in this control module improves the clarity of the program.

420-GET-INVENTORY-MASTER This module tries to read the master record that has the same control-field number as the transaction record. If the master record is read, the module checks to see whether the delete switch (the first field in the master record) is on. If it is, it means that the master is no longer active, so it's the same as if no master were found. In either of these two cases, N is moved to the master-found switch and an invalid line is printed on the invalid-transaction listing.

430-CHANGE-INVENTORY-MASTER This module is unrealistic since it will consist of only one statement when it's coded. As I have mentioned, several fields are normally changed in an actual update program. Even if this module does consist of only one statement, however, you should resist the temptation to code it in line since it represents a complete function.

460-RETURN-SORTED-TRANSACTION This module contains the RETURN statement that will return the sorted records from the sort so they can be processed by the update portion of the program. In other words, the RETURN statement is logically equivalent to a READ statement. COBOL requires that this statement be in an output-procedure section, so this program must be divided into two sections: one for all paragraphs preceding module 300, one for all paragraphs thereafter.

470-EDIT-TRANSACTION-FIELDS The extended description for this module gives the rules to be used when editing the receipt transactions.

COBOL listing

Because the coding closely follows the IPO diagrams, you should have no trouble understanding the COBOL listing. If you haven't used the SORT statement, however, you may want to note the use of sections and the use of the EXIT paragraph at the end of the program.

E17WK
38

Section

3

MODEL PROGRAMS

This section presents the four programming problems along with their complete solutions. The programs in sequence are the edit, the report extract, the sequential update, and the random update with sorting. For each program, the problem specifications are followed by the VTOC, the IPOs in sequence, the COBOL listing, and sorted cross-reference listings. The programs were compiled and tested on a System/370 Model 158 running under VS1.

The Edit Program

System flowchart:

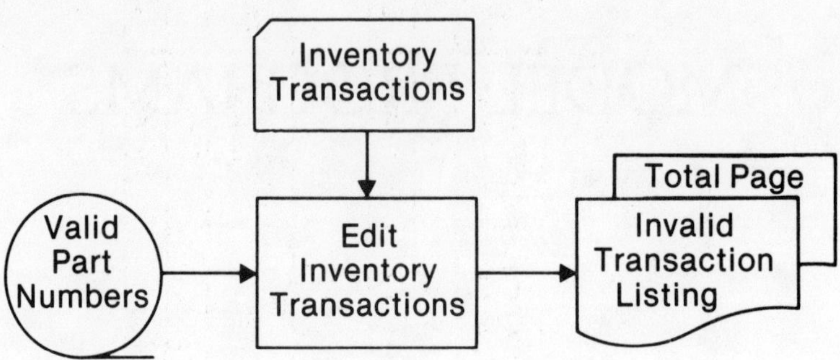

Narrative:

1. Detailed editing specifications for each type of transaction will be developed later on. For both transaction types, however, the part number must be matched against the valid part numbers in the valid-part-number file. If no match is found, the part number will be considered invalid.

2. The valid-part-number file has a maximum of 100 records in it. These records are in order of transaction frequency; the first part number has the most activity, the last part number has the least.

3. The output listing must be printed in the same order that the transactions are read.

4. The totals for this program are to be printed on a separate output page.

Record Layouts:

Valid Part Number Records

Field Name	Part Number	Date of Last Price Change	Unit Cost	Unit Price
Characteristics	X(5)	9(6)	9999V99	9999V99
Position	1–5	6–11	12–17	18–23

Sales Transactions

Field Name	Update Code	Tran. Type	Customer Order No.	Order Date	Branch Number	Salesman Number	Customer Number	Quantity	Part Number	Unused
Characteristics	C	1	X(10)	9(6)	X(2)	X(3)	X(5)	9(5)	X(5)	X(4)
Position	1	2	3–12	13–18	19–20	21–23	24–28	29–33	34–38	39- 42

Return Transactions

Field Name	Update Code	Tran. Type	Customer Memo No.	Return Date	Unused	Customer Number	Quantity	Part Number	Return Authorization Code
Characteristics	C	2	X(10)	9(6)	X(5)	X(5)	9(5)	X(5)	X(4)
Position	1	2	3–12	13–18	19–23	24–28	29–33	34–38	39–42

Output format:

```
HDG-LINE-1       99-99-99     INVALID SALES AND RETURN TRANSACTIONS   PAGE 999

HDG-LINE-2     TRAN ------------------- * INDICATES ERROR FIELDS -----------------
HDG-LINE-3     CODE    REF NO         DATE     BR SLSMN    CUST      QTY     PART    AUTH

ITL-LINE       *X1  *XXXXXXXXXX  *999999  *XX  *XXX  *XXXXX  *99999  *XXXXX

ITL-LINE       *X2  *XXXXXXXXXX  *999999              *XXXXX  *99999  *XXXXX  *XXXX

ITL-LINE       *XX   XXXXXXXXXX   999999   XX   XXX   XXXXX   99999   XXXXX   XXXX


Total page:

TOTAL-LINE-1   SUMMARY FOR SALES-RETURN VERIFICATION RUN OF 99-99-99

TOTAL-LINE-2   VALID   SALES            99,999
TOTAL-LINE-3           RETURNS          99,999
TOTAL-LINE-4               TOTAL        99,999 *

TOTAL-LINE-5   INVALID SALES            99,999
TOTAL-LINE-6           RETURNS          99,999
TOTAL-LINE-7               TOTAL        99,999 *

TOTAL-LINE-8   INVALID TRAN CODES       99,999 *

TOTAL-LINE-9   TRANSACTIONS PROCESSED   99,999 * *
```

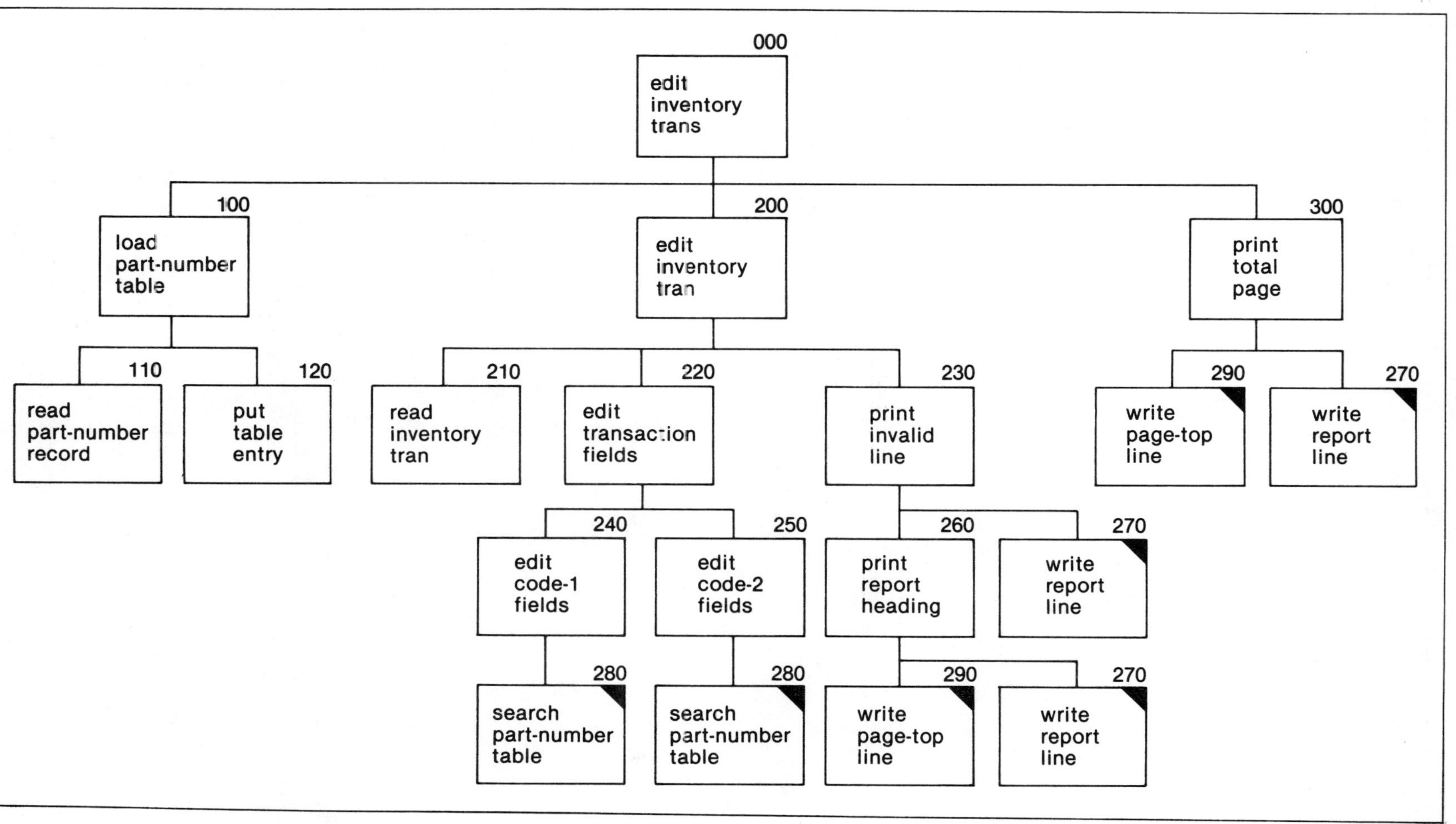
000
edit inventory trans
100
load part-number table
200
edit inventory tran
300
print total page
110
read part-number record
120
put table entry
210
read inventory tran
220
edit transaction fields
230
print invalid line
290
write page-top line
270
write report line
240
edit code-1 fields
250
edit code-2 fields
260
print report heading
270
write report line
280
search part-number table
280
search part-number table
290
write page-top line
270
write report line

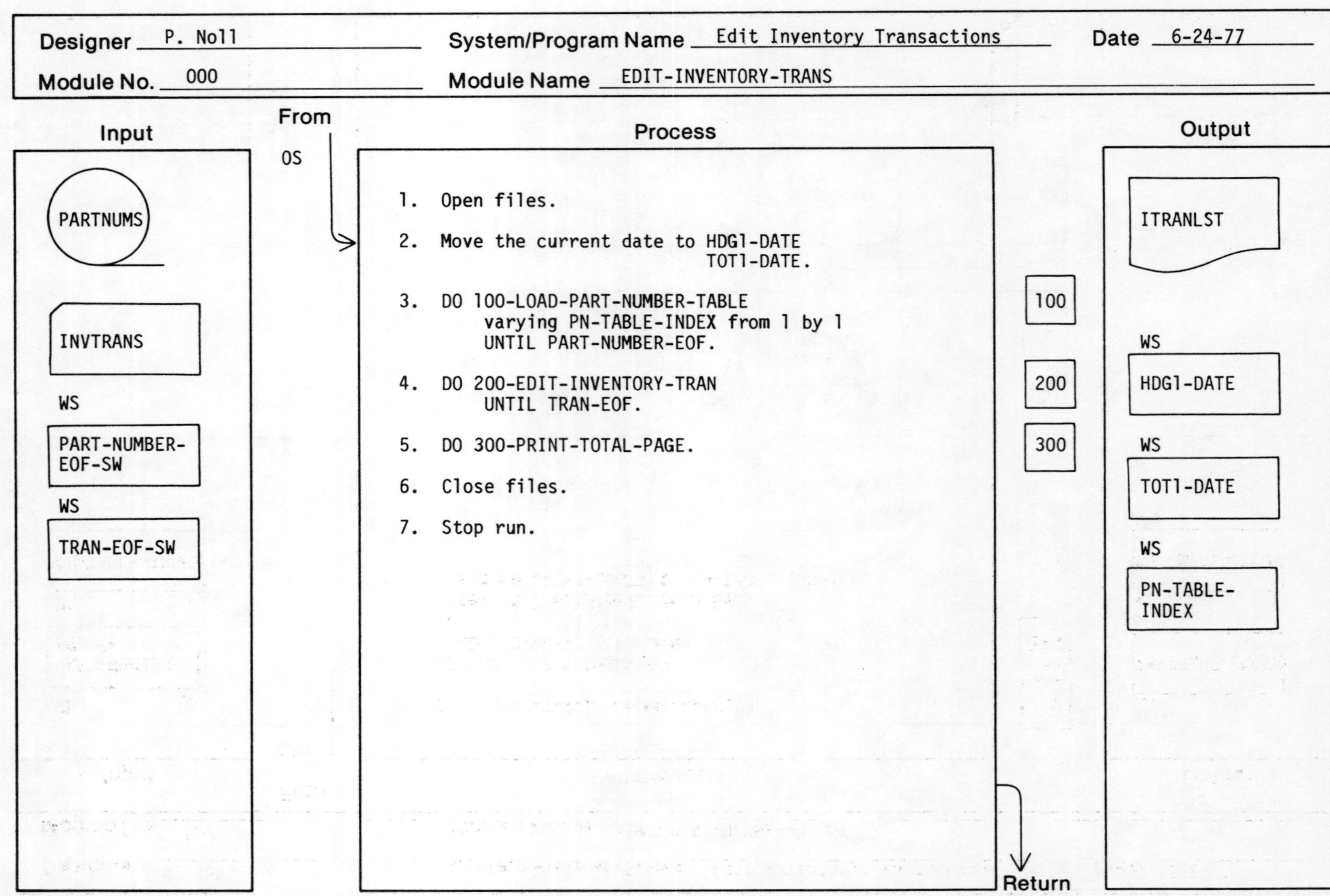
Designer P. Noll
System/Program Name Edit Inventory Transactions
Date 6-24-77
Module No. 000
Module Name EDIT-INVENTORY-TRANS
Input
PARTNUMS
INVTRANS
WS
PART-NUMBER-EOF-SW
WS
TRAN-EOF-SW
From
OS
Process
1. Open files.
2. Move the current date to HDG1-DATE
TOT1-DATE.
3. DO 100-LOAD-PART-NUMBER-TABLE
varying PN-TABLE-INDEX from 1 by 1
UNTIL PART-NUMBER-EOF.
4. DO 200-EDIT-INVENTORY-TRAN
UNTIL TRAN-EOF.
5. DO 300-PRINT-TOTAL-PAGE.
6. Close files.
7. Stop run.
100
200
300
Return
Output
ITRANLST
WS
HDG1-DATE
WS
TOT1-DATE
WS
PN-TABLE-INDEX

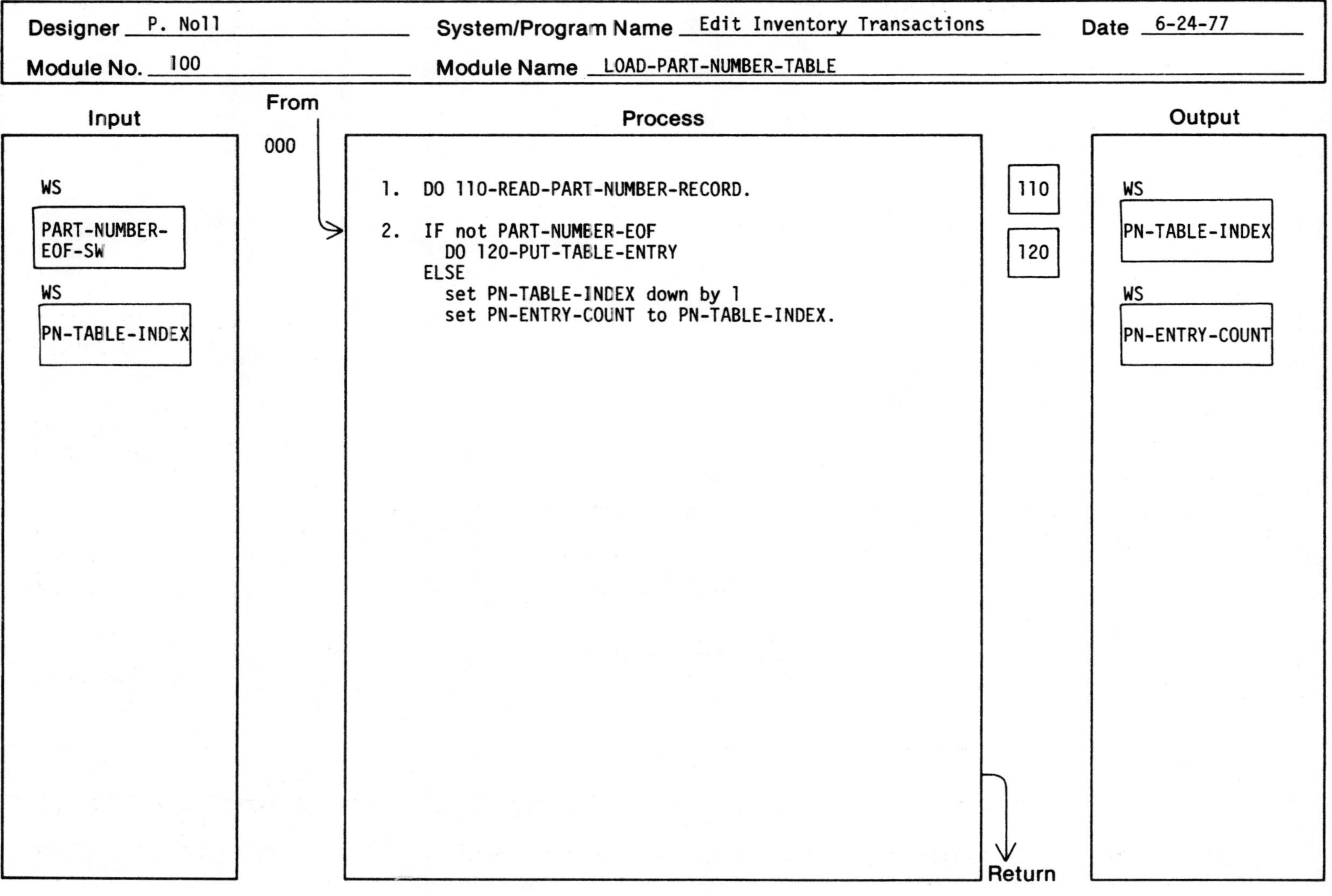

Designer P. Noll — System/Program Name Edit Inventory Transactions — Date 6-24-77

Module No. 100 — Module Name LOAD-PART-NUMBER-TABLE

Input

WS: PART-NUMBER-EOF-SW

WS: PN-TABLE-INDEX

From 000

Process

```
1.  DO 110-READ-PART-NUMBER-RECORD.

2.  IF not PART-NUMBER-EOF
      DO 120-PUT-TABLE-ENTRY
    ELSE
      set PN-TABLE-INDEX down by 1
      set PN-ENTRY-COUNT to PN-TABLE-INDEX.
```

110

120

Return

Output

WS: PN-TABLE-INDEX

WS: PN-ENTRY-COUNT

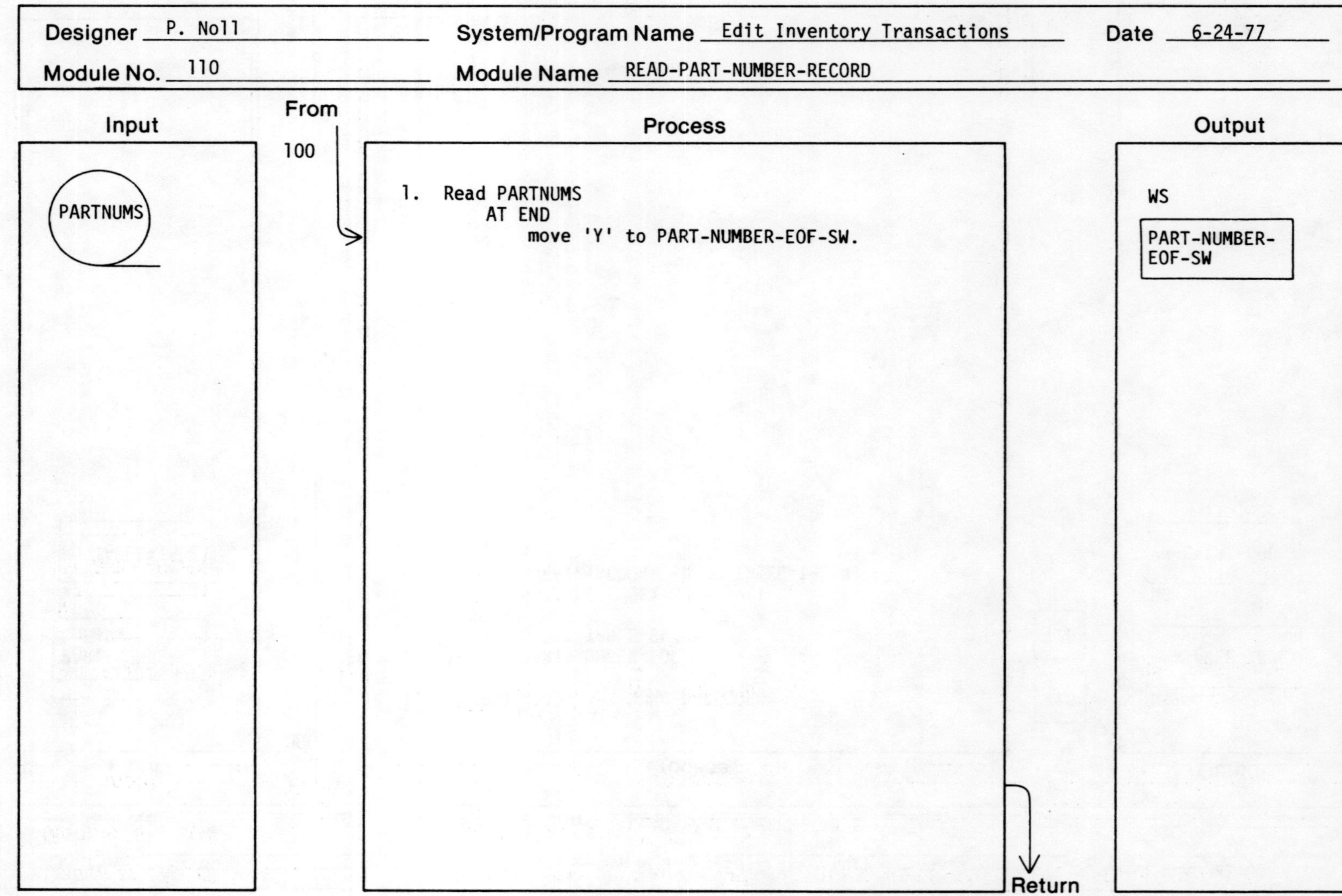

Designer P. Noll
System/Program Name Edit Inventory Transactions
Date 6-24-77
Module No. 110
Module Name READ-PART-NUMBER-RECORD
Input
PARTNUMS
From
100
Process
1. Read PARTNUMS
AT END
move 'Y' to PART-NUMBER-EOF-SW.
Return
Output
WS
PART-NUMBER-EOF-SW

Designer P. Noll   System/Program Name Edit Inventory Transactions   Date 6-24-77

Module No. 120   Module Name PUT-TABLE-ENTRY

Input	Process	Output
WS PNF-PART-NUMBER WS PN-TABLE-INDEX	From 100 1. Move PNF-PART-NUMBER to PN-TABLE-ENTRY (PN-TABLE-INDEX). Return	WS PN-TABLE-ENTRY

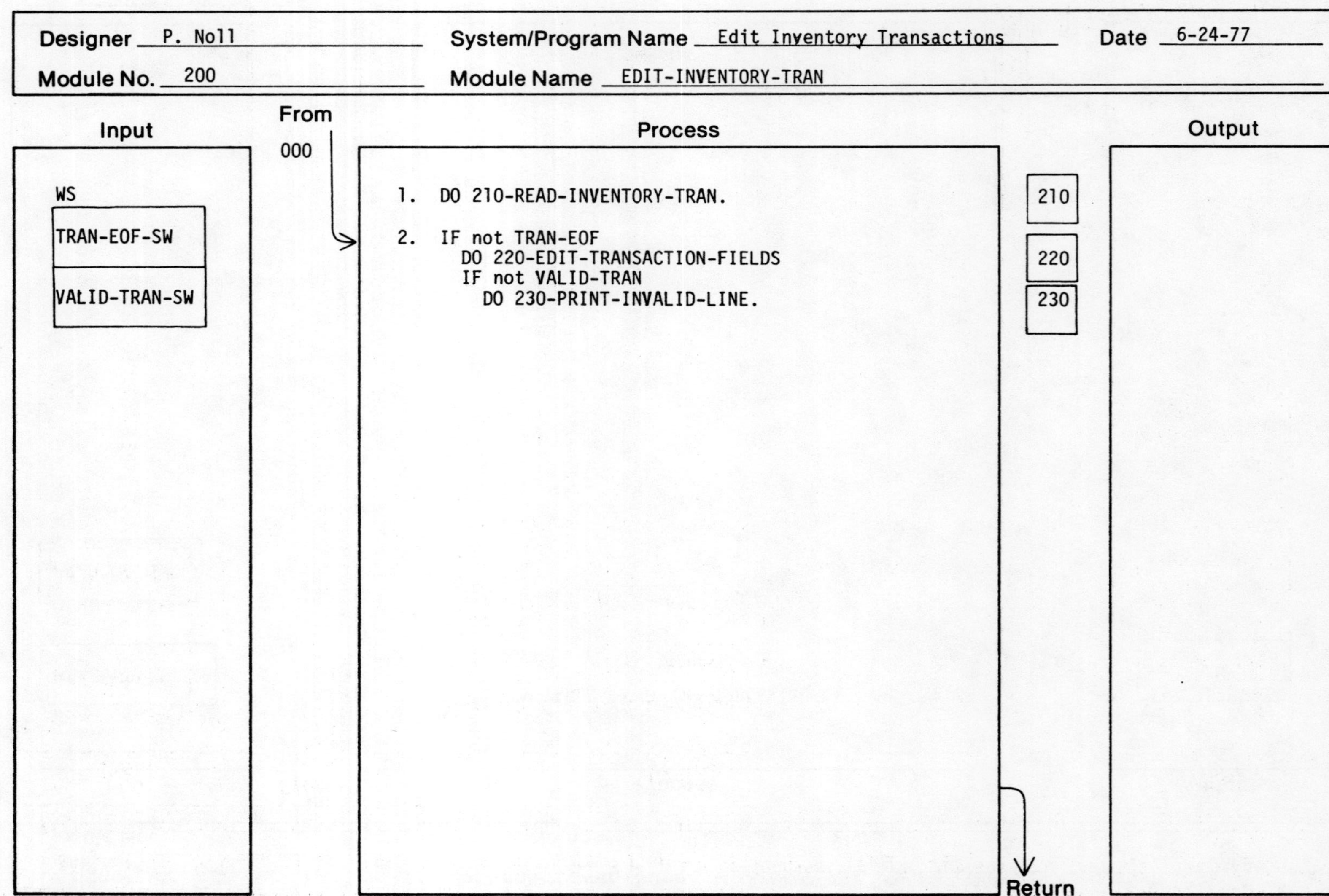

Designer P. Noll System/Program Name Edit Inventory Transactions Date 6-24-77

Module No. 200 Module Name EDIT-INVENTORY-TRAN

Input

WS

TRAN-EOF-SW
VALID-TRAN-SW

From 000

Process

```
1.  DO 210-READ-INVENTORY-TRAN.                  210

2.  IF not TRAN-EOF
      DO 220-EDIT-TRANSACTION-FIELDS             220
      IF not VALID-TRAN
        DO 230-PRINT-INVALID-LINE.               230
```

Return

Output

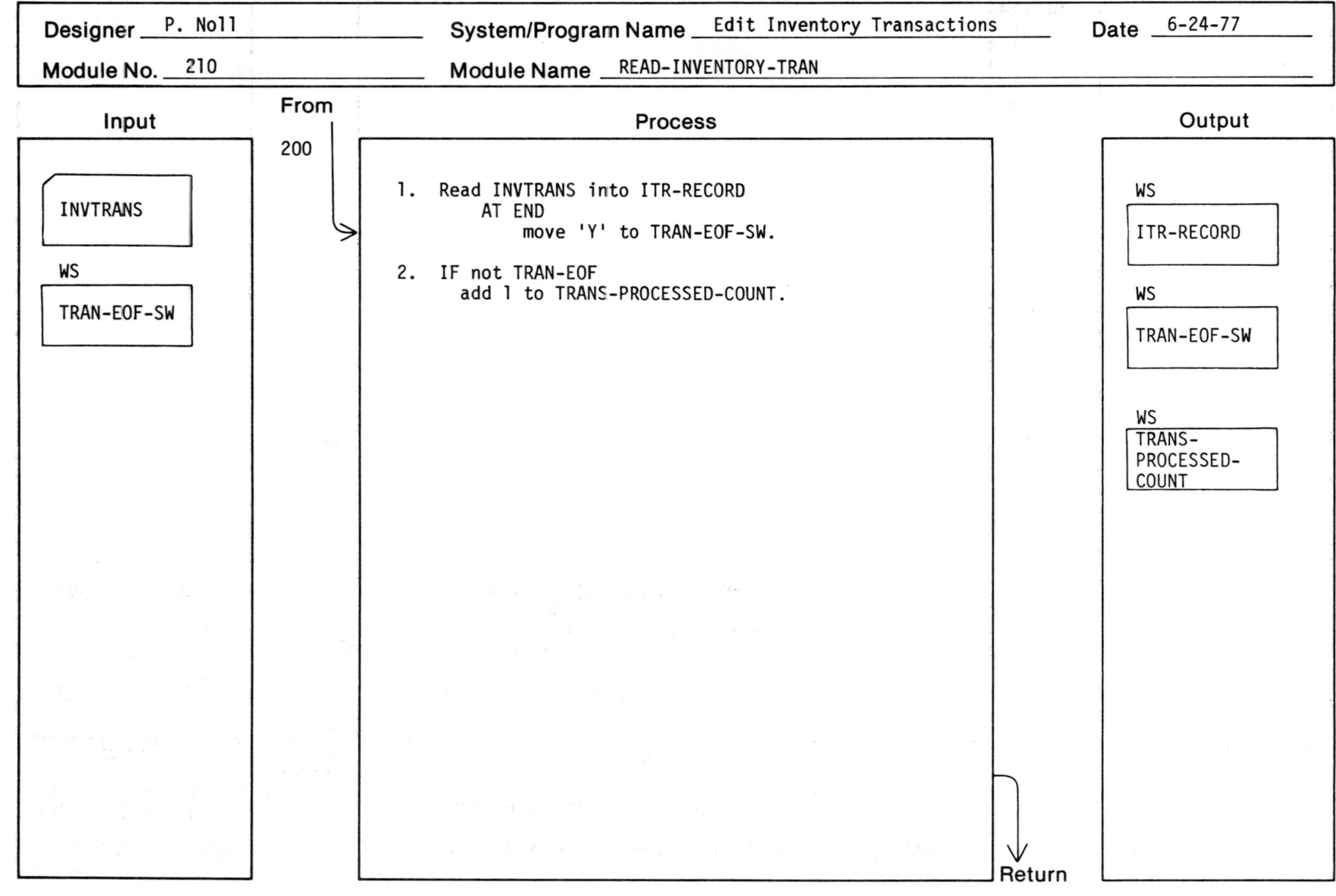
Designer P. Noll
System/Program Name Edit Inventory Transactions
Date 6-24-77
Module No. 210
Module Name READ-INVENTORY-TRAN
Input
INVTRANS
WS
TRAN-EOF-SW
From
200
Process
1. Read INVTRANS into ITR-RECORD
AT END
move 'Y' to TRAN-EOF-SW.
2. IF not TRAN-EOF
add 1 to TRANS-PROCESSED-COUNT.
Return
Output
WS
ITR-RECORD
WS
TRAN-EOF-SW
WS
TRANS-PROCESSED-COUNT

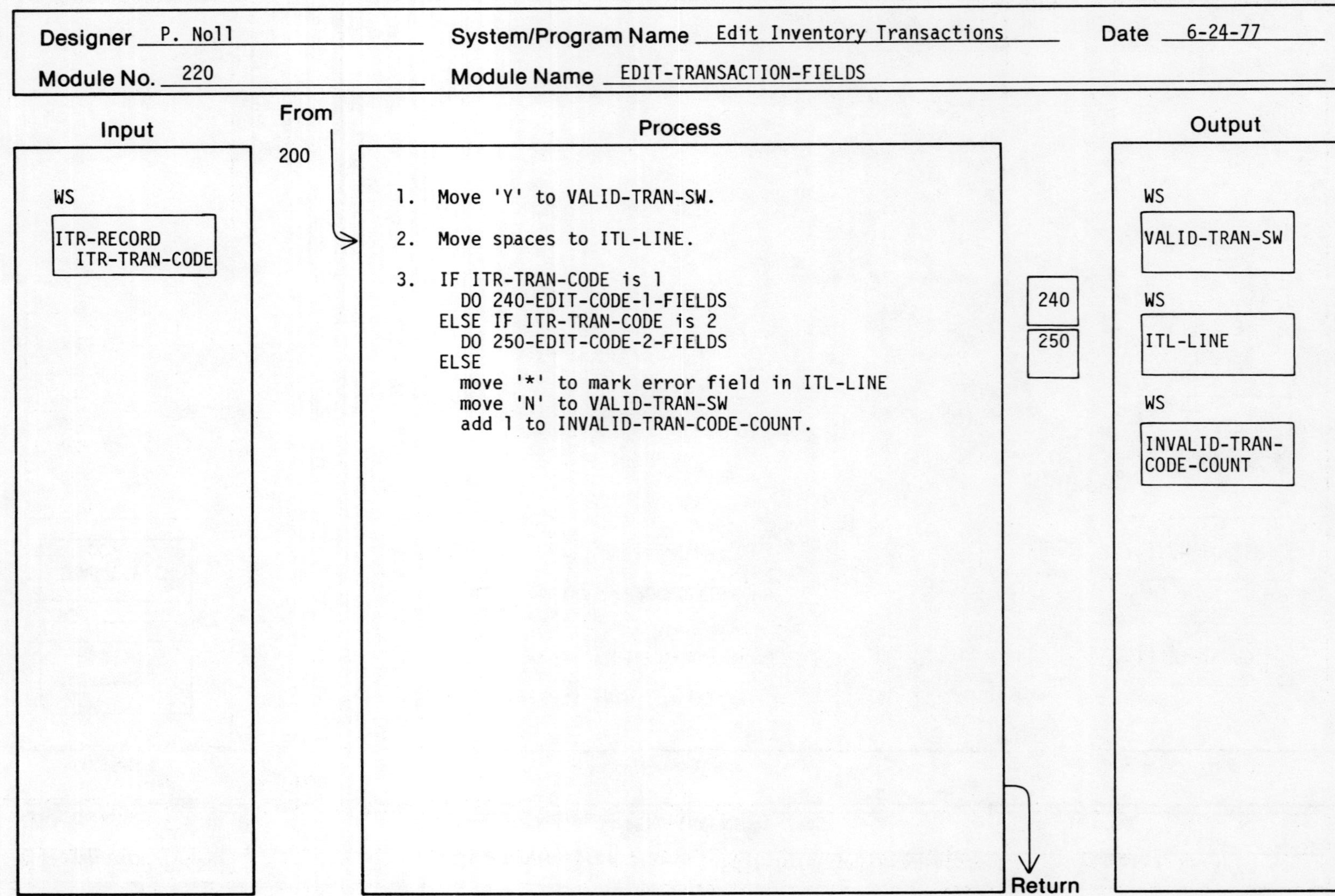
Designer P. Noll
System/Program Name Edit Inventory Transactions
Date 6-24-77
Module No. 220
Module Name EDIT-TRANSACTION-FIELDS
Input
WS
ITR-RECORD
ITR-TRAN-CODE
From
200
Process
1. Move 'Y' to VALID-TRAN-SW.
2. Move spaces to ITL-LINE.
3. IF ITR-TRAN-CODE is 1
DO 240-EDIT-CODE-1-FIELDS
ELSE IF ITR-TRAN-CODE is 2
DO 250-EDIT-CODE-2-FIELDS
ELSE
move '*' to mark error field in ITL-LINE
move 'N' to VALID-TRAN-SW
add 1 to INVALID-TRAN-CODE-COUNT.
240
250
Return
Output
WS
VALID-TRAN-SW
WS
ITL-LINE
WS
INVALID-TRAN-CODE-COUNT

Designer P. Noll System/Program Name Edit Inventory Transactions Date 6-24-77

Module No. 230 Module Name PRINT-INVALID-LINE

Input

WS
ITR-RECORD

WS
LINE-COUNT

WS
LINES-ON-PAGE

WS
ITL-LINE

From 200

Process

1. Move output fields from ITR-RECORD to ITL-LINE.
2. IF LINE-COUNT is greater than LINES-ON-PAGE
   DO 260-PRINT-REPORT-HEADING. (260)
3. Move ITL-LINE to PRINT-AREA.
4. DO 270-WRITE-REPORT-LINE. (270)

Return

Output

WS
ITL-LINE

FD
PRINT-AREA

Designer: P. Noll   System/Program Name: Edit Inventory Transactions   Date: 6-24-77

Module No.: 240   Module Name: EDIT-CODE-1-FIELDS

Input

WS
FOUND-SW

WS
ITR-RECORD

WS
CURRENT-YR

WS
VALID-TRAN-SW

From
220

Process

```
1.  DO 280-SEARCH-PART-NUMBER-TABLE.

2.  IF not FOUND
      move 'N' to VALID-TRAN-SW
      move '*' to mark error field in ITL-LINE.

3.  IF any remaining fields in ITR-RECORD are invalid
      move 'N' to VALID-TRAN-SW
      move '*' to mark error field in ITL-LINE.

4.  IF not VALID-TRAN
      add 1 to INVALID-SALES-COUNT
    ELSE
      add 1 to VALID-SALES-COUNT.
```

280

Return

Output

WS
VALID-TRAN-SW

WS
ITL-LINE

WS
INVALID-SALES-COUNT

WS
VALID-SALES-COUNT

Designer P. Noll System/Program Name Edit Inventory Transactions Date 6-24-77

Module No. 240 Module Name EDIT-CODE-1-FIELDS

Notes		Ref.
Validity is:		
ITR-UPDATE-CODE	Must be 'C'	3
ITR-CUST-ORDER-NO	Any data	3
ITR-ORDER-DATE ITR-ORDER-DAY ITR-ORDER-MONTH ITR-ORDER-YEAR	Numeric with day less than 32 month less than 13 year = current year or current year - 1	3
ITR-BRANCH-NO	Numeric and less than 25	3
ITR-SALESMAN-NO	Numeric	3
ITR-CUST-NO	Numeric	3
ITR-QUANTITY	Numeric	3
ITR-PART-NUMBER	Numeric with match in the valid-part-number file	1

NOTES:

All numeric fields must be greater than zero.

Notes	Ref.

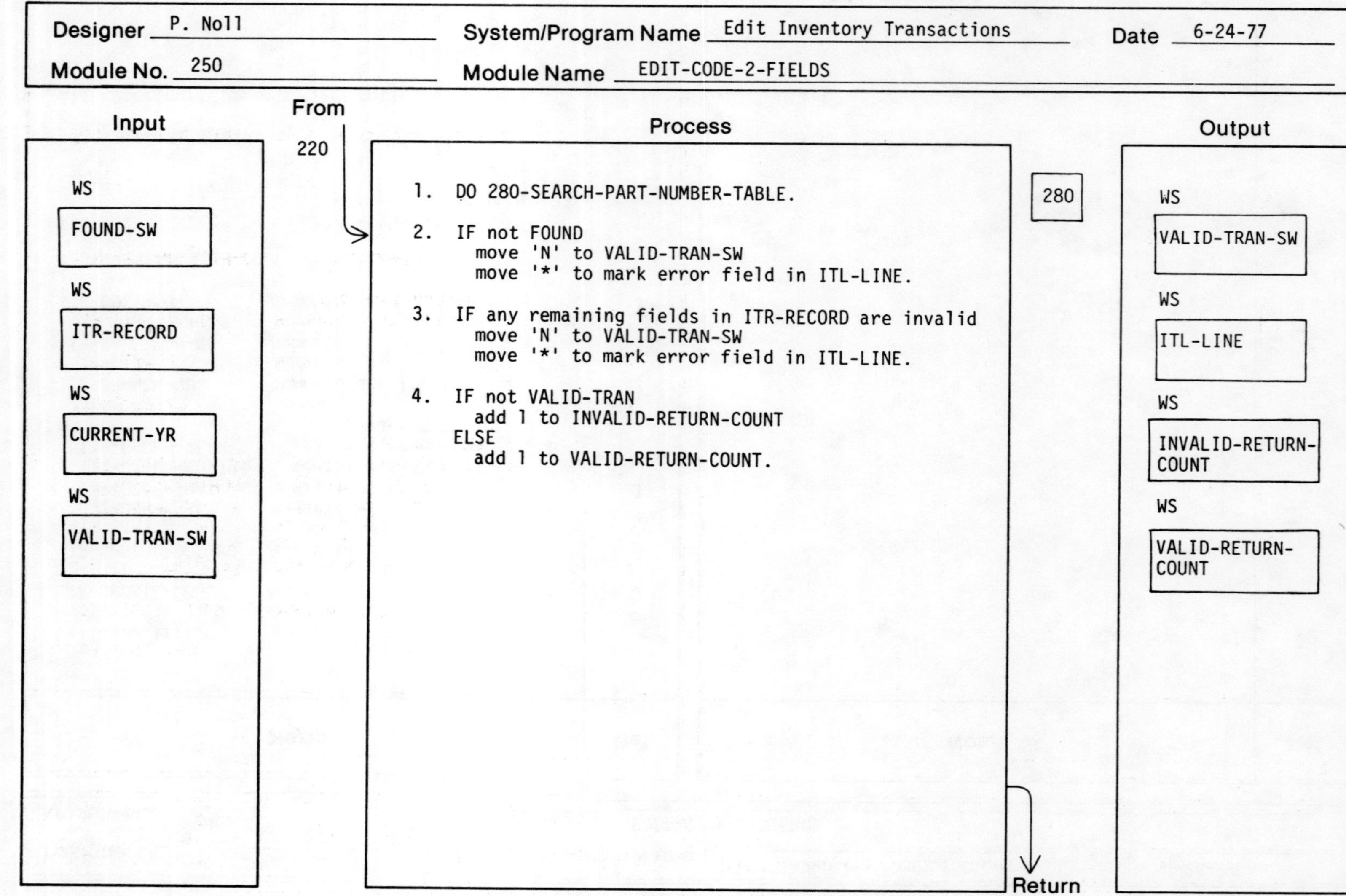

Designer P. Noll System/Program Name Edit Inventory Transactions Date 6-24-77

Module No. 250 Module Name EDIT-CODE-2-FIELDS

Input

WS FOUND-SW

WS ITR-RECORD

WS CURRENT-YR

WS VALID-TRAN-SW

From 220

Process

```
1.  DO 280-SEARCH-PART-NUMBER-TABLE.

2.  IF not FOUND
      move 'N' to VALID-TRAN-SW
      move '*' to mark error field in ITL-LINE.

3.  IF any remaining fields in ITR-RECORD are invalid
      move 'N' to VALID-TRAN-SW
      move '*' to mark error field in ITL-LINE.

4.  IF not VALID-TRAN
      add 1 to INVALID-RETURN-COUNT
    ELSE
      add 1 to VALID-RETURN-COUNT.
```

280

Return

Output

WS VALID-TRAN-SW

WS ITL-LINE

WS INVALID-RETURN-COUNT

WS VALID-RETURN-COUNT

Designer: P. Noll | System/Program Name: Edit Inventory Transactions | Date: 6-24-77

Module No.: 250 | Module Name: EDIT-CODE-2-FIELDS

Notes	Ref.
Validity is:	
ITR-UPDATE-CODE Must be 'C'	3
ITR-CUST-MEMO-NO Any data	3
ITR-RETURN-DATE Numeric with ITR-RETURN-DAY day less than 32 ITR-RETURN-MONTH month less than 13 ITR-RETURN-YEAR year = current year or current year - 1	3
ITR-CUST-NO Numeric	3
ITR-QUANTITY Numeric	3
ITR-PART-NUMBER Numeric with match in the valid-part-number file	1
ITR-RETURN-AUTH-CODE Alphabetic	3
NOTES:	
All numeric fields must be greater than zero.	

Notes	Ref.

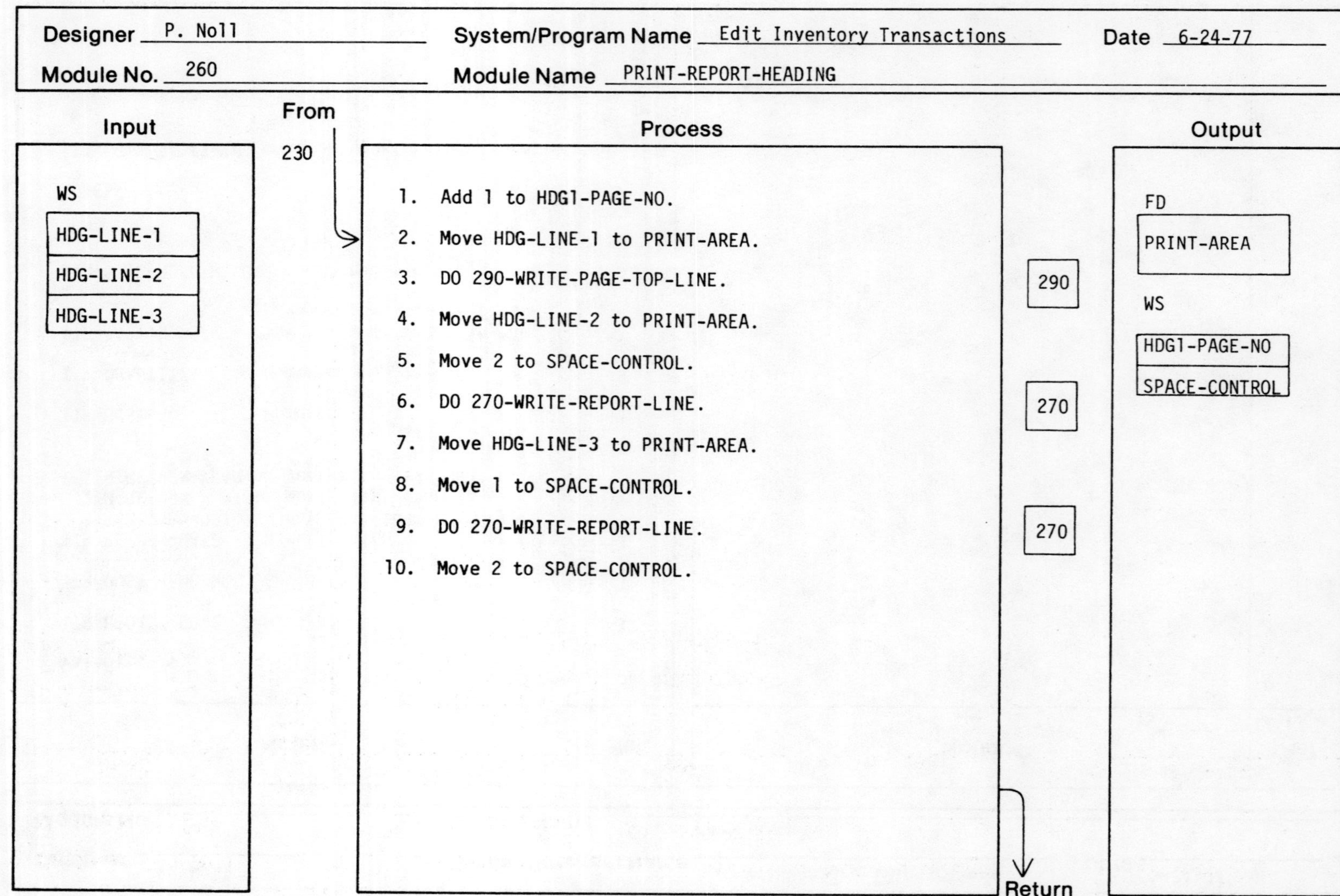
Designer P. Noll
System/Program Name Edit Inventory Transactions
Date 6-24-77
Module No. 260
Module Name PRINT-REPORT-HEADING
Input
WS
HDG-LINE-1
HDG-LINE-2
HDG-LINE-3
From 230
Process
1. Add 1 to HDG1-PAGE-NO.
2. Move HDG-LINE-1 to PRINT-AREA.
3. DO 290-WRITE-PAGE-TOP-LINE.
4. Move HDG-LINE-2 to PRINT-AREA.
5. Move 2 to SPACE-CONTROL.
6. DO 270-WRITE-REPORT-LINE.
7. Move HDG-LINE-3 to PRINT-AREA.
8. Move 1 to SPACE-CONTROL.
9. DO 270-WRITE-REPORT-LINE.
10. Move 2 to SPACE-CONTROL.
290
270
270
Return
Output
FD
PRINT-AREA
WS
HDG1-PAGE-NO
SPACE-CONTROL

Designer P. Ncll | System/Program Name Edit Inventory Transactions | Date 6-24-77

Module No. 270 | Module Name WRITE-REPORT-LINE

Input	From	Process	Output
FD PRINT-AREA WS SPACE-CONTROL	230 260 300	1. WRITE PRINT-AREA AFTER ADVANCING SPACE-CONTROL LINES. 2. ADD SPACE-CONTROL TO LINE-COUNT.	ITRANLST WS LINE-COUNT

Return

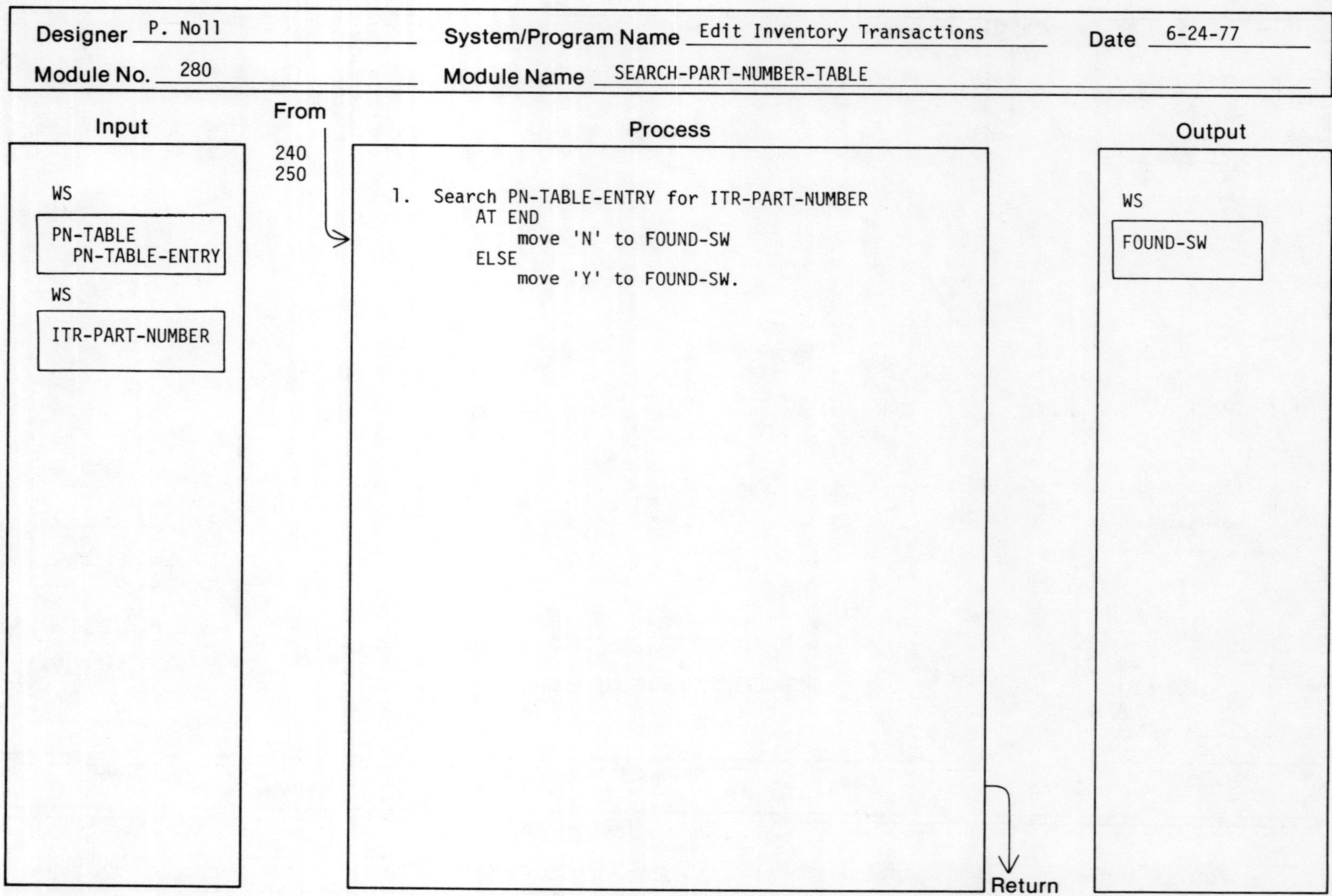
Designer P. Noll
System/Program Name Edit Inventory Transactions
Date 6-24-77
Module No. 280
Module Name SEARCH-PART-NUMBER-TABLE
Input
WS
PN-TABLE
PN-TABLE-ENTRY
WS
ITR-PART-NUMBER
From
240
250
Process
1. Search PN-TABLE-ENTRY for ITR-PART-NUMBER
AT END
move 'N' to FOUND-SW
ELSE
move 'Y' to FOUND-SW.
Return
Output
WS
FOUND-SW

Designer P. Noll System/Program Name Edit Inventory Transactions Date 6-24-77

Module No. 290 Module Name WRITE-PAGE-TOP-LINE

Input	From	Process	Output
FD PRINT-AREA	260 300	1. WRITE PRINT-AREA AFTER ADVANCING PAGE-TOP. 2. MOVE ZERO TO LINE-COUNT. Return	ITRANLST WS LINE-COUNT

Designer P. Noll | System/Program Name Edit Inventory Transactions | Date 6-24-77

Module No. 300 | Module Name PRINT-TOTAL-PAGE

Input

WS
- VALID-SALES-COUNT
- VALID-RETURN-COUNT
- INVALID-SALES-COUNT
- INVALID-RETURN-COUNT

WS
- TOTAL-LINE-1
- .
- .
- .
- TOTAL-LINE-9

From 000

Process

```
1.  Add VALID-SALES-COUNT
        VALID-RETURN-COUNT
            giving VALID-COUNT.

2.  Add INVALID-SALES-COUNT
        INVALID-RETURN-COUNT
            giving INVALID-COUNT.

3.  Move TOTAL-LINE-1 to PRINT-AREA.

4.  DO 290-WRITE-PAGE-TOP-LINE.                    290

5.  Prepare total lines 2 through 9 for printing.

6.  When each line is ready for printing
        DO 270-WRITE-REPORT-LINE.                  270
```

Return

Output

WS
- VALID-COUNT
- INVALID-COUNT

FD
- PRINT-AREA

WS
- SPACE-CONTROL

```
PP 5734-CB1 V3 RELEASE 3.2 30APR74       IBM OS AMERICAN NATIONAL STANDARD COBOL

   1

000010 IDENTIFICATION DIVISION.                                    EDIT
000020*                                                            EDIT
000030 PROGRAM-ID. EDIT.                                           EDIT
000040 AUTHOR. PAUL NOLL.                                          EDIT
000050 INSTALLATION. MM&A.                                         EDIT
000060 DATE-COMPILED. OCT 20,1977.                                 EDIT
000070*                                                            EDIT
000080 ENVIRONMENT DIVISION.                                       EDIT
000090*                                                            EDIT
000100 CONFIGURATION SECTION.                                      EDIT
000110*                                                            EDIT
000120 SPECIAL-NAMES.                                              EDIT
000130     C01 IS PAGE-TOP.                                        EDIT
000140*                                                            EDIT
000150 INPUT-OUTPUT SECTION.                                       EDIT
000160*                                                            EDIT
000170 FILE-CONTROL.                                               EDIT
000180     SELECT PARTNUMS ASSIGN TO UT-S-PARTNUMS.                EDIT
000190     SELECT INVTRANS ASSIGN TO UT-S-INVTRANS.                EDIT
000200     SELECT ITRANLST ASSIGN TO UT-S-ITRANLST.                EDIT
000210*                                                            EDIT
000220 DATA DIVISION.                                              EDIT
000230*                                                            EDIT
000240 FILE SECTION.                                               EDIT
000250*                                                            EDIT
000260 FD  PARTNUMS                                                EDIT
000270     LABEL RECORDS ARE STANDARD                              EDIT
000280     RECORDING MODE IS F                                     EDIT
000290     RECORD CONTAINS 24 CHARACTERS                           EDIT
000300     BLOCK CONTAINS 0 RECORDS.                               EDIT
000310*                                                            EDIT
000320 01  PNF-AREA                PIC X(24).                      EDIT
000330*                                                            EDIT
000340 FD  INVTRANS                                                EDIT
000350     LABEL RECORDS ARE STANDARD                              EDIT
```

```
000360         RECORDING MODE IS F                                                  EDIT
000370         RECORD CONTAINS 80 CHARACTERS                                        EDIT
000380         BLOCK CONTAINS 0 RECORDS.                                            EDIT
000390*                                                                             EDIT
000400 01   INV-AREA               PIC X(80).                                       EDIT
000410*                                                                             EDIT
000420 FD   ITRANLST                                                                EDIT
000430         LABEL RECORDS ARE STANDARD                                           EDIT
000440         RECORDING MODE IS F                                                  EDIT
000450         RECORD CONTAINS 133 CHARACTERS                                       EDIT
000460         BLOCK CONTAINS 0 RECORDS.                                            EDIT
000470*                                                                             EDIT
000480 01   PRINT-AREA             PIC X(133).                                      EDIT
000490*                                                                             EDIT
000500 WORKING-STORAGE SECTION.                                                     EDIT
000510*                                                                             EDIT
000520 01   SWITCHES.                                                               EDIT
000530*                                                                             EDIT
000540         05  PART-NUMBER-EOF-SW        PIC X          VALUE 'N'.              EDIT
000550             88  PART-NUMBER-EOF                      VALUE 'Y'.              EDIT
000560         05  TRAN-EOF-SW               PIC X          VALUE 'N'.              EDIT
000570             88  TRAN-EOF                             VALUE 'Y'.              EDIT
000580         05  VALID-TRAN-SW             PIC X.                                 EDIT
000590             88  VALID-TRAN                           VALUE 'Y'.              EDIT
000600         05  FOUND-SW                  PIC X.                                 EDIT
000610             88  FOUND                                VALUE 'Y'.              EDIT
000620*                                                                             EDIT
000630 01   COUNT-FIELDS                     COMP-3.                                EDIT
000640*                                                                             EDIT
000650         05  TRANS-PROCESSED-COUNT     PIC S9(5)      VALUE ZERO.             EDIT
000660         05  INVALID-TRAN-CODE-COUNT   PIC S9(5)      VALUE ZERO.             EDIT
000670         05  INVALID-SALES-COUNT       PIC S9(5)      VALUE ZERO.             EDIT
000680         05  VALID-SALES-COUNT         PIC S9(5)      VALUE ZERO.             EDIT
000690         05  INVALID-RETURN-COUNT      PIC S9(5)      VALUE ZERO.             EDIT
000700         05  VALID-RETURN-COUNT        PIC S9(5)      VALUE ZERO.             EDIT
000710         05  INVALID-COUNT             PIC S9(5)      VALUE ZERO.             EDIT
000720         05  VALID-COUNT               PIC S9(5)      VALUE ZERO.             EDIT
000730*                                                                             EDIT
```

```
000740 01  PRINT-FIELDS              COMP          SYNC.                     EDIT
000750*                                                                      EDIT
000760     05  LINE-COUNT            PIC S999      VALUE +999.               EDIT
000770     05  LINES-ON-PAGE         PIC S999      VALUE +57.                EDIT
000780     05  SPACE-CONTROL         PIC S9.                                 EDIT
000790*                                                                      EDIT
000800 01  DATE-FIELDS.                                                      EDIT
000810*                                                                      EDIT
000820     05  TODAYS-DATE.                                                  EDIT
000830         10  FILLER            PIC X(6).                               EDIT
000840         10  TODAYS-YEAR       PIC 99.                                 EDIT
000850     05  CURRENT-YEAR          PIC S99       COMP-3.                   EDIT
000860     05  CURRENT-YEAR-MINUS-1  PIC S99       COMP-3.                   EDIT
000870*                                                                      EDIT
000880 01  PN-TABLE.                                                         EDIT
000890*                                                                      EDIT
000900     05  PN-TABLE-ENTRY        OCCURS 100 TIMES                        EDIT
000910                               INDEXED BY PN-TABLE-INDEX               EDIT
000920                               PIC X(5).                               EDIT
000930     05  PN-ENTRY-COUNT        INDEX.                                  EDIT
000940*                                                                      EDIT
000950 01  PNF-RECORD.                                                       EDIT
000960*                                                                      EDIT
000970     05  PNF-PART-NUMBER       PIC X(5).                               EDIT
000980     05  FILLER                PIC X(19).                              EDIT
000990*                                                                      EDIT
001000 01  MARK.                                                             EDIT
001010*                                                                      EDIT
001020     05  FILLER                PIC X         VALUE '*'.                EDIT
001030*                                                                      EDIT
001040 01  ITR-RECORD.                                                       EDIT
001050*                                                                      EDIT
001060     05  ITR-TYPE-CODE.                                                EDIT
001070         10  ITR-UPDATE-CODE   PIC X.                                  EDIT
001080         10  ITR-TRAN-CODE     PIC X.                                  EDIT
001090     05  ITR-REF-NO            PIC X(10).                              EDIT
001100     05  ITR-REF-DATE.                                                 EDIT
001110         10  ITR-MONTH         PIC XX.                                 EDIT
```

```
001120                88  GOOD-ITR-MONTH              VALUES '01' THRU '12'.   EDIT
001130            10  ITR-DAY               PIC XX.                             EDIT
001140                88  GOOD-ITR-DAY                VALUES '01' THRU '31'.   EDIT
001150            10  ITR-YEAR              PIC 99.                             EDIT
001160        05  ITR-BRANCH-NO             PIC XX.                             EDIT
001170                88  GOOD-ITR-BRANCH             VALUES '01' THRU '25'.   EDIT
001180        05  ITR-SALESMAN-NO           PIC X(3).                           EDIT
001190        05  ITR-CUSTOMER-NO           PIC X(5).                           EDIT
001200        05  ITR-QUANTITY              PIC X(5).                           EDIT
001210        05  ITR-PART-NUMBER           PIC X(5).                           EDIT
001220        05  ITR-RETURN-CODE           PIC X(4).                           EDIT
001230        05  FILLER                    PIC X(38).                          EDIT
001240*                                                                         EDIT
001250 01  HDG-LINE-1.                                                          EDIT
001260*                                                                         EDIT
001270        05  HDG1-CC           PIC X.                                      EDIT
001280        05  FILLER            PIC X(3)      VALUE SPACE.                  EDIT
001290        05  HDG1-DATE         PIC X(8).                                   EDIT
001300        05  FILLER            PIC X(9)      VALUE '     INVAL'.           EDIT
001310        05  FILLER            PIC X(20)     VALUE 'ID SALES AND RETURN '.EDIT
001320        05  FILLER            PIC X(20)     VALUE 'TRANSACTIONS    PAGE '.EDIT
001330        05  HDG1-PAGE-NO      PIC 999       VALUE ZERO.                   EDIT
001340        05  FILLER            PIC X(69)     VALUE SPACE.                  EDIT
001350*                                                                         EDIT
001360 01  HDG-LINE-2.                                                          EDIT
001370*                                                                         EDIT
001380        05  HDG2-CC           PIC X.                                      EDIT
001390        05  FILLER            PIC X(20)     VALUE 'TRAN ---------------'.EDIT
001400        05  FILLER            PIC X(20)     VALUE '--- * INDICATES ERRO'.EDIT
001410        05  FILLER            PIC X(20)     VALUE 'R FIELDS -----------'.EDIT
001420        05  FILLER            PIC X(20)     VALUE '-------             '.EDIT
001430        05  FILLER            PIC X(20)     VALUE '                    '.EDIT
001440        05  FILLER            PIC X(20)     VALUE '                    '.EDIT
001450        05  FILLER            PIC X(12)     VALUE '                    EDIT
001460*                                                                         EDIT
001470 01  HDG-LINE-3.                                                          EDIT
001480*                                                                         EDIT
001490        05  HDG3-CC           PIC X.                                      EDIT
```

```
001500      05  FILLER              PIC X(20)   VALUE 'CODE    REF NO        '.EDIT
001510      05  FILLER              PIC X(20)   VALUE 'DATE    BR SLSMN    C'.EDIT
001520      05  FILLER              PIC X(20)   VALUE 'UST     QTY      PART'.EDIT
001530      05  FILLER              PIC X(20)   VALUE '    AUTH            '.EDIT
001540      05  FILLER              PIC X(20)   VALUE '                    '.EDIT
001550      05  FILLER              PIC X(32)   VALUE SPACE.                  EDIT
001560*                                                                       EDIT
001570 01   ITL-LINE                    VALUE SPACE.                          EDIT
001580*                                                                       EDIT
001590      05  ITL-CC                  PIC X.                                EDIT
001600      05  ITL-TYPE-CODE-ERR       PIC X.                                EDIT
001610      05  ITL-TYPE-CODE           PIC XX.                               EDIT
001620      05  FILLER                  PIC XX.                               EDIT
001630      05  ITL-REF-NO-ERR          PIC X.                                EDIT
001640      05  ITL-REF-NO              PIC X(10).                            EDIT
001650      05  FILLER                  PIC XX.                               EDIT
001660      05  ITL-REF-DATE-ERR        PIC X.                                EDIT
001670      05  ITL-REF-DATE            PIC X(6).                             EDIT
001680      05  FILLER                  PIC X(2).                             EDIT
001690      05  ITL-BRANCH-NO-ERR       PIC X.                                EDIT
001700      05  ITL-BRANCH-NO           PIC XX.                               EDIT
001710      05  FILLER                  PIC XX.                               EDIT
001720      05  ITL-SALESMAN-NO-ERR PIC X.                                    EDIT
001730      05  ITL-SALESMAN-NO         PIC XXX.                              EDIT
001740      05  FILLER                  PIC XX.                               EDIT
001750      05  ITL-CUSTOMER-NO-ERR PIC X.                                    EDIT
001760      05  ITL-CUSTOMER-NO         PIC X(5).                             EDIT
001770      05  FILLER                  PIC XX.                               EDIT
001780      05  ITL-QUANTITY-ERR        PIC X.                                EDIT
001790      05  ITL-QUANTITY            PIC X(5).                             EDIT
001800      05  FILLER                  PIC XX.                               EDIT
001810      05  ITL-PART-NUMBER-ERR PIC X.                                    EDIT
001820      05  ITL-PART-NUMBER         PIC X(5).                             EDIT
001830      05  FILLER                  PIC XX.                               EDIT
001840      05  ITL-RETURN-CODE-ERR PIC X.                                    EDIT
001850      05  ITL-RETURN-CODE         PIC X(4).                             EDIT
001860      05  FILLER                  PIC X(65).                            EDIT
001870*                                                                       EDIT
```

6

```
001880 01  TOTAL-LINE-1.                                                 EDIT
001890*                                                                  EDIT
001900         05  TOT1-CC             PIC X.                            EDIT
001910         05  FILLER              PIC X(20)   VALUE 'SUMMARY FOR SALES-RE'.EDIT
001920         05  FILLER              PIC X(20)   VALUE 'TURN VERIFICATION RU'.EDIT
001930         05  FILLER              PIC X(5)    VALUE 'N OF '.        EDIT
001940         05  TOT1-DATE           PIC X(8).                         EDIT
001950         05  FILLER              PIC X(79)   VALUE SPACE.          EDIT
001960*                                                                  EDIT
001970 01  TOTAL-LINE-2.                                                 EDIT
001980*                                                                  EDIT
001990         05  TOT2-CC             PIC X.                            EDIT
002000         05  FILLER              PIC X(20)   VALUE 'VALID    SALES       '.EDIT
002010         05  FILLER              PIC X(4)    VALUE '    '.         EDIT
002020         05  TOT2-VALID-SALES-COUNT          PIC ZZ,ZZ9.           EDIT
002030         05  FILLER              PIC X(102)  VALUE SPACE.          EDIT
002040*                                                                  EDIT
002050 01  TOTAL-LINE-3.                                                 EDIT
002060*                                                                  EDIT
002070         05  TOT3-CC             PIC X.                            EDIT
002080         05  FILLER              PIC X(20)   VALUE '          RETURNS     '.EDIT
002090         05  FILLER              PIC X(4)    VALUE '    '.         EDIT
002100         05  TOT3-VALID-RETURN-COUNT         PIC ZZ,ZZ9.           EDIT
002110         05  FILLER              PIC X(102)  VALUE SPACE.          EDIT
002120*                                                                  EDIT
002130 01  TOTAL-LINE-4.                                                 EDIT
002140*                                                                  EDIT
002150         05  TOT4-CC             PIC X.                            EDIT
002160         05  FILLER              PIC X(20)   VALUE '              TOTAL   '.EDIT
002170         05  FILLER              PIC X(4)    VALUE '    '.         EDIT
002180         05  TOT4-VALID-COUNT                PIC ZZ,ZZ9.           EDIT
002190         05  FILLER              PIC X(10)   VALUE ' *        '.   EDIT
002200         05  FILLER              PIC X(92)   VALUE SPACE.          EDIT
002210*                                                                  EDIT
002220 01  TOTAL-LINE-5.                                                 EDIT
002230*                                                                  EDIT
002240         05  TOT5-CC             PIC X.                            EDIT
002250         05  FILLER              PIC X(20)   VALUE 'INVALID SALES       '.EDIT
```

```
002260       05  FILLER             PIC X(4)     VALUE '    '.                 EDIT
002270       05  TOT5-INVALID-SALES-COUNT        PIC ZZ,ZZ9.                   EDIT
002280       05  FILLER             PIC X(102)   VALUE SPACE.                  EDIT
002290*                                                                        EDIT
002300 01    TOTAL-LINE-6.                                                     EDIT
002310*                                                                        EDIT
002320       05  TOT6-CC            PIC X.                                     EDIT
002330       05  FILLER             PIC X(20)    VALUE '       RETURNS      '.EDIT
002340       05  FILLER             PIC X(4)     VALUE '    '.                 EDIT
002350       05  TOT6-INVALID-RETURN-COUNT       PIC ZZ,ZZ9.                   EDIT
002360       05  FILLER             PIC X(102)   VALUE SPACE.                  EDIT
002370*                                                                        EDIT
002380 01    TOTAL-LINE-7.                                                     EDIT
002390*                                                                        EDIT
002400       05  TOT7-CC            PIC X.                                     EDIT
002410       05  FILLER             PIC X(20)    VALUE '           TOTAL    '.EDIT
002420       05  FILLER             PIC X(4)     VALUE '    '.                 EDIT
002430       05  TOT7-INVALID-COUNT              PIC ZZ,ZZ9.                   EDIT
002440       05  FILLER             PIC X(10)    VALUE ' *        '.           EDIT
002450       05  FILLER             PIC X(92)    VALUE SPACE.                  EDIT
002460*                                                                        EDIT
002470 01    TOTAL-LINE-8.                                                     EDIT
002480*                                                                        EDIT
002490       05  TOT8-CC            PIC X.                                     EDIT
002500       05  FILLER             PIC X(20)    VALUE 'INVALID TRAN CODES  '.EDIT
002510       05  FILLER             PIC X(4)     VALUE '    '.                 EDIT
002520       05  TOT8-INVALID-TRAN-CODE-COUNT PIC ZZ,ZZ9.                      EDIT
002530       05  FILLER             PIC X(10)    VALUE ' *        '.           EDIT
002540       05  FILLER             PIC X(92)    VALUE SPACE.                  EDIT
002550*                                                                        EDIT
002560 01    TOTAL-LINE-9.                                                     EDIT
002570*                                                                        EDIT
002580       05  TOT9-CC            PIC X.                                     EDIT
002590       05  FILLER             PIC X(20)    VALUE 'TRANSACTIONS PROCESS'.EDIT
002600       05  FILLER             PIC X(4)     VALUE 'ED  '.                 EDIT
002610       05  TOT9-TRANS-PROCESSED-COUNT      PIC ZZ,ZZ9.                   EDIT
002620       05  FILLER             PIC X(10)    VALUE ' * *      '.           EDIT
002630       05  FILLER             PIC X(92)    VALUE SPACE.                  EDIT
```

8

```
002640*                                                                  EDIT
002650 PROCEDURE DIVISION.                                               EDIT
002660*                                                                  EDIT
002670 000-EDIT-INVENTORY-TRANS.                                         EDIT
002680*                                                                  EDIT
002690     OPEN INPUT  PARTNUMS                                          EDIT
002700                 INVTRANS                                          EDIT
002710         OUTPUT ITRANLST.                                          EDIT
002720     MOVE CURRENT-DATE TO TODAYS-DATE.                             EDIT
002730     MOVE TODAYS-YEAR TO CURRENT-YEAR.                             EDIT
002740     SUBTRACT 1 FROM CURRENT-YEAR GIVING CURRENT-YEAR-MINUS-1.     EDIT
002750     MOVE TODAYS-DATE TO HDG1-DATE                                 EDIT
002760                         TOT1-DATE.                                EDIT
002770     PERFORM 100-LOAD-PART-NUMBER-TABLE                            EDIT
002780         VARYING PN-TABLE-INDEX FROM 1 BY 1                        EDIT
002790         UNTIL PART-NUMBER-EOF.                                    EDIT
002800     PERFORM 200-EDIT-INVENTORY-TRAN                               EDIT
002810         UNTIL TRAN-EOF.                                           EDIT
002820     PERFORM 300-PRINT-TOTAL-PAGE.                                 EDIT
002830     CLOSE PARTNUMS                                                EDIT
002840           INVTRANS                                                EDIT
002850           ITRANLST.                                               EDIT
002860     STOP RUN.                                                     EDIT
002870*                                                                  EDIT
002880 100-LOAD-PART-NUMBER-TABLE.                                       EDIT
002890*                                                                  EDIT
002900     PERFORM 110-READ-PART-NUMBER-RECORD.                          EDIT
002910     IF NOT PART-NUMBER-EOF                                        EDIT
002920         PERFORM 120-PUT-TABLE-ENTRY                               EDIT
002930     ELSE                                                          EDIT
002940         SET PN-TABLE-INDEX DOWN BY 1                              EDIT
002950         SET PN-ENTRY-COUNT TO PN-TABLE-INDEX.                     EDIT
002960*                                                                  EDIT
002970 110-READ-PART-NUMBER-RECORD.                                      EDIT
002980*                                                                  EDIT
002990     READ PARTNUMS INTO PNF-RECORD                                 EDIT
003000         AT END                                                    EDIT
003010             MOVE 'Y' TO PART-NUMBER-EOF-SW.                       EDIT
```

```
003020*                                                                    EDIT
003030 120-PUT-TABLE-ENTRY.                                                EDIT
003040*                                                                    EDIT
003050     MOVE PNF-PART-NUMBER TO PN-TABLE-ENTRY (PN-TABLE-INDEX).        EDIT
003060*                                                                    EDIT
003070 200-EDIT-INVENTORY-TRAN.                                            EDIT
003080*                                                                    EDIT
003090     PERFORM 210-READ-INVENTORY-TRAN.                                EDIT
003100     IF NOT TRAN-EOF                                                 EDIT
003110         PERFORM 220-EDIT-TRANSACTION-FIELDS                         EDIT
003120         IF NOT VALID-TRAN                                           EDIT
003130             PERFORM 230-PRINT-INVALID-LINE.                         EDIT
003140*                                                                    EDIT
003150 210-READ-INVENTORY-TRAN.                                            EDIT
003160*                                                                    EDIT
003170     READ INVTRANS INTO ITR-RECORD                                   EDIT
003180         AT END                                                      EDIT
003190             MOVE 'Y' TO TRAN-EOF-SW.                                EDIT
003200     IF NOT TRAN-EOF                                                 EDIT
003210         ADD 1 TO TRANS-PROCESSED-COUNT.                             EDIT
003220*                                                                    EDIT
003230 220-EDIT-TRANSACTION-FIELDS.                                        EDIT
003240*                                                                    EDIT
003250     MOVE 'Y' TO VALID-TRAN-SW.                                      EDIT
003260     MOVE SPACE TO ITL-LINE.                                         EDIT
003270     IF ITR-TRAN-CODE = 1                                            EDIT
003280         PERFORM 240-EDIT-CODE-1-FIELDS                              EDIT
003290     ELSE IF ITR-TRAN-CODE = 2                                       EDIT
003300         PERFORM 250-EDIT-CODE-2-FIELDS                              EDIT
003310     ELSE                                                            EDIT
003320         MOVE MARK TO ITL-TYPE-CODE-ERR                              EDIT
003330         MOVE 'N' TO VALID-TRAN-SW                                   EDIT
003340         ADD 1 TO INVALID-TRAN-CODE-COUNT.                           EDIT
003350*                                                                    EDIT
003360 230-PRINT-INVALID-LINE.                                             EDIT
003370*                                                                    EDIT
003380     MOVE ITR-TYPE-CODE   TO ITL-TYPE-CODE.                          EDIT
003390     MOVE ITR-REF-NO      TO ITL-REF-NO.                             EDIT
```

10

```
003400     MOVE ITR-REF-DATE     TO ITL-REF-DATE.                       EDIT
003410     MOVE ITR-BRANCH-NO    TO ITL-BRANCH-NO.                      EDIT
003420     MOVE ITR-SALESMAN-NO TO ITL-SALESMAN-NO.                     EDIT
003430     MOVE ITR-CUSTOMER-NO TO ITL-CUSTOMER-NO.                     EDIT
003440     MOVE ITR-QUANTITY     TO ITL-QUANTITY.                       EDIT
003450     MOVE ITR-PART-NUMBER TO ITL-PART-NUMBER.                     EDIT
003460     MOVE ITR-RETURN-CODE TO ITL-RETURN-CODE.                     EDIT
003470     IF LINE-COUNT GREATER THAN LINES-ON-PAGE                     EDIT
003480         PERFORM 260-PRINT-REPORT-HEADING.                        EDIT
003490     MOVE ITL-LINE TO PRINT-AREA.                                 EDIT
003500     PERFORM 270-WRITE-REPORT-LINE.                               EDIT
003510*                                                                 EDIT
003520 240-EDIT-CODE-1-FIELDS.                                          EDIT
003530*                                                                 EDIT
003540     PERFORM 280-SEARCH-PART-NUMBER-TABLE.                        EDIT
003550     IF NOT FOUND                                                 EDIT
003560         MOVE MARK TO ITL-PART-NUMBER-ERR.                        EDIT
003570     IF ITR-UPDATE-CODE NOT = 'C'                                 EDIT
003580         MOVE MARK TO ITL-TYPE-CODE-ERR.                          EDIT
003590     IF          ITR-REF-DATE NUMERIC                             EDIT
003600           AND GOOD-ITR-DAY                                       EDIT
003610           AND GOOD-ITR-MONTH                                     EDIT
003620           AND (ITR-YEAR = (CURRENT-YEAR OR CURRENT-YEAR-MINUS-1))EDIT
003630         NEXT SENTENCE                                            EDIT
003640     ELSE                                                         EDIT
003650         MOVE MARK TO ITL-REF-DATE-ERR.                           EDIT
003660     IF          ITR-BRANCH-NO NOT NUMERIC                        EDIT
003670            OR NOT GOOD-ITR-BRANCH                                EDIT
003680         MOVE MARK TO ITL-BRANCH-NO-ERR.                          EDIT
003690     IF          ITR-SALESMAN-NO NOT NUMERIC                      EDIT
003700            OR ITR-SALESMAN-NO = ZERO                             EDIT
003710         MOVE MARK TO ITL-SALESMAN-NO-ERR.                        EDIT
003720     IF          ITR-CUSTOMER-NO NOT NUMERIC                      EDIT
003730            OR ITR-CUSTOMER-NO = ZERO                             EDIT
003740         MOVE MARK TO ITL-CUSTOMER-NO-ERR.                        EDIT
003750     IF          ITR-QUANTITY NOT NUMERIC                         EDIT
003760            OR ITR-QUANTITY = ZERO                                EDIT
003770         MOVE MARK TO ITL-QUANTITY-ERR.                           EDIT
```

```
003780     IF ITL-LINE NOT = SPACE                                       EDIT
003790         MOVE 'N' TO VALID-TRAN-SW                                 EDIT
003800         ADD 1 TO INVALID-SALES-COUNT                              EDIT
003810     ELSE                                                          EDIT
003820         ADD 1 TO VALID-SALES-COUNT.                               EDIT
003830*                                                                  EDIT
003840 250-EDIT-CODE-2-FIELDS.                                           EDIT
003850*                                                                  EDIT
003860     PERFORM 280-SEARCH-PART-NUMBER-TABLE.                         EDIT
003870     IF NOT FOUND                                                  EDIT
003880         MOVE MARK TO ITL-PART-NUMBER-ERR.                         EDIT
003890     IF ITR-UPDATE-CODE NOT = 'C'                                  EDIT
003900         MOVE MARK TO ITL-TYPE-CODE-ERR.                           EDIT
003910     IF          ITR-REF-DATE NUMERIC                              EDIT
003920            AND GOOD-ITR-DAY                                       EDIT
003930            AND GOOD-ITR-MONTH                                     EDIT
003940            AND (ITR-YEAR = (CURRENT-YEAR OR CURRENT-YEAR-MINUS-1))EDIT
003950         NEXT SENTENCE                                             EDIT
003960     ELSE                                                          EDIT
003970         MOVE MARK TO ITL-REF-DATE-ERR.                            EDIT
003980     IF          ITR-CUSTOMER-NO NOT NUMERIC                       EDIT
003990             OR ITR-CUSTOMER-NO = ZERO                             EDIT
004000         MOVE MARK TO ITL-CUSTOMER-NO-ERR.                         EDIT
004010     IF          ITR-QUANTITY NOT NUMERIC                          EDIT
004020             OR ITR-QUANTITY = ZERO                                EDIT
004030         MOVE MARK TO ITL-QUANTITY-ERR.                            EDIT
004040     IF          ITR-RETURN-CODE NOT ALPHABETIC                    EDIT
004050             OR ITR-RETURN-CODE = SPACE                            EDIT
004060         MOVE MARK TO ITL-RETURN-CODE-ERR.                         EDIT
004070     IF ITL-LINE NOT = SPACE                                       EDIT
004080         MOVE 'N' TO VALID-TRAN-SW                                 EDIT
004090         ADD 1 TO INVALID-RETURN-COUNT                             EDIT
004100     ELSE                                                          EDIT
004110         ADD 1 TO VALID-RETURN-COUNT.                              EDIT
004120*                                                                  EDIT
004130 260-PRINT-REPORT-HEADING.                                         EDIT
004140*                                                                  EDIT
004150     ADD 1 TO HDG1-PAGE-NO.                                        EDIT
```

```
004160     MOVE HDG-LINE-1 TO PRINT-AREA.                              EDIT
004170     PERFORM 290-WRITE-PAGE-TOP-LINE.                            EDIT
004180     MOVE HDG-LINE-2 TO PRINT-AREA.                              EDIT
004190     MOVE 2 TO SPACE-CONTROL.                                    EDIT
004200     PERFORM 270-WRITE-REPORT-LINE.                              EDIT
004210     MOVE HDG-LINE-3 TO PRINT-AREA.                              EDIT
004220     MOVE 1 TO SPACE-CONTROL.                                    EDIT
004230     PERFORM 270-WRITE-REPORT-LINE.                              EDIT
004240     MOVE 2 TO SPACE-CONTROL.                                    EDIT
004250*                                                                EDIT
004260 270-WRITE-REPORT-LINE.                                          EDIT
004270*                                                                EDIT
004280     WRITE PRINT-AREA                                            EDIT
004290         AFTER ADVANCING SPACE-CONTROL LINES.                    EDIT
004300     ADD SPACE-CONTROL TO LINE-COUNT.                            EDIT
004310*                                                                EDIT
004320 280-SEARCH-PART-NUMBER-TABLE.                                   EDIT
004330*                                                                EDIT
004340     SET PN-TABLE-INDEX TO 1.                                    EDIT
004350     SEARCH PN-TABLE-ENTRY                                       EDIT
004360         AT END                                                  EDIT
004370             MOVE 'N' TO FOUND-SW                                EDIT
004380         WHEN ITR-PART-NUMBER = PN-TABLE-ENTRY (PN-TABLE-INDEX)  EDIT
004390             MOVE 'Y' TO FOUND-SW                                EDIT
004400         WHEN PN-TABLE-INDEX GREATER PN-ENTRY-COUNT              EDIT
004410             MOVE 'N' TO FOUND-SW.                               EDIT
004420*                                                                EDIT
004430 290-WRITE-PAGE-TOP-LINE.                                        EDIT
004440*                                                                EDIT
004450     WRITE PRINT-AREA                                            EDIT
004460         AFTER ADVANCING PAGE-TOP.                               EDIT
004470     MOVE ZERO TO LINE-COUNT.                                    EDIT
004480*                                                                EDIT
004490 300-PRINT-TOTAL-PAGE.                                           EDIT
004500*                                                                EDIT
004510     ADD VALID-SALES-COUNT    VALID-RETURN-COUNT                 EDIT
004520         GIVING  VALID-COUNT.                                    EDIT
004530     ADD INVALID-SALES-COUNT  INVALID-RETURN-COUNT               EDIT
```

```
          GIVING  INVALID-COUNT.                                     EDIT
      MOVE TOTAL-LINE-1 TO PRINT-AREA.                               EDIT
      PERFORM 290-WRITE-PAGE-TOP-LINE.                               EDIT
      MOVE VALID-SALES-COUNT TO TOT2-VALID-SALES-COUNT.              EDIT
      MOVE TOTAL-LINE-2 TO PRINT-AREA.                               EDIT
      MOVE 2 TO SPACE-CONTROL.                                       EDIT
      PERFORM 270-WRITE-REPORT-LINE.                                 EDIT
      MOVE VALID-RETURN-COUNT TO TOT3-VALID-RETURN-COUNT             EDIT
      MOVE TOTAL-LINE-3 TO PRINT-AREA.                               EDIT
      MOVE 1 TO SPACE-CONTROL.                                       EDIT
      PERFORM 270-WRITE-REPORT-LINE.                                 EDIT
      MOVE VALID-COUNT TO TOT4-VALID-COUNT.                          EDIT
      MOVE TOTAL-LINE-4 TO PRINT-AREA.                               EDIT
      MOVE 1 TO SPACE-CONTROL.                                       EDIT
      PERFORM 270-WRITE-REPORT-LINE.                                 EDIT
      MOVE INVALID-SALES-COUNT TO TOT5-INVALID-SALES-COUNT.          EDIT
      MOVE TOTAL-LINE-5 TO PRINT-AREA.                               EDIT
      MOVE 2 TO SPACE-CONTROL.                                       EDIT
      PERFORM 270-WRITE-REPORT-LINE.                                 EDIT
      MOVE INVALID-RETURN-COUNT TO TOT6-INVALID-RETURN-COUNT.        EDIT
      MOVE TOTAL-LINE-6 TO PRINT-AREA.                               EDIT
      MOVE 1 TO SPACE-CONTROL.                                       EDIT
      PERFORM 270-WRITE-REPORT-LINE.                                 EDIT
      MOVE INVALID-COUNT TO TOT7-INVALID-COUNT.                      EDIT
      MOVE TOTAL-LINE-7 TO PRINT-AREA.                               EDIT
      MOVE 1 TO SPACE-CONTROL.                                       EDIT
      PERFORM 270-WRITE-REPORT-LINE.                                 EDIT
      MOVE INVALID-TRAN-CODE-COUNT TO TOT8-INVALID-TRAN-CODE-COUNT.EDIT
      MOVE TOTAL-LINE-8 TO PRINT-AREA.                               EDIT
      MOVE 2 TO SPACE-CONTROL.                                       EDIT
      PERFORM 270-WRITE-REPORT-LINE.                                 EDIT
      MOVE TRANS-PROCESSED-COUNT TO TOT9-TRANS-PROCESSED-COUNT.      EDIT
      MOVE TOTAL-LINE-9 TO PRINT-AREA.                               EDIT
      MOVE 2 TO SPACE-CONTROL.                                       EDIT
      PERFORM 270-WRITE-REPORT-LINE.                                 EDIT
```

```
23

                          CROSS-REFERENCE DICTIONARY

DATA NAMES                      DEFN     REFERENCE


COUNT-FIELDS                    000063
CURRENT-YEAR                    000085   000273   000274   000359   000391
CURRENT-YEAR-MINUS-1            000086   000274   000359   000391
DATE-FIELDS                     000080
FOUND-SW                        000060   000437   000439   000441
HDG-LINE-1                      000125   000416
HDG-LINE-2                      000136   000418
HDG-LINE-3                      000147   000421
HDG1-CC                         000127
HDG1-DATE                       000129   000275
HDG1-PAGE-NO                    000133   000415
HDG2-CC                         000138
HDG3-CC                         000149
INV-AREA                        000040   000317
INVALID-COUNT                   000071   000453   000477
INVALID-RETURN-COUNT            000069   000409   000453   000473
INVALID-SALES-COUNT             000067   000380   000453   000469
INVALID-TRAN-CODE-CUUNT         000066   000334   000481
INVTRANS                        000019   000269   000283   000317
ITL-BRANCH-NO                   000170   000341
ITL-BRANCH-NO-ERR               000169   000368
ITL-CC                          000159
ITL-CUSTOMER-NO                 000176   000343
ITL-CUSTOMER-NO-ERR             000175   000374   000400
ITL-LINE                        000157   000326   000349   000378   000407
ITL-PART-NUMBER                 000182   000345
ITL-PART-NUMBER-ERR             000181   000356   000388
ITL-QUANTITY                    000179   000344
ITL-QUANTITY-ERR                000178   000377   000403
ITL-REF-DATE                    000167   000340
ITL-REF-DATE-ERR                000166   000365   000397
ITL-REF-NO                      000164   000339
```

```
ITL-REF-NO-ERR          000163
ITL-RETURN-CODE         000185  000346
ITL-RETURN-CODE-ERR     000184  000406
ITL-SALESMAN-NO         000173  000342
ITL-SALESMAN-NO-ERR     000172  000371
ITL-TYPE-CODE           000161  000338
ITL-TYPE-CODE-ERR       000160  000332  000358  000390
ITR-BRANCH-NO           000116  000341  000366
ITR-CUSTOMER-NO         000119  000343  000372  000398
ITR-DAY                 000113
ITR-MONTH               000111
ITR-PART-NUMBER         000121  000345  000437
ITR-QUANTITY            000120  000344  000375  000401
ITR-RECORD              000104  000317
ITR-REF-DATE            000110  000340  000359  000391
ITR-REF-NO              000109  000339
ITR-RETURN-CODE         000122  000346  000404
ITR-SALESMAN-NO         000118  000342  000369
ITR-TRAN-CODE           000108  000327  000329
ITR-TYPE-CODE           000106  000338
ITR-UPDATE-CODE         000107  000357  000389
ITR-YEAR                000115  000359  000391
ITRANLST                000020  000269  000283  000428  000445
LINE-COUNT              000076  000347  000430  000447
LINES-ON-PAGE           000077  000347
MARK                    000100  000332  000356  000358  000365  000368  000371  000374  000377  000388  000390
                                000397  000400  000403  000406
PART-NUMBER-EOF-SW      000054  000301
PARTNUMS                000018  000269  000283  000299
PN-ENTRY-COUNT          000093  000295  000439
PN-TABLE                000088
PN-TABLE-ENTRY          000090  000305  000437
PN-TABLE-INDEX          000090  000277  000294  000295  000305  000434  000437  000439  000441
PNF-AREA                000032  000299
PNF-PART-NUMBER         000097  000305
PNF-RECORD              000095  000299
PRINT-AREA              000048  000349  000416  000418  000421  000428  000445  000455  000458  000462  000466
                                000470  000474  000478  000482  000486
```

```
 25

PRINT-FIELDS                    000074
SPACE-CONTROL                   000078   000419  000422  000424  000428  000430  000459  000463  000467  000471  000475
                                         000479  000483  000487
SWITCHES                        000052
TODAYS-DATE                     000082   000272  000275
TODAYS-YEAR                     000084   000273
TOTAL-LINE-1                    000188   000455
TOTAL-LINE-2                    000197   000458
TOTAL-LINE-3                    000205   000462
TOTAL-LINE-4                    000213   000466
TOTAL-LINE-5                    000222   000470
TOTAL-LINE-6                    000230   000474
TOTAL-LINE-7                    000238   000478
TOTAL-LINE-8                    000247   000482
TOTAL-LINE-9                    000256   000486
TOT1-CC                         000190
TOT1-DATE                       000194   000275
TOT2-CC                         000199
TOT2-VALID-SALES-COUNT          000202   000457
TOT3-CC                         000207
TOT3-VALID-RETURN-COUNT         000210   000461
TOT4-CC                         000215
TOT4-VALID-COUNT                000218   000465
TOT5-CC                         000224
TOT5-INVALID-SALES-COUNT        000227   000469
TOT6-CC                         000232
TOT6-INVALID-RETURN-COUNT       000235   000473
TOT7-CC                         000240
TOT7-INVALID-COUNT              000243   000477
TOT8-CC                         000249
TOT8-INVALID-TRAN-CODE-COUNT    000252   000481
TOT9-CC                         000258
TOT9-TRANS-PROCESSED-COUNT      000261   000485
TRAN-EOF-SW                     000056   000319
TRANS-PROCESSED-COUNT           000065   000321  000485
VALID-COUNT                     000072   000451  000465
VALID-RETURN-COUNT              000070   000411  000451  000461
VALID-SALES-COUNT               000068   000382  000451  000457
```

```
 26

VALID-TRAN-SW                          000058   000325   000333   000379   000408




 27

PROCEDURE NAMES                        DEFN     REFERENCE


000-EDIT-INVENTORY-TRANS               000267
100-LOAD-PART-NUMBER-TABLE             000288   000277
110-READ-PART-NUMBER-RECORD            000297   000290
120-PUT-TABLE-ENTRY                    000303   000292
200-EDIT-INVENTORY-TRAN                000307   000280
210-READ-INVENTORY-TRAN                000315   000309
220-EDIT-TRANSACTION-FIELDS            000323   000311
230-PRINT-INVALID-LINE                 000336   000313
240-EDIT-CODE-1-FIELDS                 000352   000328
250-EDIT-CODE-2-FIELDS                 000384   000330
260-PRINT-REPORT-HEADING               000413   000348
270-WRITE-REPORT-LINE                  000426   000350   000420   000423   000460   000464   000468   000472   000476   000480   000484
                                                000488
280-SEARCH-PART-NUMBER-TABLE           000432   000354   000386
290-WRITE-PAGE-TOP-LINE                000443   000417   000456
300-PRINT-TOTAL-PAGE                   000449   000282
```

The Extract Program

System flowchart:

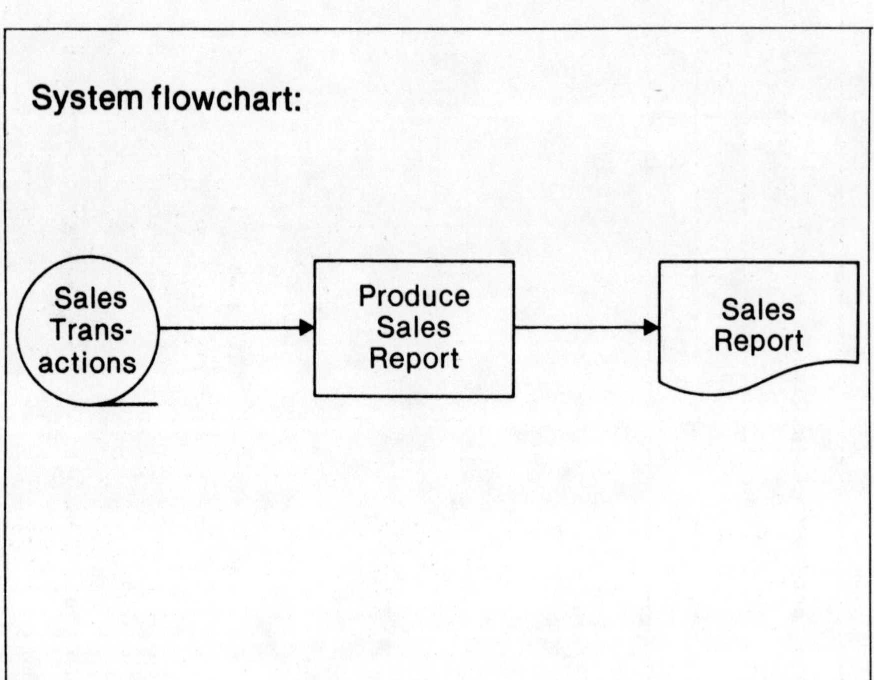

Narrative:

1. The input records have been sorted in customer-number within salesman-number sequence. There will be one or more records for each customer line printed on the report.

2. The sales amount printed for each customer is the sum of the extensions for each customer; the extension is quantity multiplied by unit price.

3. Totals will be printed for each salesman. At the end of the report, the grand total of all sales will be printed.

Transaction record layout:

Field Name	Order Number	Order Date	Salesman Number	Customer Number	Quantity	Item Number	Unit Cost	Unit Price
Characteristics	X(5)	9(6)	X(2)	X(5)	9(3)	X(5)	999V99	999V99
Position	1–5	6–11	12–13	14–18	19–21	22–26	27–31	32–36

Output format:

```
                          1111111111222222222233333333334
                 1234567890123456789012345678901234567890
HDG-LINE-1               SALES REPORT    PAGE 999

HDG-LINE-2       SALESMAN    CUST.        SALES
HDG-LINE-3         NO.        NO.        AMOUNT

CUSTOMER-TOTAL-LINE  XX          XXXXX     99,999.99
                     XX          XXXXX     99,999.99
SALESMAN-TOTAL-LINE                       999,999.99 *

                     XX          XXXXX     99,999.99
                     XX          XXXXX     99,999.99
                     XX          XXXXX     99,999.99
                     XX          XXXXX     99,999.99
                                          999,999.99 *

GRAND-TOTAL-LINE      GRAND TOTAL  $9,999,999.99 * *
```

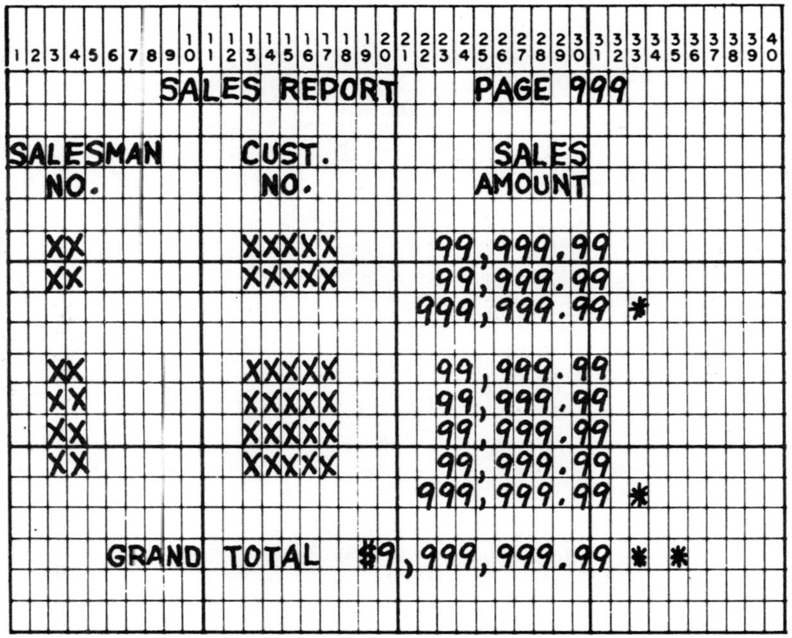

Sample output:

```
                  SALES REPORT     PAGE    1

      SALESMAN     CUST.           SALES
        NO.         NO.           AMOUNT

        31          1052         1,376.75
        31         13498         1,024.00
        31         19763         4,875.00
        31         24291           188.75
                                 7,464.50 *

        37          1940         1,125.00
        37         22341           913.00
                                 2,038.00 *

        44         26888           295.25
        44         27430           175.43
        44         31284         2,257.39
        44         32290           874.50
        44         32292         1,573.20
        44         33480           985.20
        44         49200         1,354.95
        44         58111           540.75
                                 8,056.67 *

             GRAND TOTAL      $17,559.17 * *
```

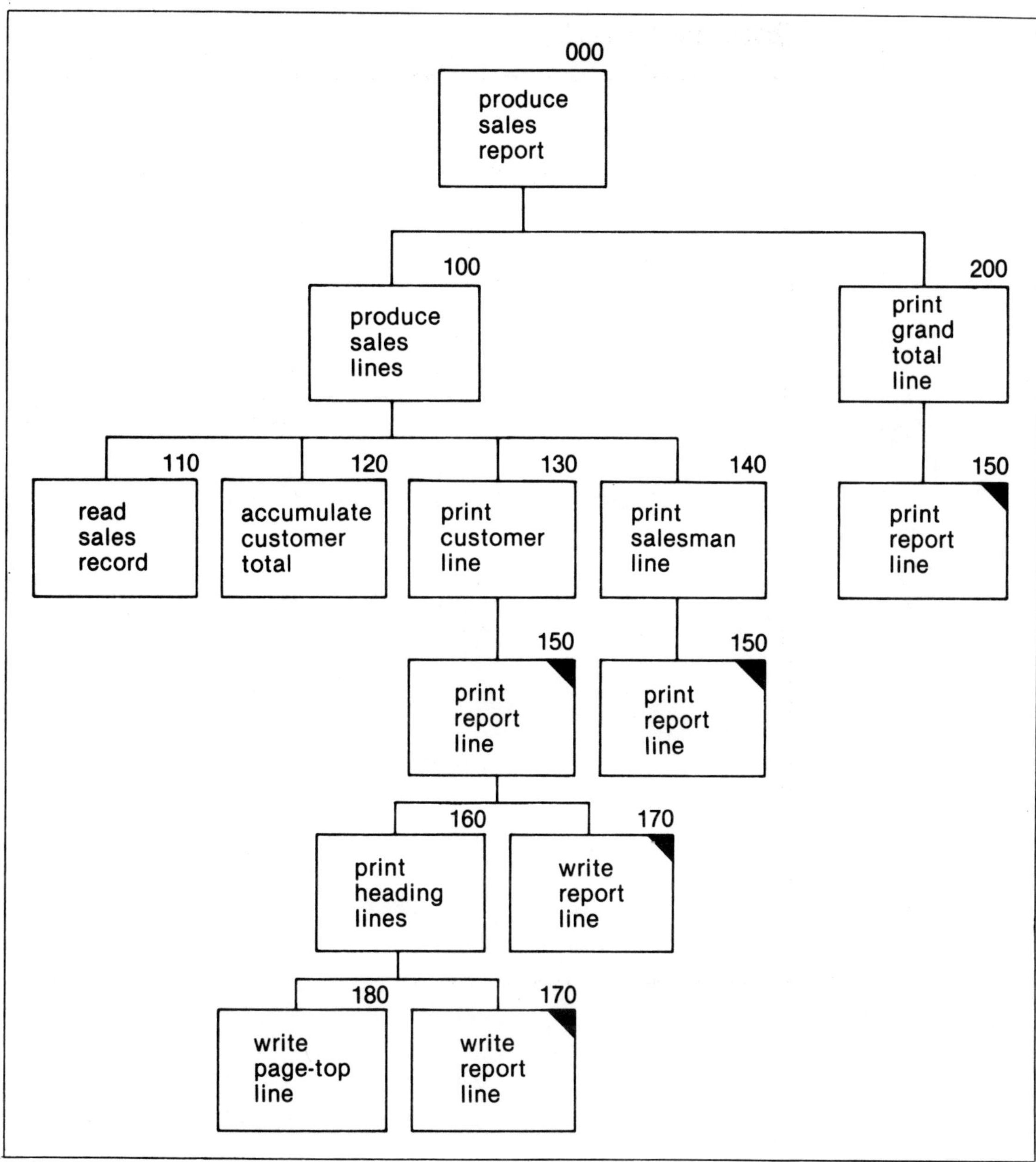
000
produce sales report
100
produce sales lines
200
print grand total line
110
read sales record
120
accumulate customer total
130
print customer line
140
print salesman line
150
print report line
150
print report line
150
print report line
160
print heading lines
170
write report line
180
write page-top line
170
write report line

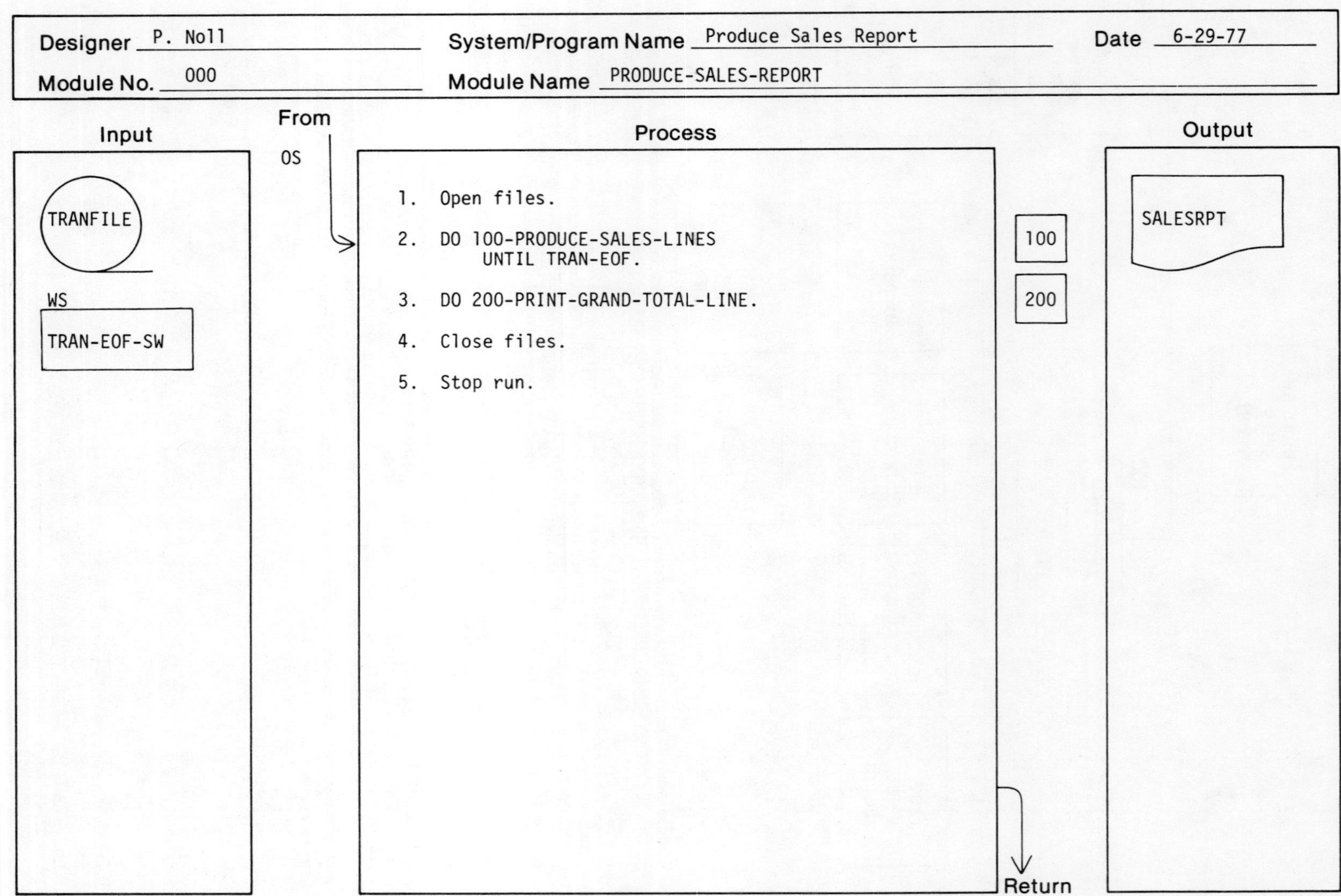
Designer P. Noll
System/Program Name Produce Sales Report
Date 6-29-77
Module No. 000
Module Name PRODUCE-SALES-REPORT
Input
TRANFILE
WS
TRAN-EOF-SW
From
OS
Process
1. Open files.
2. DO 100-PRODUCE-SALES-LINES
UNTIL TRAN-EOF.
3. DO 200-PRINT-GRAND-TOTAL-LINE.
4. Close files.
5. Stop run.
100
200
Return
Output
SALESRPT

Designer P. Noll — System/Program Name Produce Sales Report — Date 6-29-77

Module No. 100 — Module Name PRODUCE-SALES-LINES

Input

WS

FIRST-RECORD-SW

WS

TR-SALESMAN-NO

TR-CUSTOMER-NO

WS

OLD-SALESMAN-NO

OLD-CUSTOMER-NO

WS

TRAN-EOF-SW

From 000

Process

```
1.  DO 110-READ-SALES-RECORD.                                      110

2.  IF FIRST-RECORD
      move TR-SALESMAN-NO to OLD-SALESMAN-NO
      move TR-CUSTOMER-NO to OLD-CUSTOMER-NO
      move 'N' to FIRST-RECORD-SW
    ELSE
      IF TR-SALESMAN-NO is greater than
          OLD-SALESMAN-NO
        DO 130-PRINT-CUSTOMER-LINE                                 130
        DO 140-PRINT-SALESMAN-LINE                                 140
        move TR-CUSTOMER-NO to OLD-CUSTOMER-NO
        move TR-SALESMAN-NO to OLD-SALESMAN-NO
      ELSE
        IF TR-CUSTOMER-NO is greater than
            OLD-CUSTOMER-NO
          DO 130-PRINT-CUSTOMER-LINE                               130
          move TR-CUSTOMER-NO to OLD-CUSTOMER-NO.

3.  IF not TRAN-EOF
      DO 120-ACCUMULATE-CUSTOMER-TOTAL.                            120
```

Return

Output

WS

OLD-SALESMAN-NO

OLD-CUSTOMER-NO

WS

FIRST-RECORD-SW

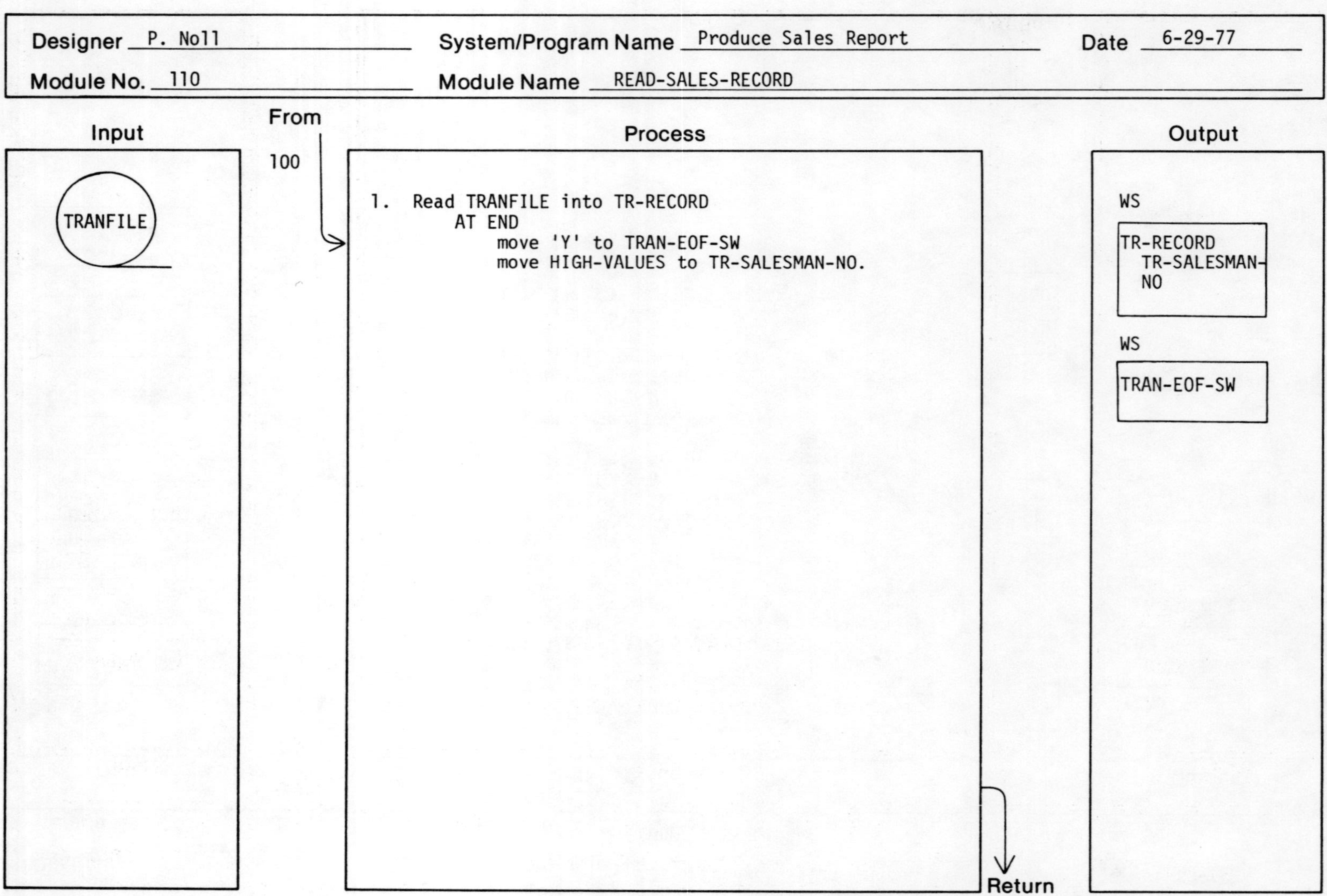

Designer P. Noll — System/Program Name Produce Sales Report — Date 6-29-77

Module No. 110 — Module Name READ-SALES-RECORD

Input

From 100

Process

```
1.  Read TRANFILE into TR-RECORD
        AT END
            move 'Y' to TRAN-EOF-SW
            move HIGH-VALUES to TR-SALESMAN-NO.
```

Return

Output

WS

TR-RECORD
  TR-SALESMAN-NO

WS

TRAN-EOF-SW

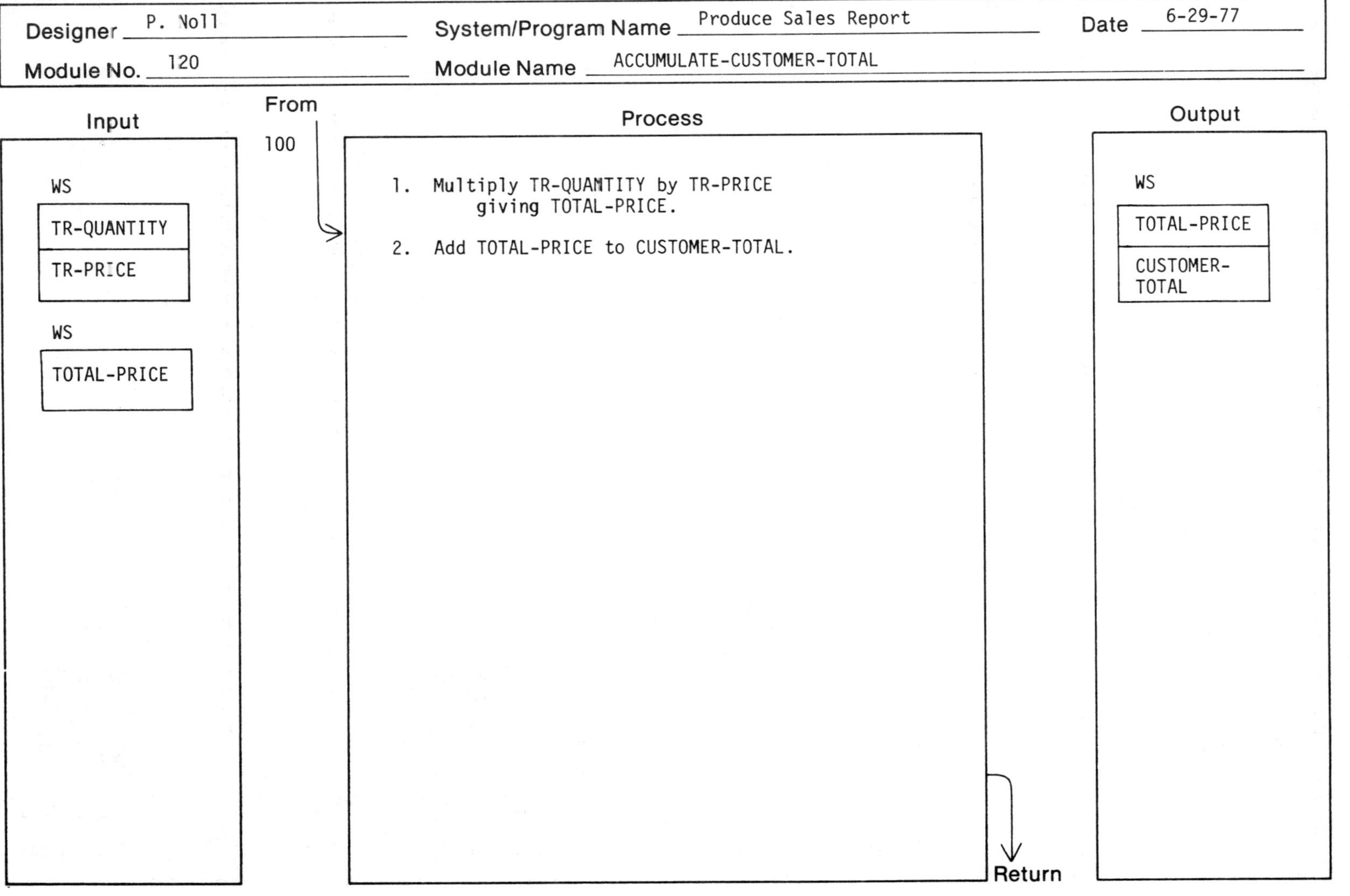
Designer P. Noll
System/Program Name Produce Sales Report
Date 6-29-77
Module No. 120
Module Name ACCUMULATE-CUSTOMER-TOTAL
Input
WS
TR-QUANTITY
TR-PRICE
WS
TOTAL-PRICE
From
100
Process
1. Multiply TR-QUANTITY by TR-PRICE giving TOTAL-PRICE.
2. Add TOTAL-PRICE to CUSTOMER-TOTAL.
Return
Output
WS
TOTAL-PRICE
CUSTOMER-TOTAL

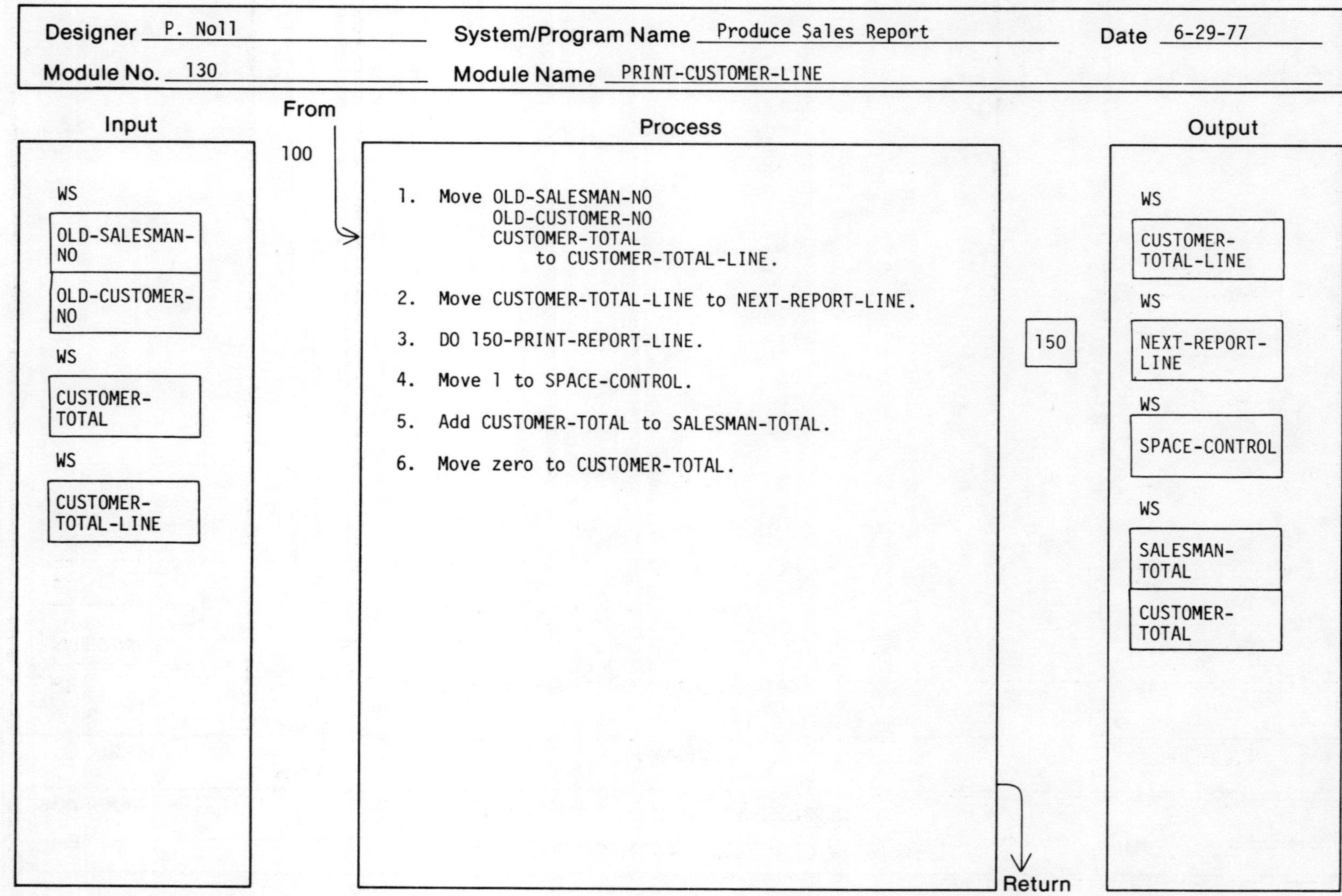
Designer P. Noll
System/Program Name Produce Sales Report
Date 6-29-77
Module No. 130
Module Name PRINT-CUSTOMER-LINE
Input
WS
OLD-SALESMAN-NO
OLD-CUSTOMER-NO
WS
CUSTOMER-TOTAL
WS
CUSTOMER-TOTAL-LINE
From
100
Process
1. Move OLD-SALESMAN-NO
OLD-CUSTOMER-NO
CUSTOMER-TOTAL
to CUSTOMER-TOTAL-LINE.
2. Move CUSTOMER-TOTAL-LINE to NEXT-REPORT-LINE.
3. DO 150-PRINT-REPORT-LINE.
4. Move 1 to SPACE-CONTROL.
5. Add CUSTOMER-TOTAL to SALESMAN-TOTAL.
6. Move zero to CUSTOMER-TOTAL.
150
Return
Output
WS
CUSTOMER-TOTAL-LINE
WS
NEXT-REPORT-LINE
WS
SPACE-CONTROL
WS
SALESMAN-TOTAL
CUSTOMER-TOTAL

Designer: P. Noll	System/Program Name: Produce Sales Report	Date: 6-29-77
Module No.: 140	Module Name: PRINT-SALESMAN-LINE	

Input

WS

SALESMAN-TOTAL

WS

SALESMAN-TOTAL-LINE

From 100

Process

1. Move SALESMAN-TOTAL to SALESMAN-TOTAL-LINE.
2. Move SALESMAN-TOTAL-LINE to NEXT-REPORT-LINE.
3. DO 150-PRINT-REPORT-LINE.
4. Move 2 to SPACE-CONTROL.
5. Add SALESMAN-TOTAL to GRAND-TOTAL.
6. Move zero to SALESMAN-TOTAL.

150

Return

Output

WS

SALESMAN-TOTAL-LINE

WS

NEXT-REPORT-LINE

WS

SPACE-CONTROL

WS

GRAND-TOTAL

SALESMAN-TOTAL

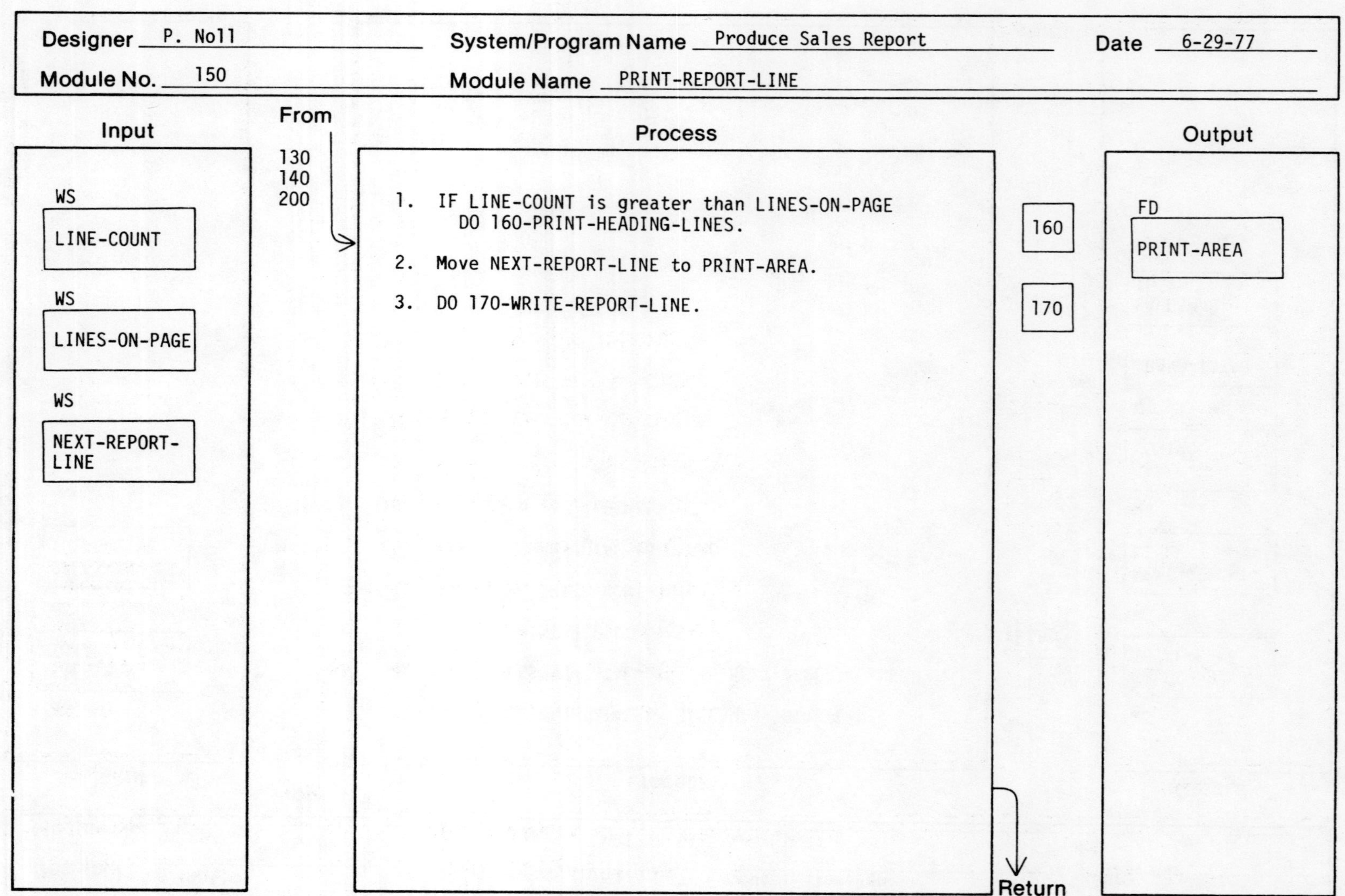

Designer: P. Noll
System/Program Name: Produce Sales Report
Date: 6-29-77
Module No.: 150
Module Name: PRINT-REPORT-LINE

From: 130, 140, 200

Input

WS: LINE-COUNT

WS: LINES-ON-PAGE

WS: NEXT-REPORT-LINE

Process

1. IF LINE-COUNT is greater than LINES-ON-PAGE
   DO 160-PRINT-HEADING-LINES.
2. Move NEXT-REPORT-LINE to PRINT-AREA.
3. DO 170-WRITE-REPORT-LINE.

160

170

Return

Output

FD: PRINT-AREA

Designer P. Noll | System/Program Name Produce Sales Report | Date 6-29-77

Module No. 160 | Module Name PRINT-HEADING-LINES

Input

WS

- HDG-LINE-1
- HDG-LINE-2
- HDG-LINE-3

From 150

Process

1. Add 1 to HDG1-PAGE-NO.
2. Move HDG-LINE-1 to PRINT-AREA.
3. DO 180-WRITE-PAGE-TOP-LINE. [180]
4. Move HDG-LINE-2 to PRINT-AREA.
5. Move 2 to SPACE-CONTROL.
6. DO 170-WRITE-REPORT-LINE. [170]
7. Move HDG-LINE-3 to PRINT-AREA.
8. Move 1 to SPACE-CONTROL.
9. DO 170-WRITE-REPORT-LINE. [170]
10. Move 2 to SPACE-CONTROL.

Return

Output

WS

- HDG1-PAGE-NO

FD

- PRINT-AREA

WS

- SPACE-CONTROL

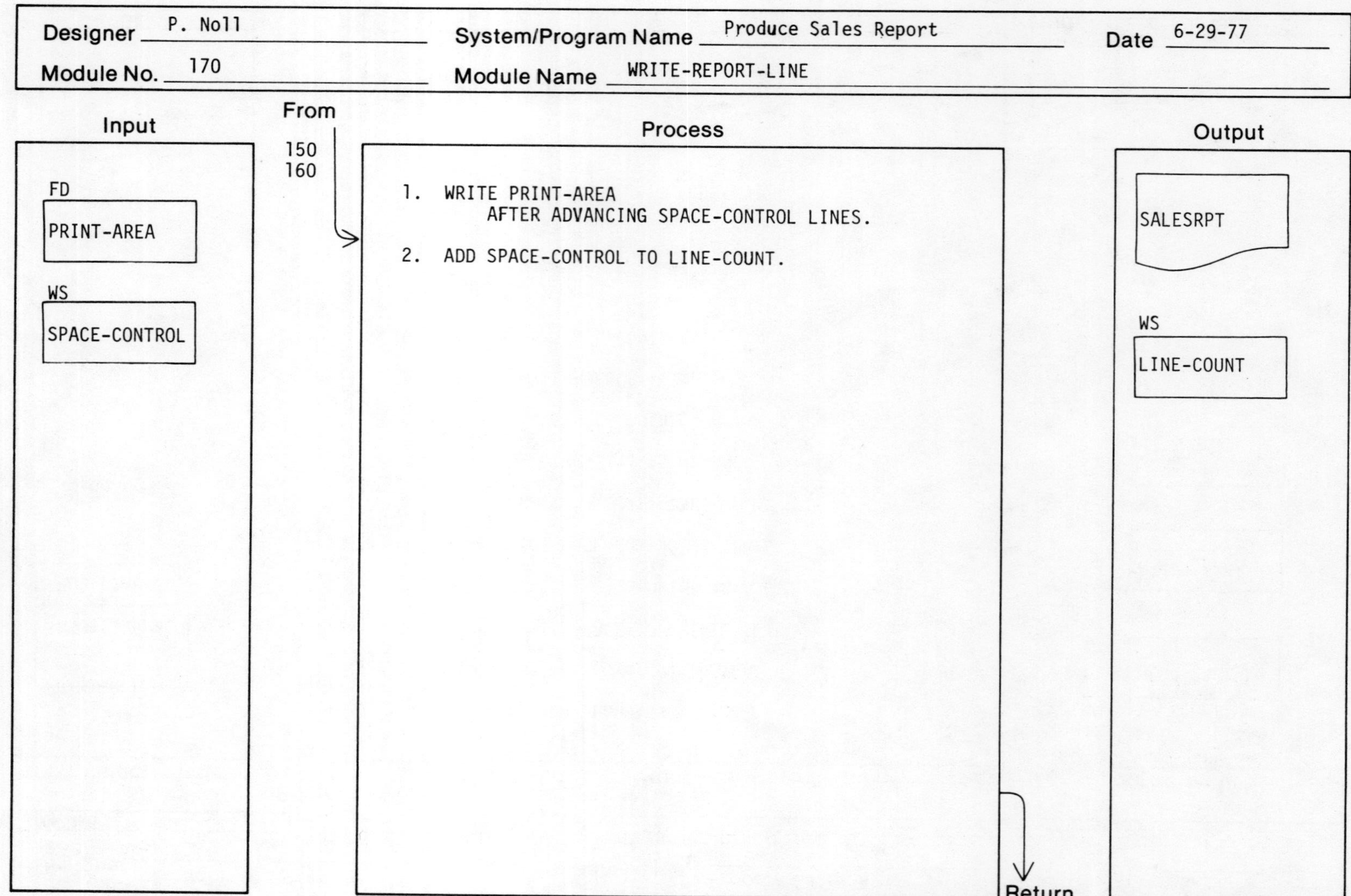
Designer P. Noll
System/Program Name Produce Sales Report
Date 6-29-77
Module No. 170
Module Name WRITE-REPORT-LINE
Input
FD
PRINT-AREA
WS
SPACE-CONTROL
From
150
160
Process
1. WRITE PRINT-AREA
AFTER ADVANCING SPACE-CONTROL LINES.
2. ADD SPACE-CONTROL TO LINE-COUNT.
Return
Output
SALESRPT
WS
LINE-COUNT

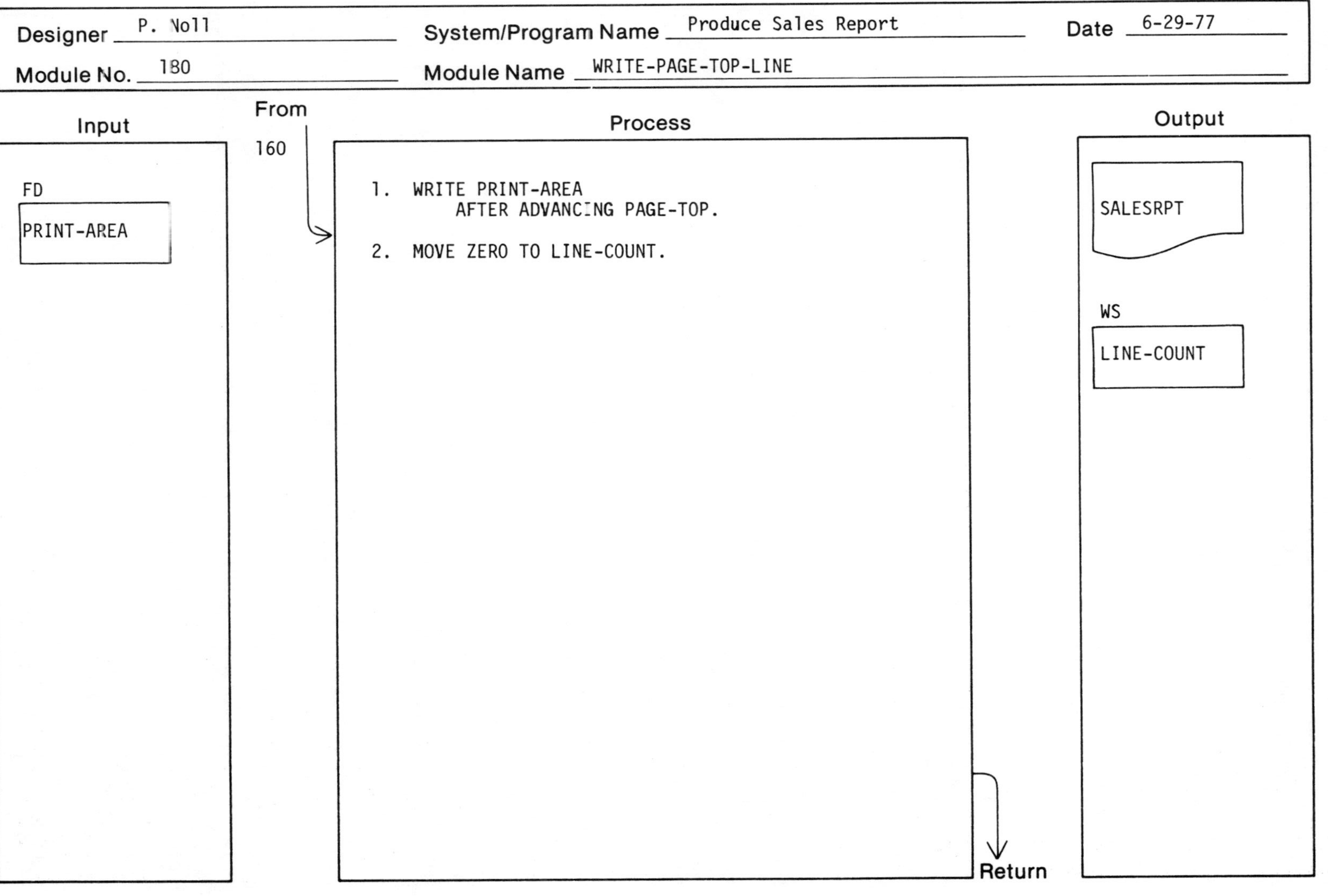
Designer P. Noll
System/Program Name Produce Sales Report
Date 6-29-77
Module No. 180
Module Name WRITE-PAGE-TOP-LINE
Input
FD
PRINT-AREA
From
160
Process
1. WRITE PRINT-AREA
AFTER ADVANCING PAGE-TOP.
2. MOVE ZERO TO LINE-COUNT.
Return
Output
SALESRPT
WS
LINE-COUNT

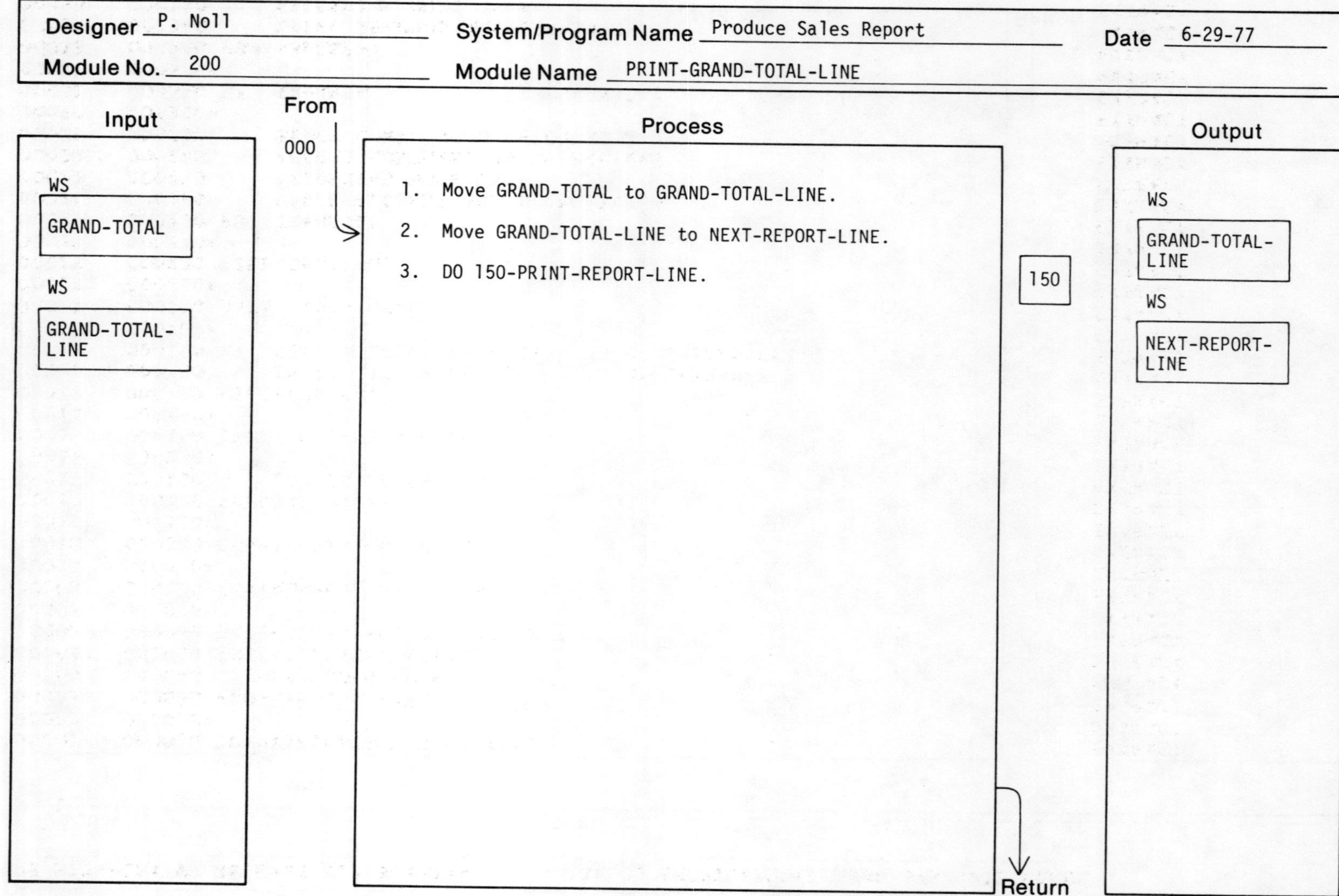

Designer P. Noll
System/Program Name Produce Sales Report
Date 6-29-77
Module No. 200
Module Name PRINT-GRAND-TOTAL-LINE
Input
WS
GRAND-TOTAL
WS
GRAND-TOTAL-LINE
From
000
Process
1. Move GRAND-TOTAL to GRAND-TOTAL-LINE.
2. Move GRAND-TOTAL-LINE to NEXT-REPORT-LINE.
3. DO 150-PRINT-REPORT-LINE.
150
Return
Output
WS
GRAND-TOTAL-LINE
WS
NEXT-REPORT-LINE

```
000010 IDENTIFICATION DIVISION.                                         EXTRACT
000020*                                                                 EXTRACT
000030 PROGRAM-ID. EXTRACT.                                             EXTRACT
000040 AUTHOR. DOUG LOWE.                                               EXTRACT
000050 INSTALLATION. MM&A.                                              EXTRACT
000060 DATE-COMPILED. OCT 20,1977.                                      EXTRACT
000070*                                                                 EXTRACT
000080 ENVIRONMENT DIVISION.                                            EXTRACT
000090*                                                                 EXTRACT
000100 CONFIGURATION SECTION.                                           EXTRACT
000110*                                                                 EXTRACT
000120 SPECIAL-NAMES.                                                   EXTRACT
000130     C01 IS PAGE-TOP.                                             EXTRACT
000140*                                                                 EXTRACT
000150 INPUT-OUTPUT SECTION.                                            EXTRACT
000160*                                                                 EXTRACT
000170 FILE-CONTROL.                                                    EXTRACT
000180     SELECT TRANFILE ASSIGN TO UT-S-TRANFILE.                     EXTRACT
000190     SELECT SALESRPT ASSIGN TO UT-S-SALESRPT.                     EXTRACT
000200*                                                                 EXTRACT
000210 DATA DIVISION.                                                   EXTRACT
000220*                                                                 EXTRACT
000230 FILE SECTION.                                                    EXTRACT
000240*                                                                 EXTRACT
000250 FD  TRANFILE                                                     EXTRACT
000260     LABEL RECORDS ARE STANDARD                                   EXTRACT
000270     RECORDING MODE IS F                                          EXTRACT
000280     RECORD CONTAINS 36 CHARACTERS                                EXTRACT
000290     BLOCK CONTAINS 0 RECORDS.                                    EXTRACT
000300*                                                                 EXTRACT
000310 01  TR-AREA                PIC X(36).                            EXTRACT
000320*                                                                 EXTRACT
000330 FD  SALESRPT                                                     EXTRACT
000340     LABEL RECORDS ARE STANDARD                                   EXTRACT
000350     RECORDING MODE IS F                                          EXTRACT
```

2

```
000360            RECORD CONTAINS 133 CHARACTERS                               EXTRACT
000370            BLOCK CONTAINS 0 RECORDS.                                    EXTRACT
000380*                                                                        EXTRACT
000390 01   PRINT-AREA              PIC X(133).                                EXTRACT
000400*                                                                        EXTRACT
000410 WORKING-STORAGE SECTION.                                                EXTRACT
000420*                                                                        EXTRACT
000430 01   SWITCHES.                                                          EXTRACT
000440*                                                                        EXTRACT
000450      05  TRAN-EOF-SW      PIC X    VALUE 'N'.                           EXTRACT
000460          88  TRAN-EOF              VALUE 'Y'.                           EXTRACT
000470      05  FIRST-RECORD-SW  PIC X    VALUE 'Y'.                           EXTRACT
000480          88  FIRST-RECORD          VALUE 'Y'.                           EXTRACT
000490*                                                                        EXTRACT
000500 01   CONTROL-FIELDS.                                                    EXTRACT
000510*                                                                        EXTRACT
000520      05  OLD-CUSTOMER-NO        PIC X(5).                               EXTRACT
000530      05  OLD-SALESMAN-NO        PIC XX.                                 EXTRACT
000540*                                                                        EXTRACT
000550 01   TOTAL-FIELDS         COMP-3.                                       EXTRACT
000560*                                                                        EXTRACT
000570      05  TOTAL-PRICE      PIC S9(5)V99     VALUE ZERO.                  EXTRACT
000580      05  CUSTOMER-TOTAL   PIC S9(5)V99     VALUE ZERO.                  EXTRACT
000590      05  SALESMAN-TOTAL   PIC S9(7)V99     VALUE ZERO.                  EXTRACT
000600      05  GRAND-TOTAL      PIC S9(7)V99     VALUE ZERO.                  EXTRACT
000610*                                                                        EXTRACT
000620 01   PRINT-FIELDS         COMP             SYNC.                        EXTRACT
000630*                                                                        EXTRACT
000640      05  LINE-COUNT       PIC S999         VALUE +58.                   EXTRACT
000650      05  LINES-ON-PAGE    PIC S999         VALUE +57.                   EXTRACT
000660      05  PAGE-NUMBER      PIC S999         VALUE ZERO.                  EXTRACT
000670      05  SPACE-CONTROL    PIC S9.                                       EXTRACT
000680*                                                                        EXTRACT
000690 01   TR-RECORD.                                                         EXTRACT
000700*                                                                        EXTRACT
000710      05  FILLER           PIC X(11).                                    EXTRACT
000720      05  TR-SALESMAN-NO   PIC XX.                                       EXTRACT
000730      05  TR-CUSTOMER-NO   PIC X(5).                                     EXTRACT
```

```
000740       05  TR-QUANTITY      PIC 999.                             EXTRACT
000750       05  FILLER           PIC X(10).                           EXTRACT
000760       05  TR-PRICE         PIC 999V99.                          EXTRACT
000770*                                                                EXTRACT
000780 01    HDG-LINE-1.                                               EXTRACT
000790*                                                                EXTRACT
000800       05  HDG1-CC          PIC X.                               EXTRACT
000810       05  FILLER           PIC X(20)   VALUE '        SALES REPORT'.EXTRACT
000820       05  FILLER           PIC X(9)    VALUE '    PAGE '.       EXTRACT
000830       05  HDG1-PAGE-NO     PIC ZZ9.                             EXTRACT
000840       05  FILLER           PIC X(100)  VALUE SPACE.             EXTRACT
000850*                                                                EXTRACT
000860 01    HDG-LINE-2.                                               EXTRACT
000870*                                                                EXTRACT
000880       05  HDG2-CC          PIC X.                               EXTRACT
000890       05  FILLER           PIC X(20)   VALUE 'SALESMAN    CUST.   '.EXTRACT
000900       05  FILLER           PIC X(20)   VALUE '     SALES          '.EXTRACT
000910       05  FILLER           PIC X(92)   VALUE SPACE.             EXTRACT
000920*                                                                EXTRACT
000930 01    HDG-LINE-3.                                               EXTRACT
000940*                                                                EXTRACT
000950       05  HDG3-CC          PIC X.                               EXTRACT
000960       05  FILLER           PIC X(20)   VALUE '  NO.        NO.    '.EXTRACT
000970       05  FILLER           PIC X(20)   VALUE '    AMOUNT          '.EXTRACT
000980       05  FILLER           PIC X(92)   VALUE SPACE.             EXTRACT
000990*                                                                EXTRACT
001000 01    NEXT-REPORT-LINE     PIC X(133).                          EXTRACT
001010*                                                                EXTRACT
001020 01    CUSTOMER-TOTAL-LINE.                                      EXTRACT
001030*                                                                EXTRACT
001040       05  CTL-CC                 PIC X.                         EXTRACT
001050       05  FILLER                 PIC XX          VALUE SPACE.   EXTRACT
001060       05  CTL-SALESMAN-NO        PIC Z9.                        EXTRACT
001070       05  FILLER                 PIC X(8)        VALUE SPACE.   EXTRACT
001080       05  CTL-CUSTOMER-NO        PIC Z(4)9.                     EXTRACT
001090       05  FILLER                 PIC X(5)        VALUE SPACE.   EXTRACT
001100       05  CTL-CUSTOMER-TOTAL     PIC ZZ,ZZ9.99.                 EXTRACT
001110       05  FILLER                 PIC X(101)      VALUE SPACE.   EXTRACT
```

4

```
001120*                                                              EXTRACT
001130 01  SALESMAN-TOTAL-LINE.                                      EXTRACT
001140*                                                              EXTRACT
001150     05  STL-CC                  PIC X.                        EXTRACT
001160     05  FILLER                  PIC X(19)       VALUE SPACE.  EXTRACT
001170     05  STL-SALESMAN-TOTAL      PIC Z,ZZZ,ZZ9.99.             EXTRACT
001180     05  FILLER                  PIC XX          VALUE ' *'.   EXTRACT
001190     05  FILLER                  PIC X(99)       VALUE SPACE.  EXTRACT
001200*                                                              EXTRACT
001210 01  GRAND-TOTAL-LINE.                                         EXTRACT
001220*                                                              EXTRACT
001230     05  GTL-CC              PIC X.                            EXTRACT
001240     05  FILLER              PIC X(18)   VALUE '     GRAND TOTAL  EXTRACT
001250     05  GTL-GRAND-TOTAL PIC $$,$$$,$$9.99.                    EXTRACT
001260     05  FILLER              PIC X(4)    VALUE ' * *'.         EXTRACT
001270     05  FILLER              PIC X(97)   VALUE SPACE.          EXTRACT
001280*                                                              EXTRACT
001290 PROCEDURE DIVISION.                                           EXTRACT
001300*                                                              EXTRACT
001310 000-PRODUCE-SALES-REPORT.                                     EXTRACT
001320*                                                              EXTRACT
001330     OPEN INPUT  TRANFILE                                      EXTRACT
001340          OUTPUT SALESRPT.                                     EXTRACT
001350     PERFORM 100-PRODUCE-SALES-LINES                           EXTRACT
001360         UNTIL TRAN-EOF.                                       EXTRACT
001370     PERFORM 200-PRINT-GRAND-TOTAL-LINE.                       EXTRACT
001380     CLOSE TRANFILE                                            EXTRACT
001390           SALESRPT.                                           EXTRACT
001400     STOP RUN.                                                 EXTRACT
001410*                                                              EXTRACT
001420 100-PRODUCE-SALES-LINES.                                      EXTRACT
001430*                                                              EXTRACT
001440     PERFORM 110-READ-SALES-RECORD.                            EXTRACT
001450     IF FIRST-RECORD                                           EXTRACT
001460         MOVE TR-SALESMAN-NO TO OLD-SALESMAN-NO                EXTRACT
001470         MOVE TR-CUSTOMER-NO TO OLD-CUSTOMER-NO                EXTRACT
001480         MOVE 'N' TO FIRST-RECORD-SW                           EXTRACT
001490     ELSE                                                      EXTRACT
```

```
001500         IF TR-SALESMAN-NO GREATER THAN OLD-SALESMAN-NO            EXTRACT
001510             PERFORM 130-PRINT-CUSTOMER-LINE                       EXTRACT
001520             PERFORM 140-PRINT-SALESMAN-LINE                       EXTRACT
001530             MOVE TR-SALESMAN-NO TO OLD-SALESMAN-NO                EXTRACT
001540             MOVE TR-CUSTOMER-NO TO OLD-CUSTOMER-NO                EXTRACT
001550         ELSE                                                      EXTRACT
001560             IF TR-CUSTOMER-NO GREATER THAN OLD-CUSTOMER-NO        EXTRACT
001570                 PERFORM 130-PRINT-CUSTOMER-LINE                   EXTRACT
001580                 MOVE TR-CUSTOMER-NO TO OLD-CUSTOMER-NO.           EXTRACT
001590     IF NOT TRAN-EOF                                               EXTRACT
001600         PERFORM 120-ACCUMULATE-CUSTOMER-TOTAL.                    EXTRACT
001610*                                                                  EXTRACT
001620 110-READ-SALES-RECORD.                                            EXTRACT
001630*                                                                  EXTRACT
001640     READ TRANFILE INTO TR-RECORD                                  EXTRACT
001650         AT END                                                    EXTRACT
001660             MOVE 'Y' TO TRAN-EOF-SW                               EXTRACT
001670             MOVE HIGH-VALUES TO TR-SALESMAN-NO.                   EXTRACT
001680*                                                                  EXTRACT
001690 120-ACCUMULATE-CUSTOMER-TOTAL.                                    EXTRACT
001700*                                                                  EXTRACT
001710     MULTIPLY TR-QUANTITY BY TR-PRICE                              EXTRACT
001720         GIVING TOTAL-PRICE.                                       EXTRACT
001730     ADD TOTAL-PRICE TO CUSTOMER-TOTAL.                            EXTRACT
001740*                                                                  EXTRACT
001750 130-PRINT-CUSTOMER-LINE.                                          EXTRACT
001760*                                                                  EXTRACT
001770     MOVE OLD-SALESMAN-NO      TO CTL-SALESMAN-NO.                 EXTRACT
001780     MOVE OLD-CUSTOMER-NO      TO CTL-CUSTOMER-NO.                 EXTRACT
001790     MOVE CUSTOMER-TOTAL       TO CTL-CUSTOMER-TOTAL.              EXTRACT
001800     MOVE CUSTOMER-TOTAL-LINE TO NEXT-REPORT-LINE.                 EXTRACT
001810     PERFORM 150-PRINT-REPORT-LINE.                                EXTRACT
001820     MOVE 1 TO SPACE-CONTROL.                                      EXTRACT
001830     ADD CUSTOMER-TOTAL TO SALESMAN-TOTAL.                         EXTRACT
001840     MOVE ZERO TO CUSTOMER-TOTAL.                                  EXTRACT
001850*                                                                  EXTRACT
001860 140-PRINT-SALESMAN-LINE.                                          EXTRACT
001870*                                                                  EXTRACT
```

6

```
001880     MOVE SALESMAN-TOTAL      TO STL-SALESMAN-TOTAL.             EXTRACT
001890     MOVE SALESMAN-TOTAL-LINE TO NEXT-REPORT-LINE.               EXTRACT
001900     PERFORM 150-PRINT-REPORT-LINE.                              EXTRACT
001910     MOVE 2 TO SPACE-CONTROL.                                    EXTRACT
001920     ADD SALESMAN-TOTAL TO GRAND-TOTAL.                          EXTRACT
001930     MOVE ZERO TO SALESMAN-TOTAL.                                EXTRACT
001940*                                                                EXTRACT
001950 150-PRINT-REPORT-LINE.                                          EXTRACT
001960*                                                                EXTRACT
001970     IF LINE-COUNT GREATER THAN LINES-ON-PAGE                    EXTRACT
001980         PERFORM 160-PRINT-HEADING-LINES.                        EXTRACT
001990     MOVE NEXT-REPORT-LINE TO PRINT-AREA.                        EXTRACT
002000     PERFORM 170-WRITE-REPORT-LINE.                              EXTRACT
002010*                                                                EXTRACT
002020 160-PRINT-HEADING-LINES.                                        EXTRACT
002030*                                                                EXTRACT
002040     ADD 1 TO PAGE-NUMBER.                                       EXTRACT
002050     MOVE PAGE-NUMBER TO HDG1-PAGE-NO.                           EXTRACT
002060     MOVE HDG-LINE-1 TO PRINT-AREA.                              EXTRACT
002070     PERFORM 180-WRITE-PAGE-TOP-LINE.                            EXTRACT
002080     MOVE HDG-LINE-2 TO PRINT-AREA.                              EXTRACT
002090     MOVE 2 TO SPACE-CONTROL.                                    EXTRACT
002100     PERFORM 170-WRITE-REPORT-LINE.                              EXTRACT
002110     MOVE HDG-LINE-3 TO PRINT-AREA.                              EXTRACT
002120     MOVE 1 TO SPACE-CONTROL.                                    EXTRACT
002130     PERFORM 170-WRITE-REPORT-LINE.                              EXTRACT
002140     MOVE 2 TO SPACE-CONTROL.                                    EXTRACT
002150*                                                                EXTRACT
002160 170-WRITE-REPORT-LINE.                                          EXTRACT
002170*                                                                EXTRACT
002180     WRITE PRINT-AREA                                            EXTRACT
002190         AFTER ADVANCING SPACE-CONTROL LINES.                    EXTRACT
002200     ADD SPACE-CONTROL TO LINE-COUNT.                            EXTRACT
002210*                                                                EXTRACT
002220 180-WRITE-PAGE-TOP-LINE.                                        EXTRACT
002230*                                                                EXTRACT
002240     WRITE PRINT-AREA                                            EXTRACT
002250         AFTER ADVANCING PAGE-TOP.                               EXTRACT
```

7

```
002260     MOVE ZERO TO LINE-COUNT.                                 EXTRACT
002270*                                                             EXTRACT
002280 200-PRINT-GRAND-TOTAL-LINE.                                  EXTRACT
002290*                                                             EXTRACT
002300     MOVE GRAND-TOTAL TO GTL-GRAND-TOTAL.                     EXTRACT
002310     MOVE GRAND-TOTAL-LINE TO NEXT-REPORT-LINE.               EXTRACT
002320     PERFORM 150-PRINT-REPORT-LINE.                           EXTRACT
002330*                                                             EXTRACT
```

```
14

                                  CROSS-REFERENCE DICTIONARY

DATA NAMES                   DEFN     REFERENCE

CONTROL-FIELDS               000050
CTL-CC                       000104
CTL-CUSTOMER-NO              000108   000178
CTL-CUSTOMER-TOTAL           000110   000179
CTL-SALESMAN-NO              000106   000177
CUSTOMER-TOTAL               000058   000173  000179  000183  000184
CUSTOMER-TOTAL-LINE          000102   000180
FIRST-RECORD-SW              000047   000148
GRAND-TOTAL                  000060   000192  000230
GRAND-TOTAL-LINE             000121   000231
GTL-CC                       000123
GTL-GRAND-TOTAL              000125   000230
HDG-LINE-1                   000078   000206
HDG-LINE-2                   000086   000208
HDG-LINE-3                   000093   000211
HDG1-CC                      000080
HDG1-PAGE-NO                 000083   000205
HDG2-CC                      000088
HDG3-CC                      000095
LINE-COUNT                   000064   000197  000220  000226
LINES-ON-PAGE                000065   000197
NEXT-REPORT-LINE             000100   000180  000189  000199  000231
OLD-CUSTOMER-NO              000052   000147  000154  000156  000158  000178
OLD-SALESMAN-NO              000053   000146  000150  000153  000177
PAGE-NUMBER                  000066   000204  000205
PRINT-AREA                   000039   000199  000206  000208  000211  000218  000224
PRINT-FIELDS                 000062
SALESMAN-TOTAL               000059   000183  000188  000192  000193
SALESMAN-TOTAL-LINE          000113   000189
SALESRPT                     000019   000133  000138  000218  000224
SPACE-CONTROL                000067   000182  000191  000209  000212  000214  000218  000220
STL-CC                       000115
```

```
15

STL-SALESMAN-TOTAL                    000117   000188
SWITCHES                              000043
TOTAL-FIELDS                          000055
TOTAL-PRICE                           000057   000171   000173
TR-AREA                               000031   000164
TR-CUSTOMER-NO                        000073   000147   000154   000156   000158
TR-PRICE                              000076   000171
TR-QUANTITY                           000074   000171
TR-RECORD                             000069   000164
TR-SALESMAN-NO                        000072   000146   000150   000153   000167
TRAN-EOF-SW                           000045   000166
TRANFILE                              000018   000133   000138   000164



16

PROCEDURE NAMES                       DEFN     REFERENCE


000-PRODUCE-SALES-REPORT              000131
100-PRODUCE-SALES-LINES               000142   000135
110-READ-SALES-RECORD                 000162   000144
120-ACCUMULATE-CUSTOMER-TOTAL         000169   000160
130-PRINT-CUSTOMER-LINE               000175   000151   000157
140-PRINT-SALESMAN-LINE               000186   000152
150-PRINT-REPORT-LINE                 000195   000181   000190   000232
160-PRINT-HEADING-LINES               000202   000198
170-WRITE-REPORT-LINE                 000216   000200   000210   000213
180-WRITE-PAGE-TOP-LINE               000222   000207
200-PRINT-GRAND-TOTAL-LINE            000228   000137
```

The Sequential-Update Program

System flowchart:

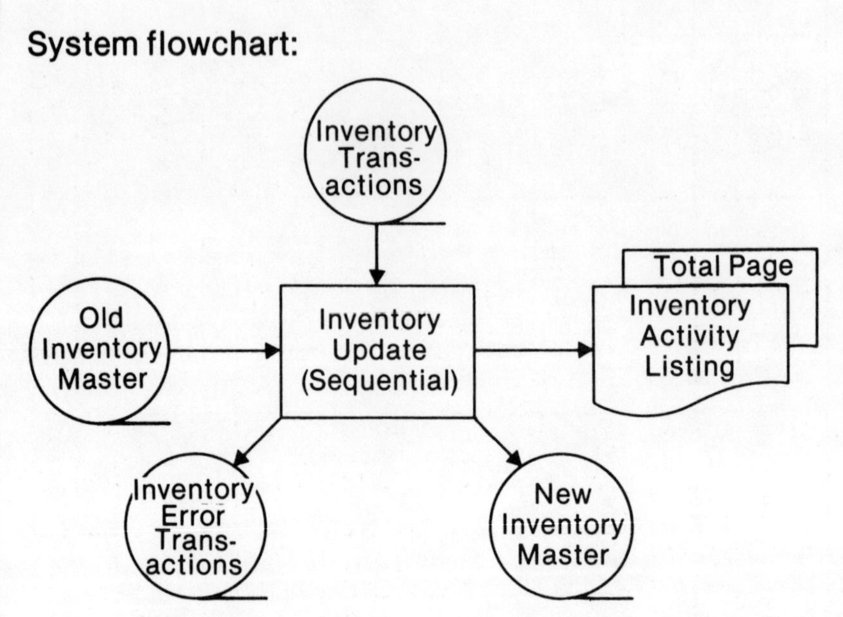

Narrative:

1. Use transaction records to update master records. A transaction record may change, add, or delete a master file record. There may be none, one, or several transactions for each master, and both files are in item-number sequence.

2. Print an update report with one line for each valid transaction record as shown in the print chart. The totals for the program are to be printed on a separate output page.

3. Write a record on the error tape if an unmatched transaction or an invalid action code is detected. The error record should have the same format as the transaction record.

Record layouts:

Inventory Master Records

Field Name	Item No.	Item Description	Unit Cost	Unit Price	On-hand Balance
Characteristics	X(5)	X(20)	999V99	999V99	9(3)
Position	1-5	6-25	26-30	31-35	36-38

Transaction Record for a Master-File Addition

Field Name	Action Code	Item No.	Item Description	Unit Cost	Unit Price	On-hand Balance
Characteristics	A	X(5)	X(20)	999V99	999V99	9(3)
Position	1	2-6	7-26	27-31	32-36	37-39

Transaction Record for a Master-File Change (Only fields that need to be changed are given in the transaction)

Field Name	Action Code	Item No.	Item Description	Unit Cost	Unit Price	On-hand Balance
Characteristics	C	X(5)	X(20)	999V99	999V99	9(3)
Position	1	2-6	7-26	27-31	32-36	37-39

Transaction Record for a Master-File Deletion

Field Name	Action Code	Item No.	Unused
Characteristics	D	X(5)	X(33)
Position	1	2-6	7-39

Output format:

```
HDG-LINE-1          99-99-99                            UPDATE LISTING                           PAGE 999

HDG-LINE-2          ITEM NO.   ITEM DESCRIPTION         UNIT COST    UNIT PRICE    ON HAND    ACTION

NEXT-UPDATE-LINE     XXXXX     XXXXXXXXXXXXXXXXXXXX      999.99        999.99       999       CHANGED
                     XXXXX     XXXXXXXXXXXXXXXXXXXX      999.99        999.99       999       ADDED
                     XXXXX     XXXXXXXXXXXXXXXXXXXX      999.99        999.99       999       DELETED


Total page:

TOTAL-LINE-1        SUMMARY FOR UPDATE RUN OF 99-99-99

TOTAL-LINE-2        CHANGES                   99,999
TOTAL-LINE-3        ADDITIONS                 99,999
TOTAL-LINE-4        DELETIONS                 99,999
TOTAL-LINE-5        TOTAL UPDATES             99,999 *

TOTAL-LINE-6        ERRORS                    99,999

TOTAL-LINE-7        TRANSACTIONS PROCESSED   999,999 * *
```

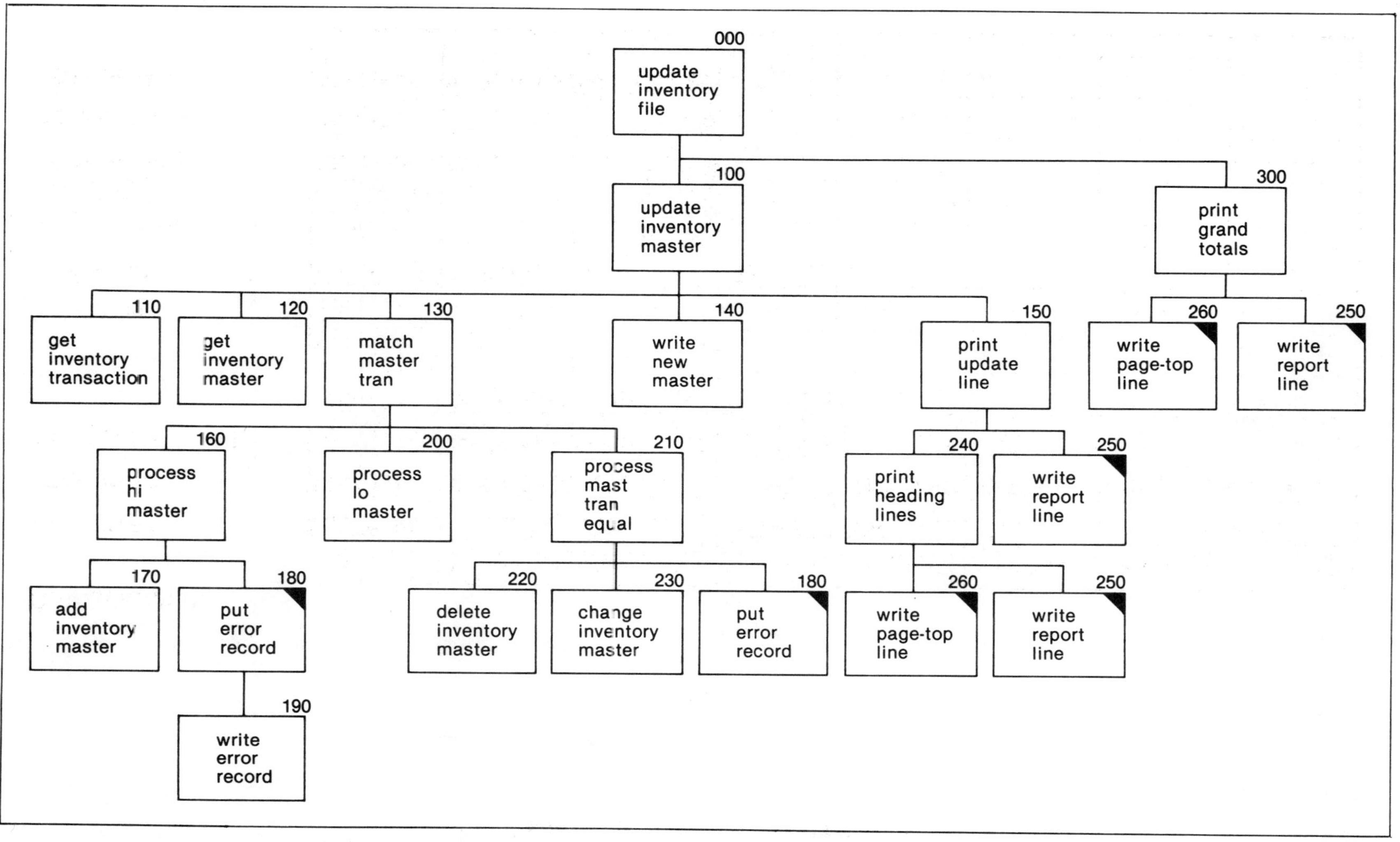
000
update inventory file
100
update inventory master
300
print grand totals
110
get inventory transaction
120
get inventory master
130
match master tran
140
write new master
150
print update line
260
write page-top line
250
write report line
160
process hi master
200
process lo master
210
process mast tran equal
240
print heading lines
250
write report line
170
add inventory master
180
put error record
220
delete inventory master
230
change inventory master
180
put error record
260
write page-top line
250
write report line
190
write error record

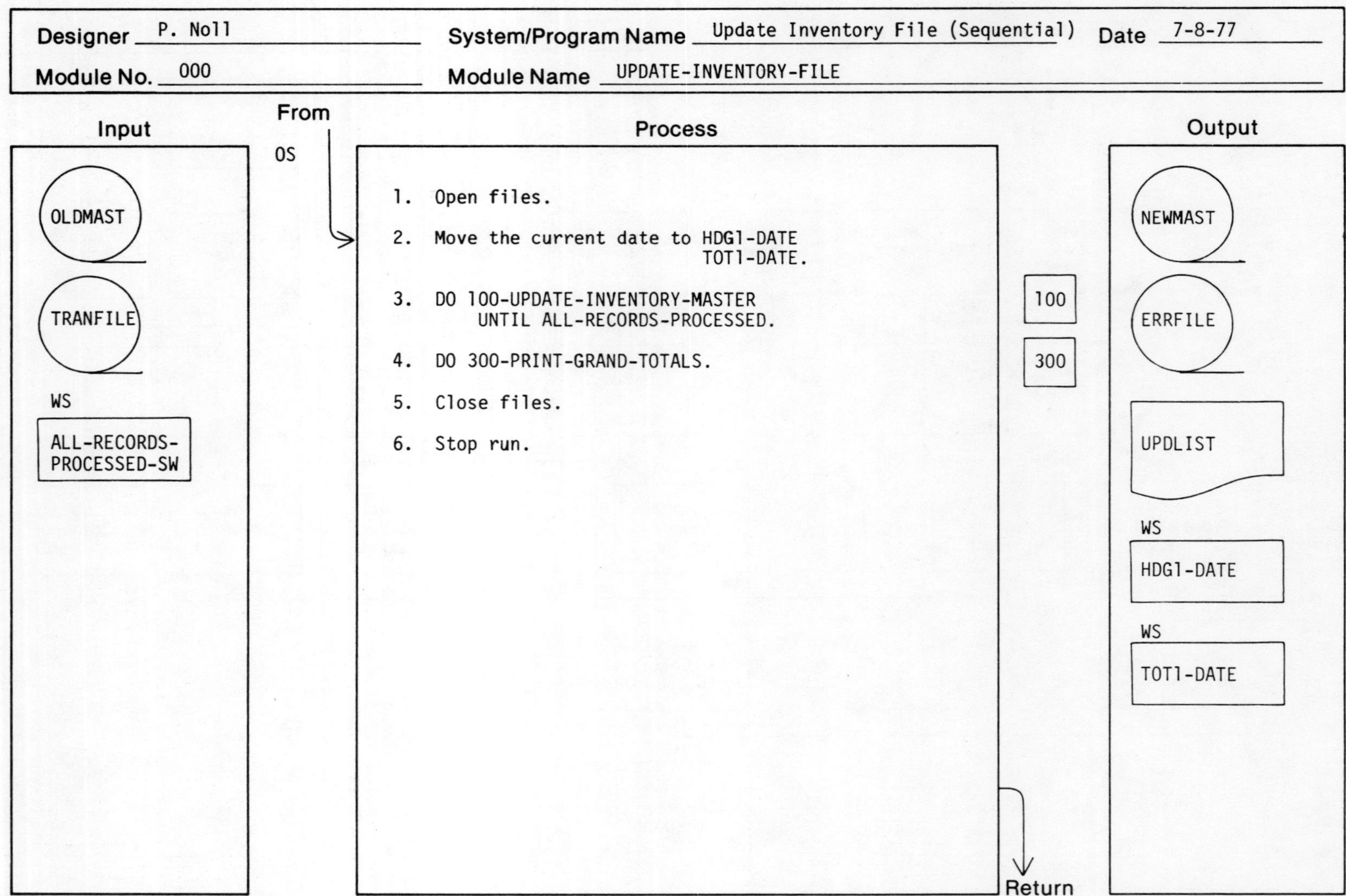

Designer P. Noll System/Program Name Update Inventory File (Sequential) Date 7-8-77

Module No. 000 Module Name UPDATE-INVENTORY-FILE

Input

OLDMAST

TRANFILE

WS

ALL-RECORDS-PROCESSED-SW

From

OS

Process

1. Open files.
2. Move the current date to HDG1-DATE
   TOT1-DATE.
3. DO 100-UPDATE-INVENTORY-MASTER
   UNTIL ALL-RECORDS-PROCESSED.
4. DO 300-PRINT-GRAND-TOTALS.
5. Close files.
6. Stop run.

100

300

Return

Output

NEWMAST

ERRFILE

UPDLIST

WS

HDG1-DATE

WS

TOT1-DATE

Designer P. Noll   System/Program Name Update Inventory File (Sequential)   Date 7-8-77

Module No. 100   Module Name UPDATE-INVENTORY-MASTER

Input	From	Process		Output
WS NEED-TRANSACTION-SW NEED-MASTER-SW WRITE-MASTER-SW PRINT-UPDATE-SW	000	1. IF NEED-TRANSACTION DO 110-GET-INVENTORY-TRANSACTION move 'N' to NEED-TRANSACTION-SW.	110	WS NEED-TRANSACTION-SW NEED-MASTER-SW WRITE-MASTER-SW PRINT-UPDATE-SW
		2. IF NEED-MASTER DO 120-GET-INVENTORY-MASTER move 'N' to NEED-MASTER-SW.	120	
		3. DO 130-MATCH-MASTER-TRAN.	130	
		4. IF WRITE-MASTER DO 140-WRITE-NEW-MASTER move 'N' to WRITE-MASTER-SW.	140	
		5. IF PRINT-UPDATE DO 150-PRINT-UPDATE-LINE move 'N' to PRINT-UPDATE-SW.	150	
			Return	

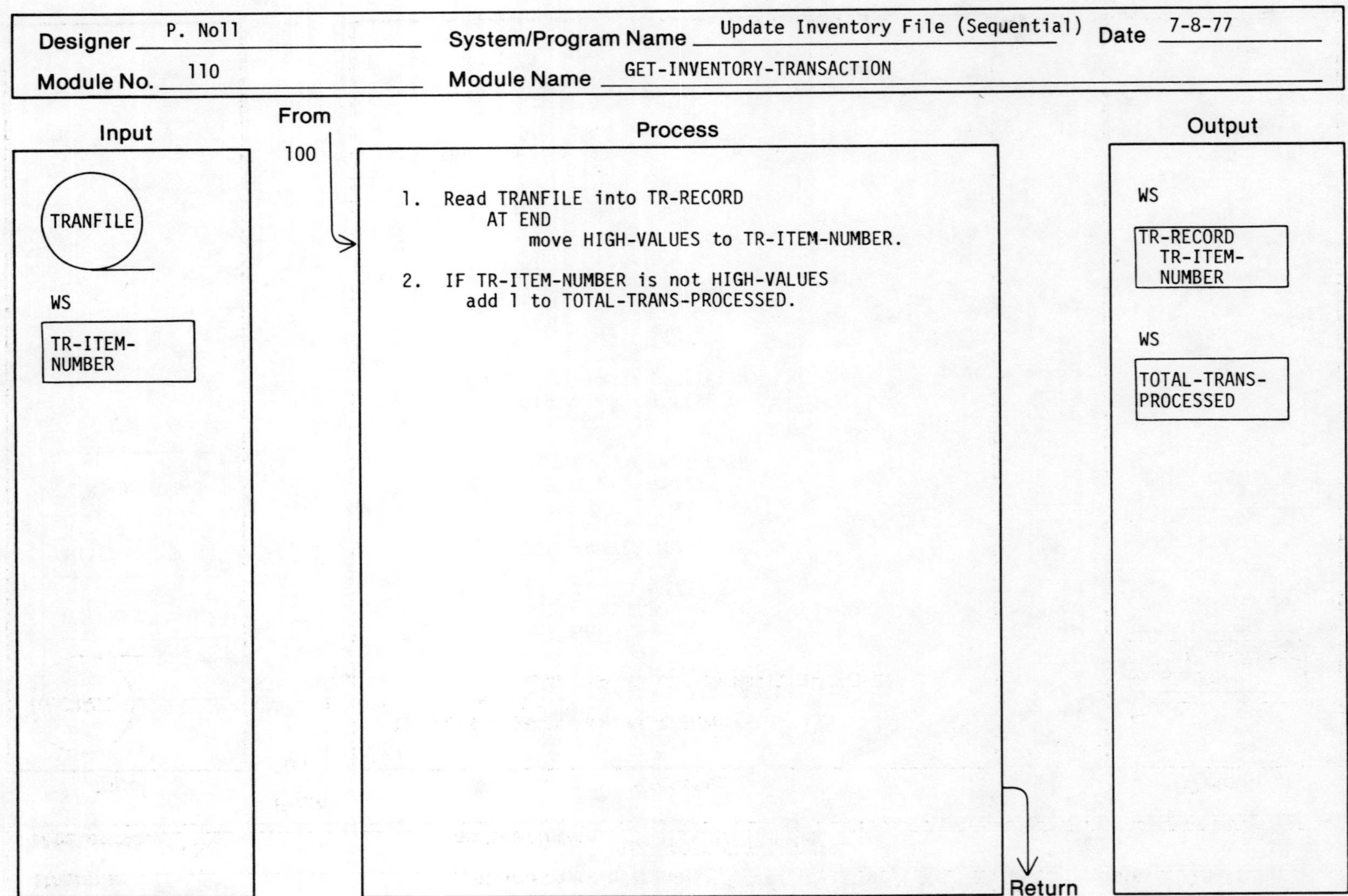
Designer P. Noll
System/Program Name Update Inventory File (Sequential)
Date 7-8-77
Module No. 110
Module Name GET-INVENTORY-TRANSACTION
Input
TRANFILE
WS
TR-ITEM-NUMBER
From 100
Process
1. Read TRANFILE into TR-RECORD
AT END
move HIGH-VALUES to TR-ITEM-NUMBER.
2. IF TR-ITEM-NUMBER is not HIGH-VALUES
add 1 to TOTAL-TRANS-PROCESSED.
Return
Output
WS
TR-RECORD
TR-ITEM-NUMBER
WS
TOTAL-TRANS-PROCESSED

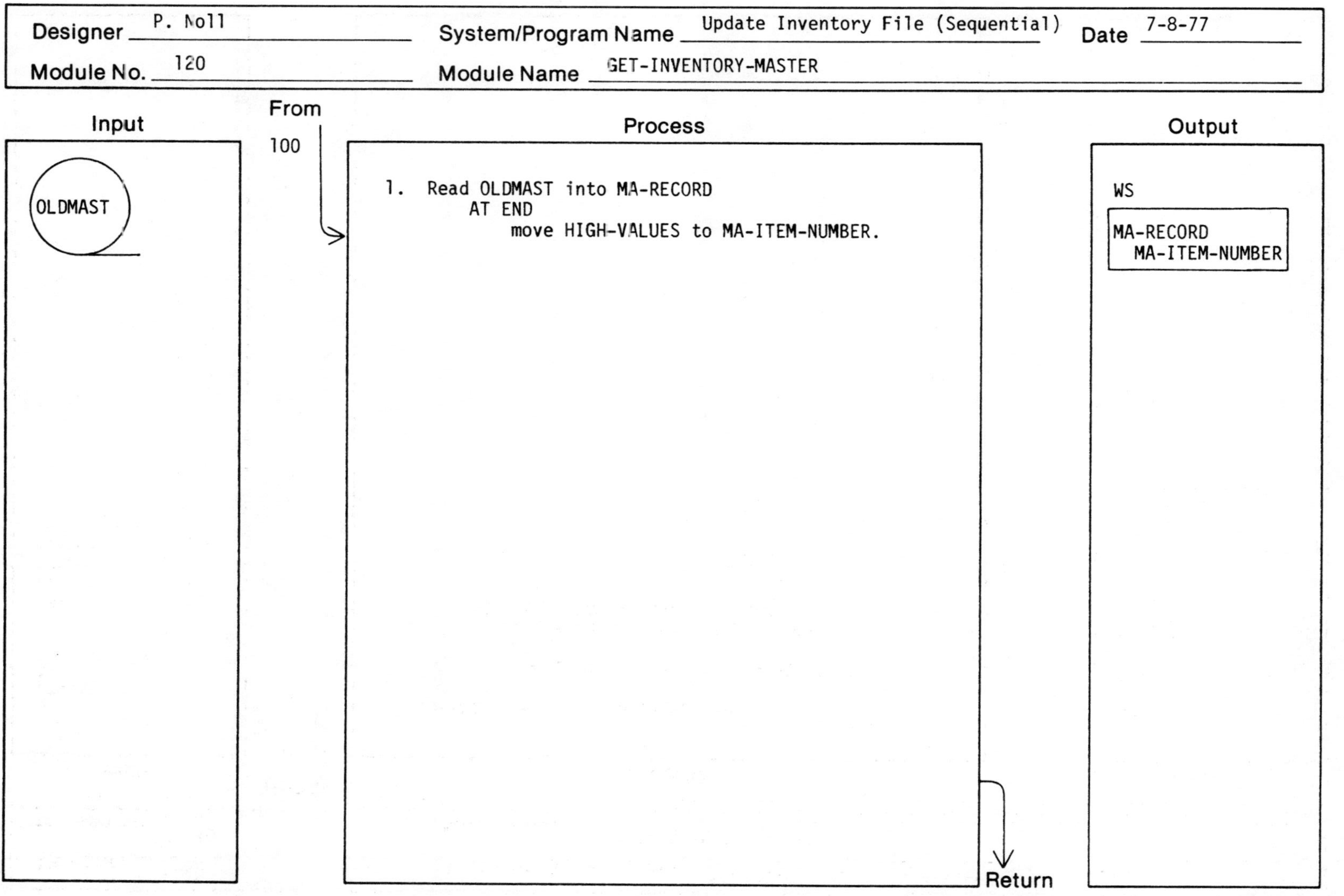
Designer P. Noll
System/Program Name Update Inventory File (Sequential)
Date 7-8-77
Module No. 120
Module Name GET-INVENTORY-MASTER
Input
OLDMAST
From
100
Process
1. Read OLDMAST into MA-RECORD
AT END
move HIGH-VALUES to MA-ITEM-NUMBER.
Return
Output
WS
MA-RECORD
MA-ITEM-NUMBER

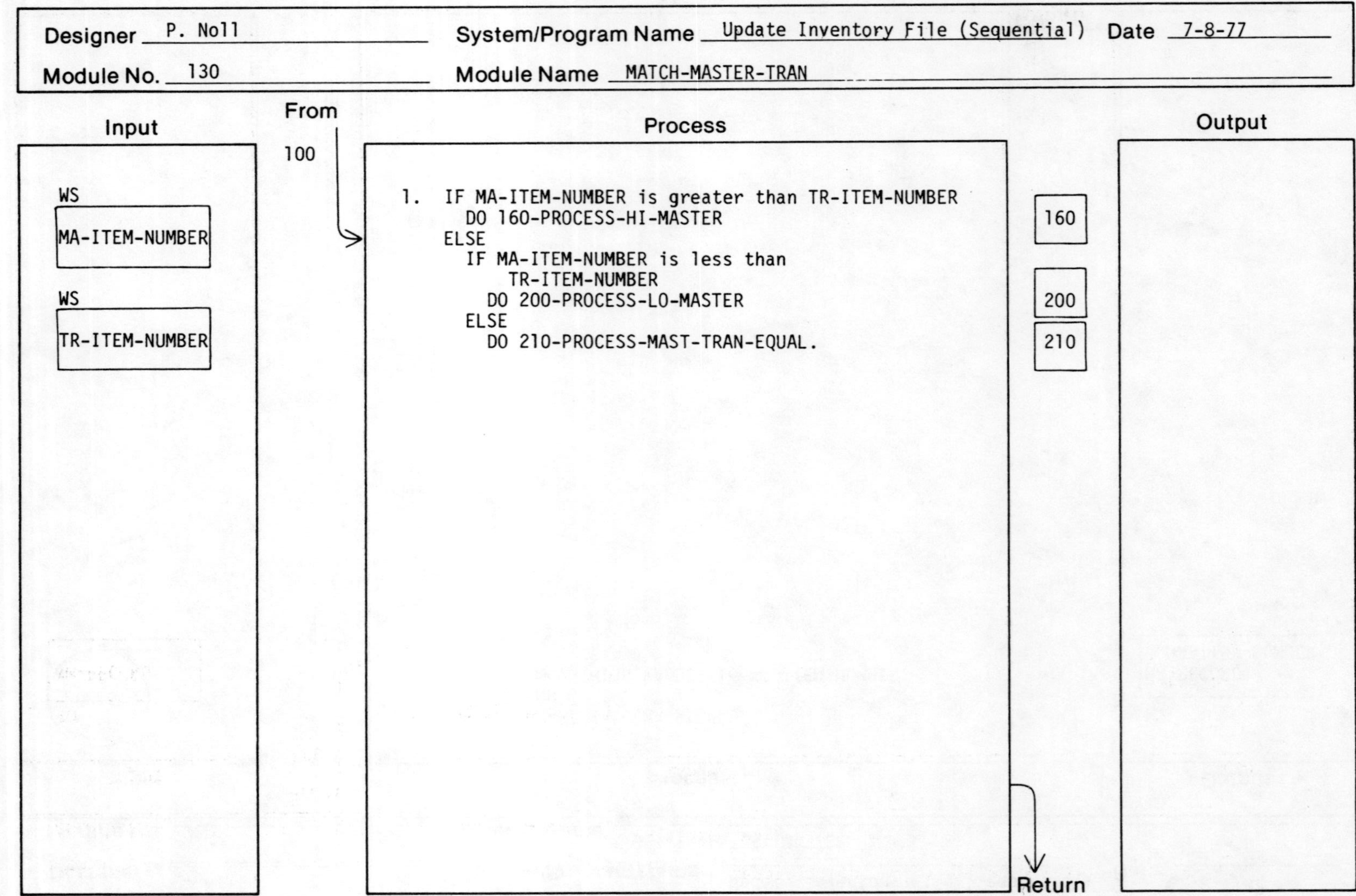

Designer P. Noll — System/Program Name Update Inventory File (Sequential) — Date 7-8-77

Module No. 130 — Module Name MATCH-MASTER-TRAN

Input

WS
MA-ITEM-NUMBER

WS
TR-ITEM-NUMBER

From 100

Process

```
1.  IF MA-ITEM-NUMBER is greater than TR-ITEM-NUMBER        160
      DO 160-PROCESS-HI-MASTER
    ELSE
      IF MA-ITEM-NUMBER is less than
          TR-ITEM-NUMBER
        DO 200-PROCESS-LO-MASTER                            200
      ELSE
        DO 210-PROCESS-MAST-TRAN-EQUAL.                     210
```

Return

Output

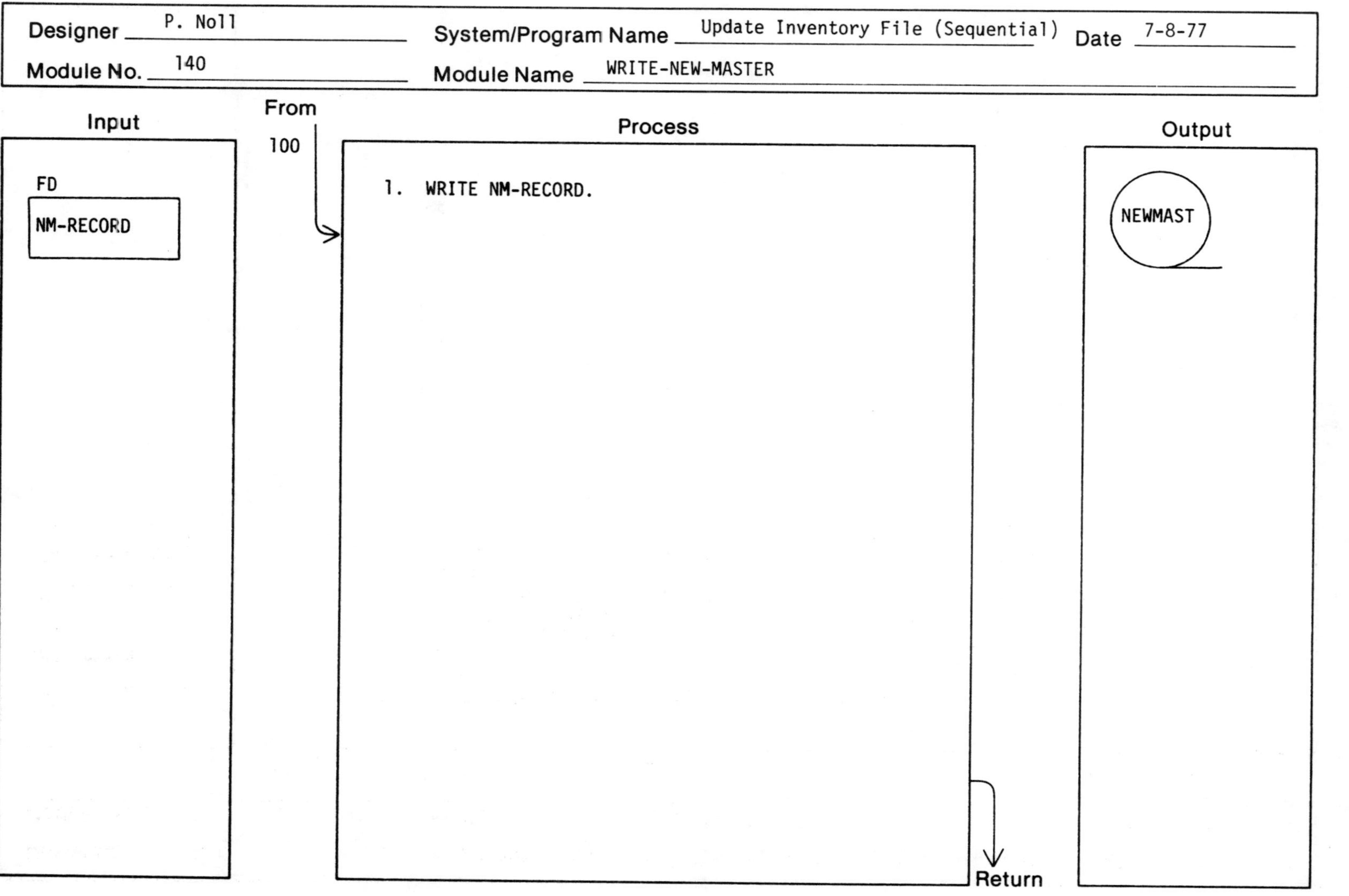
Designer P. Noll
System/Program Name Update Inventory File (Sequential)
Date 7-8-77
Module No. 140
Module Name WRITE-NEW-MASTER
Input
FD
NM-RECORD
From
100
Process
1. WRITE NM-RECORD.
Return
Output
NEWMAST

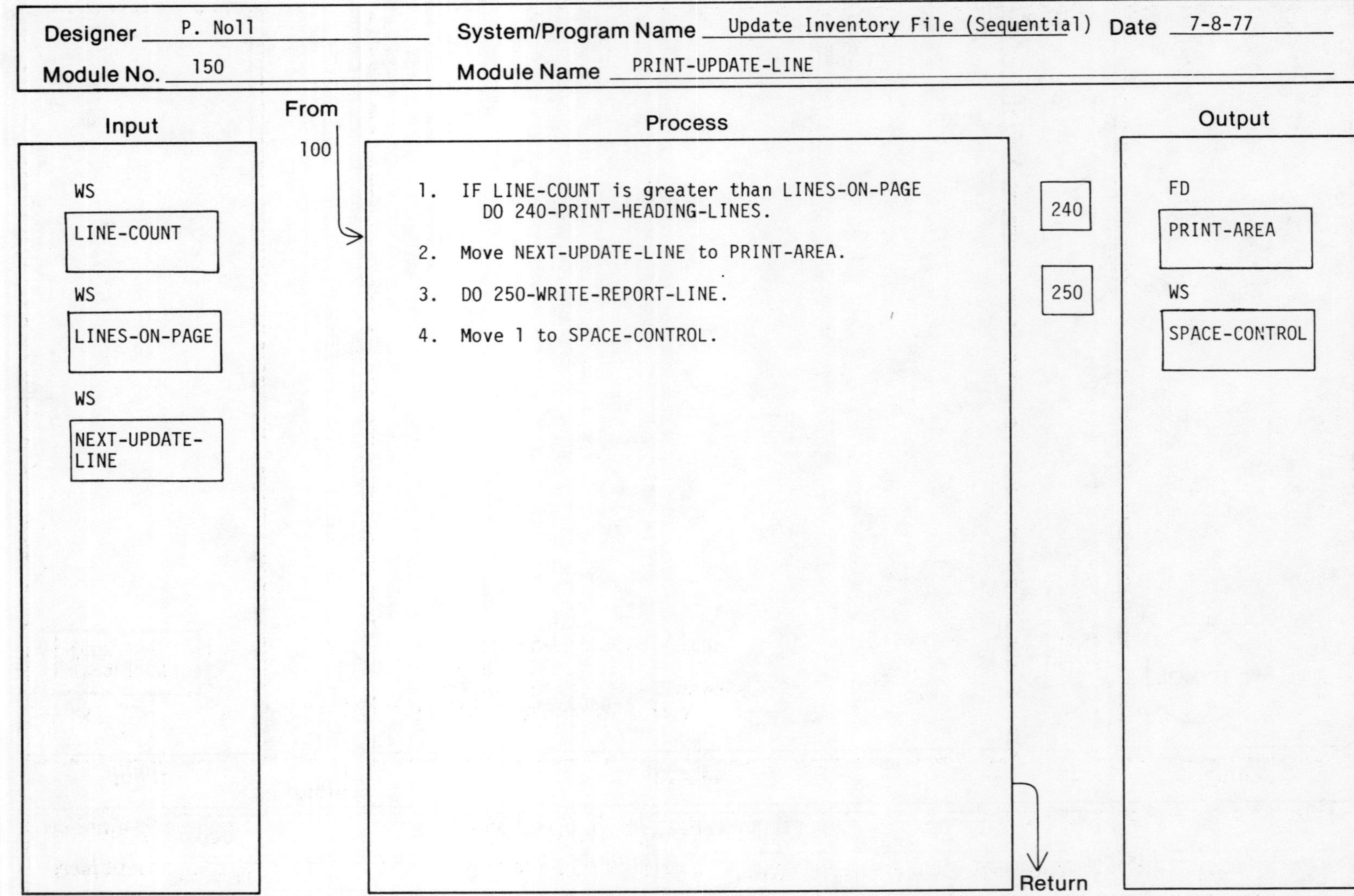

Designer: P. Noll System/Program Name: Update Inventory File (Sequential) Date: 7-8-77

Module No.: 150 Module Name: PRINT-UPDATE-LINE

Input	Process	Output
WS LINE-COUNT WS LINES-ON-PAGE WS NEXT-UPDATE-LINE	From 100 1. IF LINE-COUNT is greater than LINES-ON-PAGE DO 240-PRINT-HEADING-LINES. [240] 2. Move NEXT-UPDATE-LINE to PRINT-AREA. 3. DO 250-WRITE-REPORT-LINE. [250] 4. Move 1 to SPACE-CONTROL. Return	FD PRINT-AREA WS SPACE-CONTROL

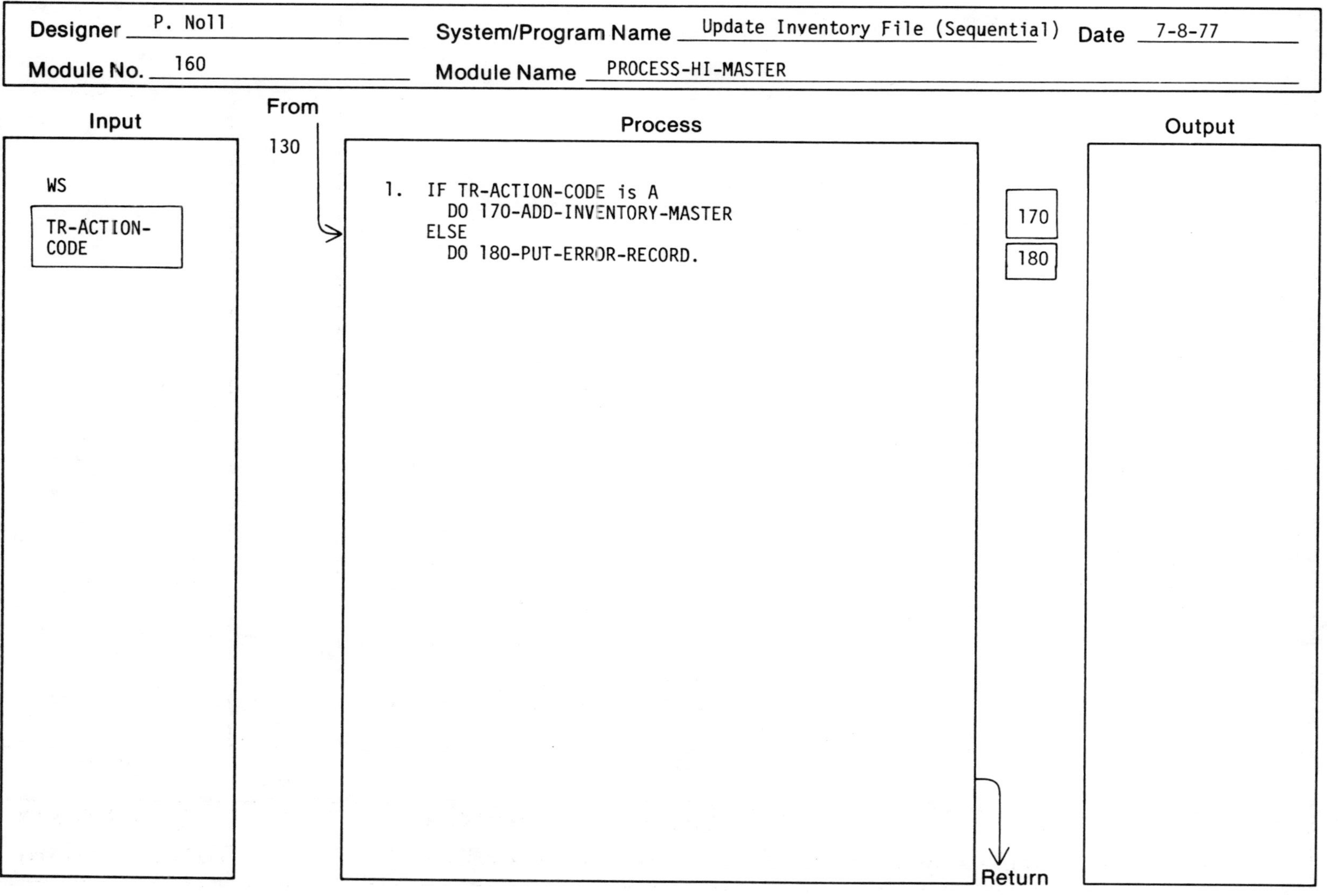
Designer P. Noll
System/Program Name Update Inventory File (Sequential)
Date 7-8-77
Module No. 160
Module Name PROCESS-HI-MASTER
Input
WS
TR-ACTION-CODE
From
130
Process
1. IF TR-ACTION-CODE is A
DO 170-ADD-INVENTORY-MASTER
ELSE
DO 180-PUT-ERROR-RECORD.
170
180
Return
Output

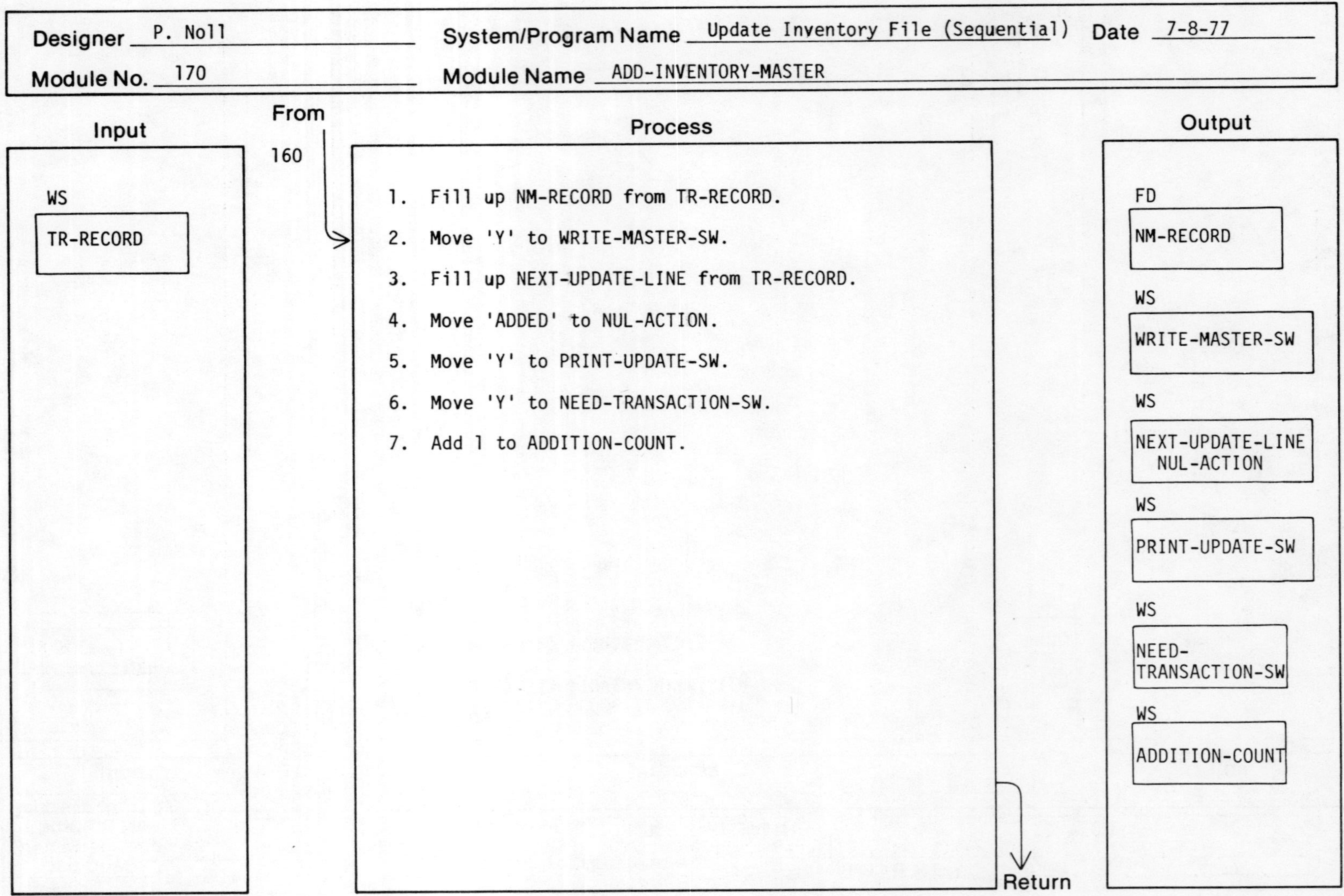
Designer P. Noll
System/Program Name Update Inventory File (Sequential)
Date 7-8-77
Module No. 170
Module Name ADD-INVENTORY-MASTER
Input
WS
TR-RECORD
From
160
Process
1. Fill up NM-RECORD from TR-RECORD.
2. Move 'Y' to WRITE-MASTER-SW.
3. Fill up NEXT-UPDATE-LINE from TR-RECORD.
4. Move 'ADDED' to NUL-ACTION.
5. Move 'Y' to PRINT-UPDATE-SW.
6. Move 'Y' to NEED-TRANSACTION-SW.
7. Add 1 to ADDITION-COUNT.
Return
Output
FD
NM-RECORD
WS
WRITE-MASTER-SW
WS
NEXT-UPDATE-LINE
NUL-ACTION
WS
PRINT-UPDATE-SW
WS
NEED-
TRANSACTION-SW
WS
ADDITION-COUNT

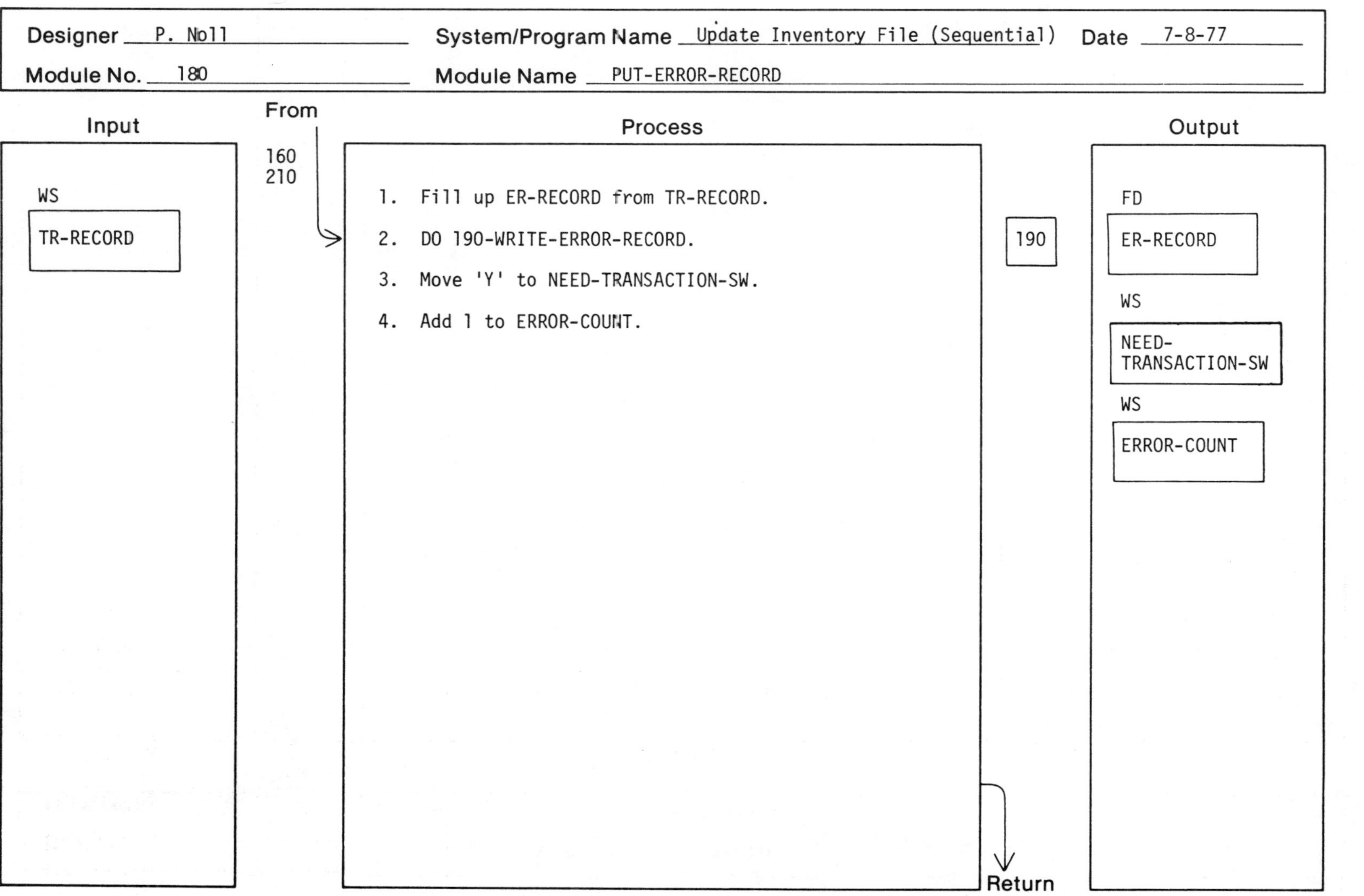

Sequential-Update Program

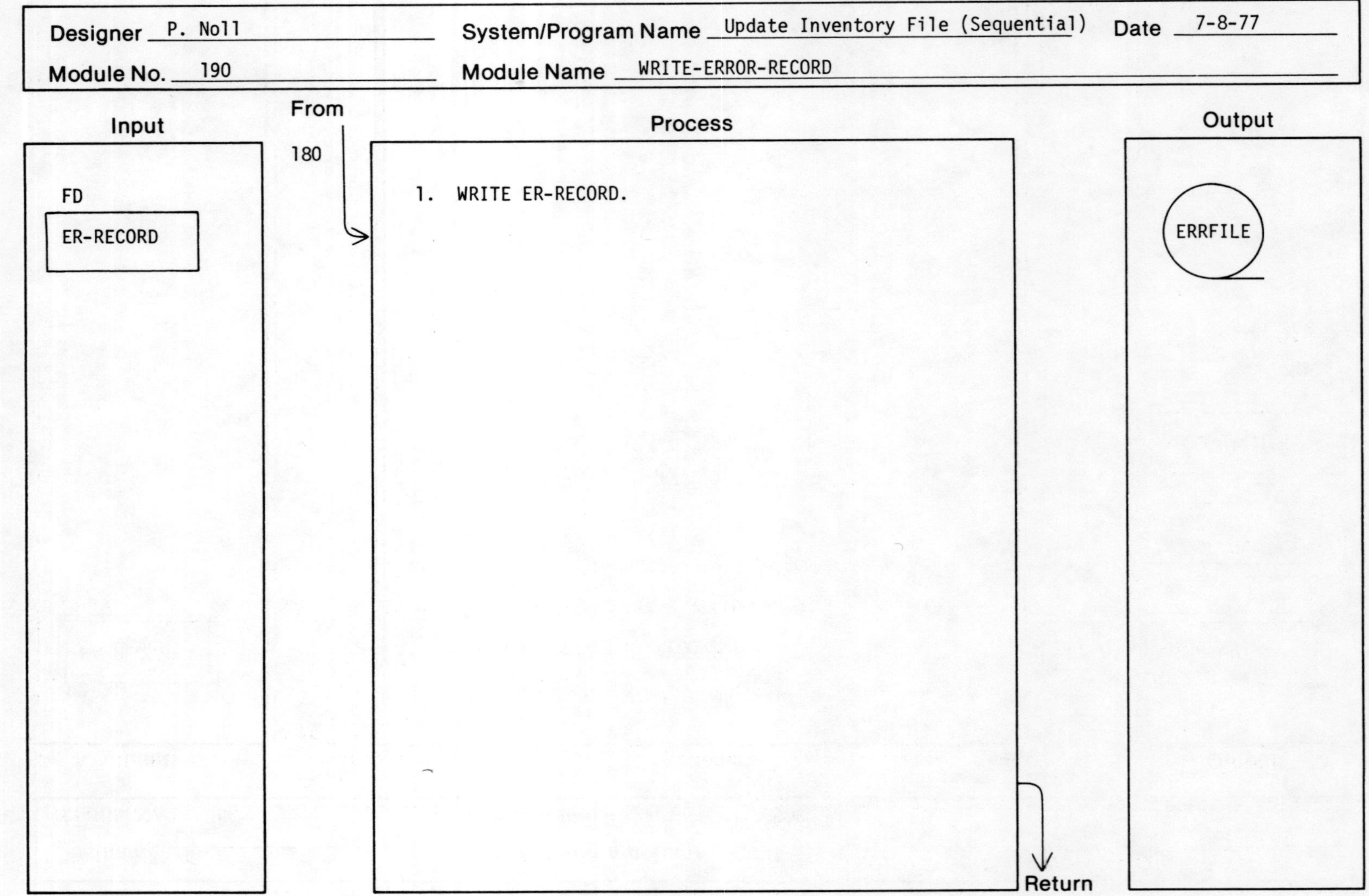
Designer P. Noll
System/Program Name Update Inventory File (Sequential)
Date 7-8-77
Module No. 190
Module Name WRITE-ERROR-RECORD
Input
From
180
Process
Output
FD
ER-RECORD
1. WRITE ER-RECORD.
ERRFILE
Return

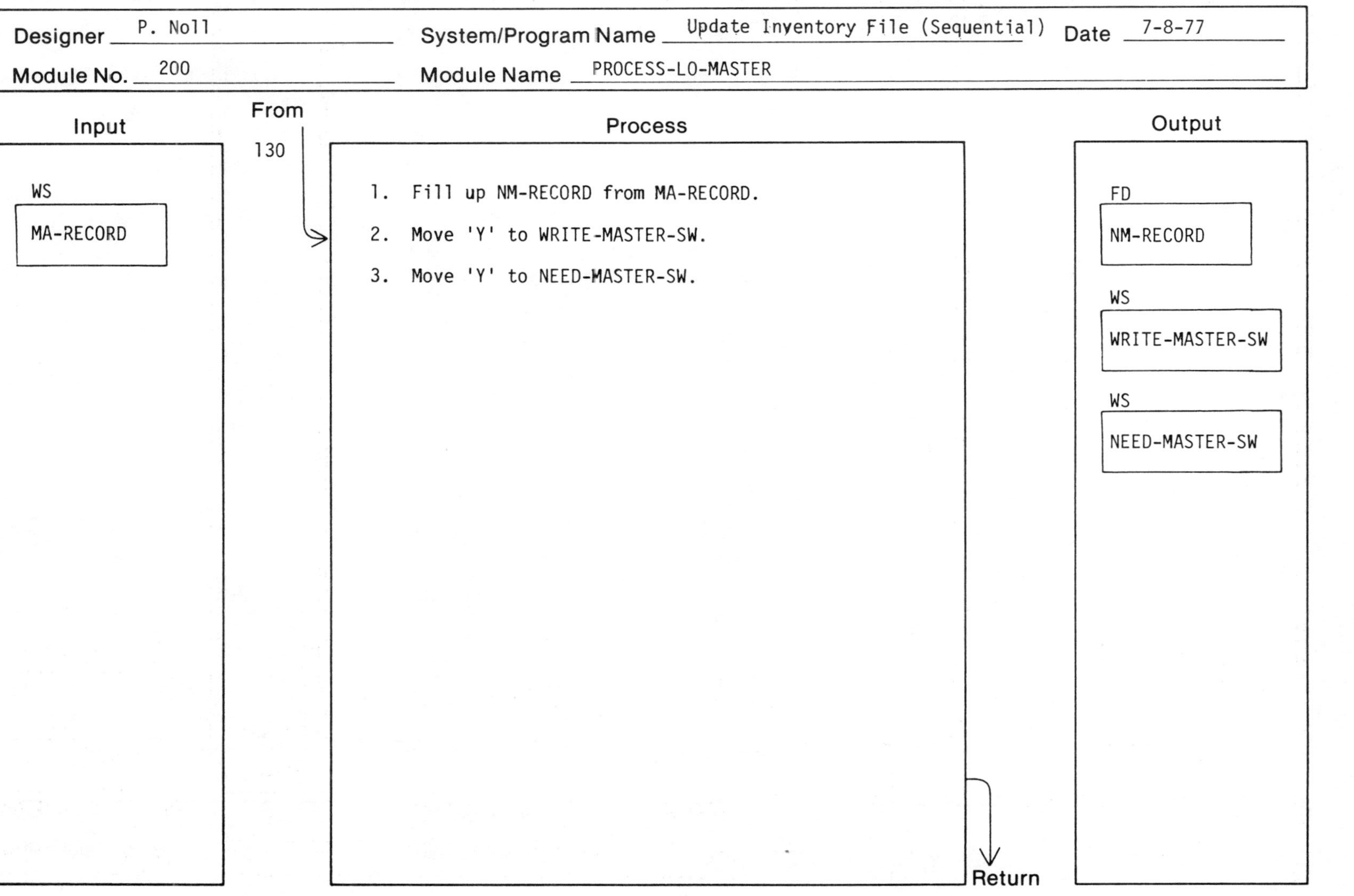

Sequential-Update Program

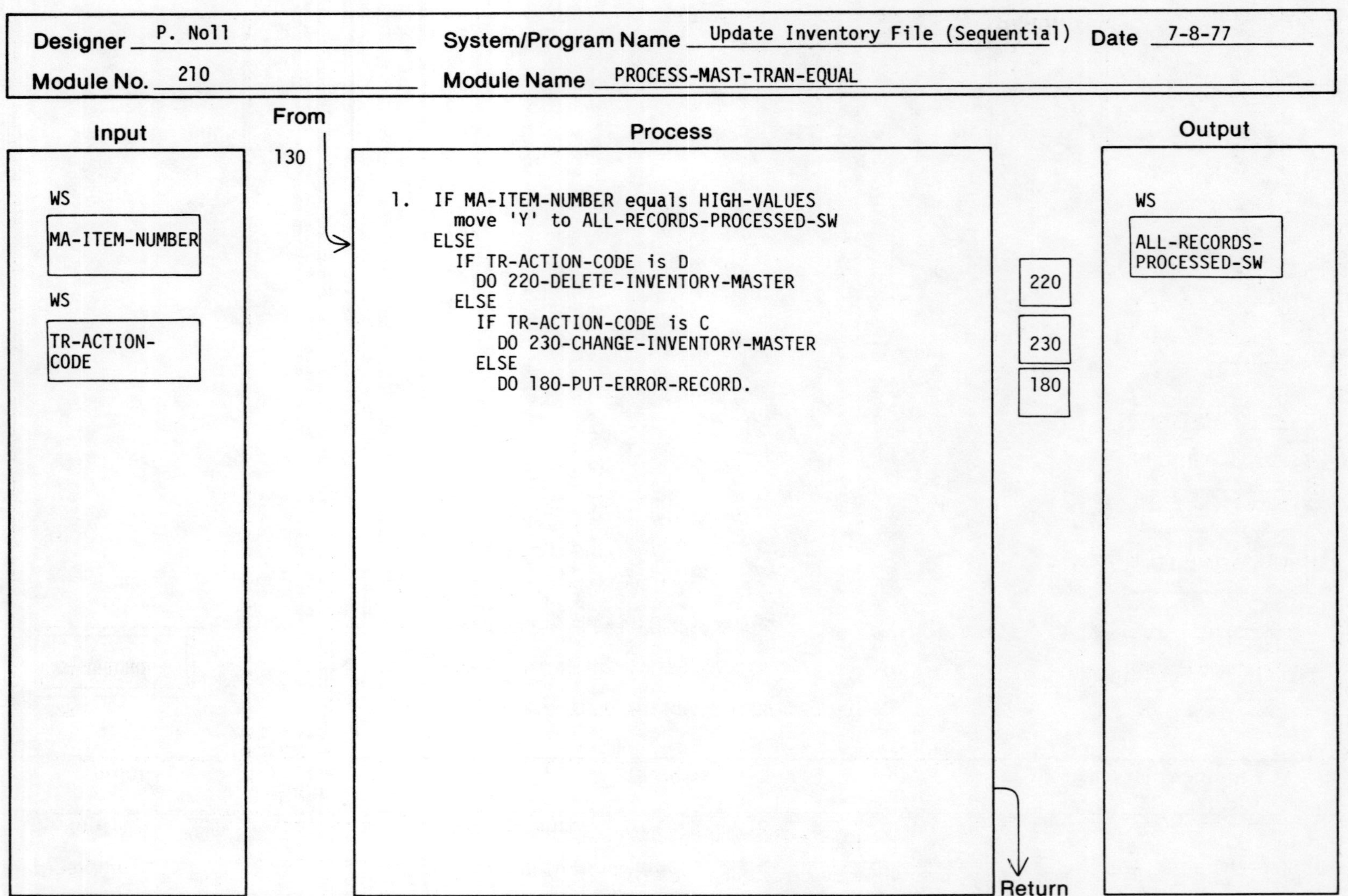

Designer P. Noll System/Program Name Update Inventory File (Sequential) Date 7-8-77

Module No. 210 Module Name PROCESS-MAST-TRAN-EQUAL

Input

WS: MA-ITEM-NUMBER

WS: TR-ACTION-CODE

From 130

Process

```
1.  IF MA-ITEM-NUMBER equals HIGH-VALUES
      move 'Y' to ALL-RECORDS-PROCESSED-SW
    ELSE
      IF TR-ACTION-CODE is D
        DO 220-DELETE-INVENTORY-MASTER        220
      ELSE
        IF TR-ACTION-CODE is C
          DO 230-CHANGE-INVENTORY-MASTER      230
        ELSE
          DO 180-PUT-ERROR-RECORD.            180
```

Return

Output

WS: ALL-RECORDS-PROCESSED-SW

Designer: P. Noll | System/Program Name: Update Inventory File (Sequential) | Date: 7-8-77

Module No.: 220 | Module Name: DELETE-INVENTORY-MASTER

Input	Process	Output
WS MA-RECORD	From 210 1. Fill up NEXT-UPDATE-LINE from MA-RECORD. 2. Move 'DELETED' to NUL-ACTION. 3. Move 'Y' to PRINT-UPDATE-SW. 4. Move 'Y' to NEED-MASTER-SW. 5. Move 'Y' to NEED-TRANSACTION-SW. 6. Add 1 to DELETION-COUNT. Return	WS NEXT-UPDATE-LINE NUL-ACTION WS PRINT-UPDATE-SW NEED-MASTER-SW NEED-TRANSACTION-SW WS DELETION-COUNT

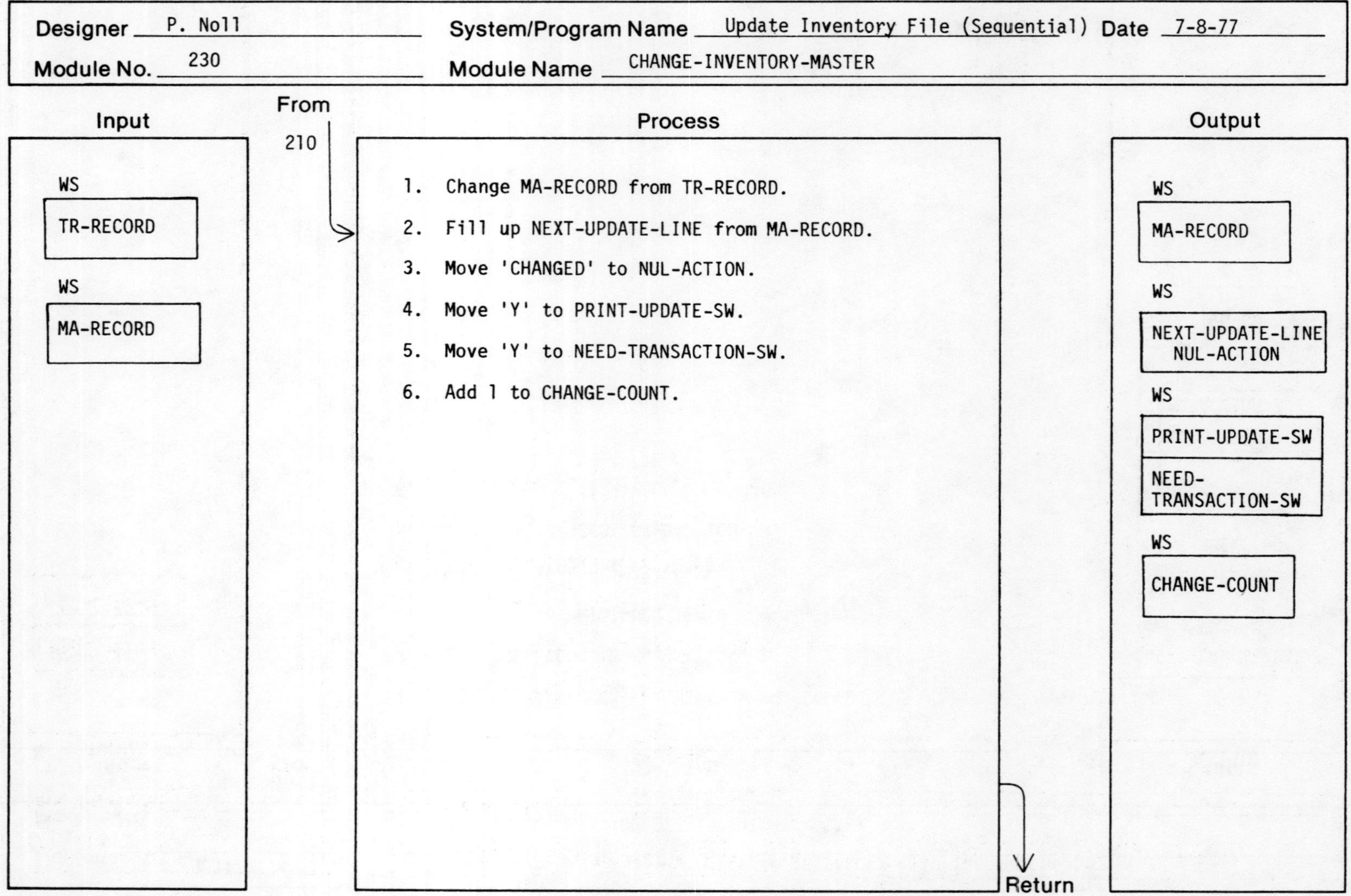

Designer P. Noll System/Program Name Update Inventory File (Sequential) Date 7-8-77

Module No. 230 Module Name CHANGE-INVENTORY-MASTER

Input

WS
TR-RECORD

WS
MA-RECORD

From 210

Process

1. Change MA-RECORD from TR-RECORD.
2. Fill up NEXT-UPDATE-LINE from MA-RECORD.
3. Move 'CHANGED' to NUL-ACTION.
4. Move 'Y' to PRINT-UPDATE-SW.
5. Move 'Y' to NEED-TRANSACTION-SW.
6. Add 1 to CHANGE-COUNT.

Return

Output

WS
MA-RECORD

WS
NEXT-UPDATE-LINE
NUL-ACTION

WS
PRINT-UPDATE-SW
NEED-TRANSACTION-SW

WS
CHANGE-COUNT

Designer: P. Noll | System/Program Name: Update Inventory File (Sequential) | Date: 7-8-77

Module No.: 240 | Module Name: PRINT-HEADING-LINES

Input	From	Process		Output
WS HDG-LINE-1 HDG-LINE-2	150	1. Add 1 to HDG1-PAGE-NO. 2. Move HDG-LINE-1 to PRINT-AREA. 3. DO 260-WRITE-PAGE-TOP-LINE. 4. Move HDG-LINE-2 to PRINT-AREA. 5. Move 2 to SPACE-CONTROL. 6. DO 250-WRITE-REPORT-LINE.	260 250 Return	WS HDG1-PAGE-NO FD PRINT-AREA WS SPACE-CONTROL

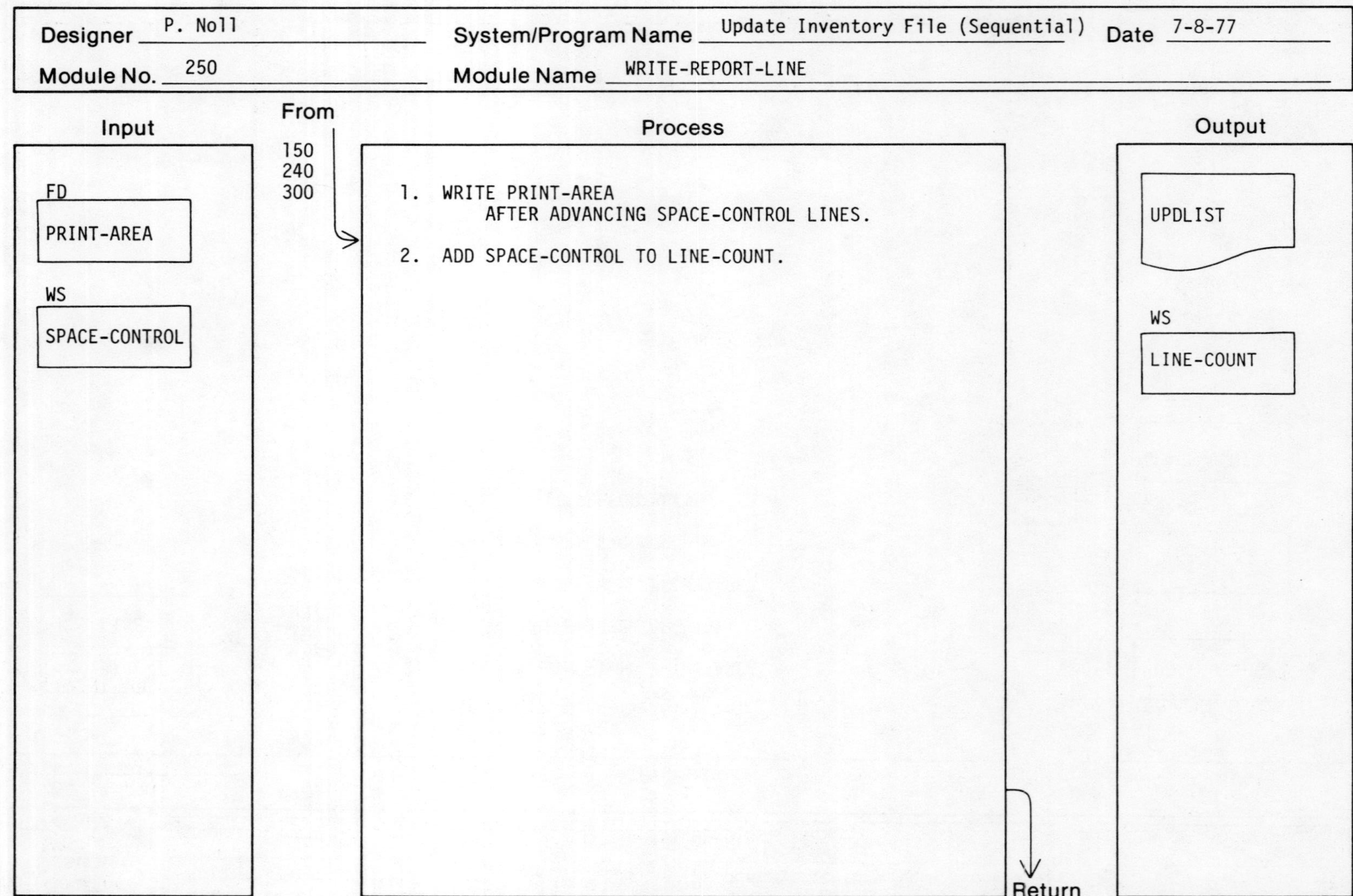
Designer P. Noll
System/Program Name Update Inventory File (Sequential)
Date 7-8-77
Module No. 250
Module Name WRITE-REPORT-LINE
Input
FD
PRINT-AREA
WS
SPACE-CONTROL
From
150
240
300
Process
1. WRITE PRINT-AREA
AFTER ADVANCING SPACE-CONTROL LINES.
2. ADD SPACE-CONTROL TO LINE-COUNT.
Return
Output
UPDLIST
WS
LINE-COUNT

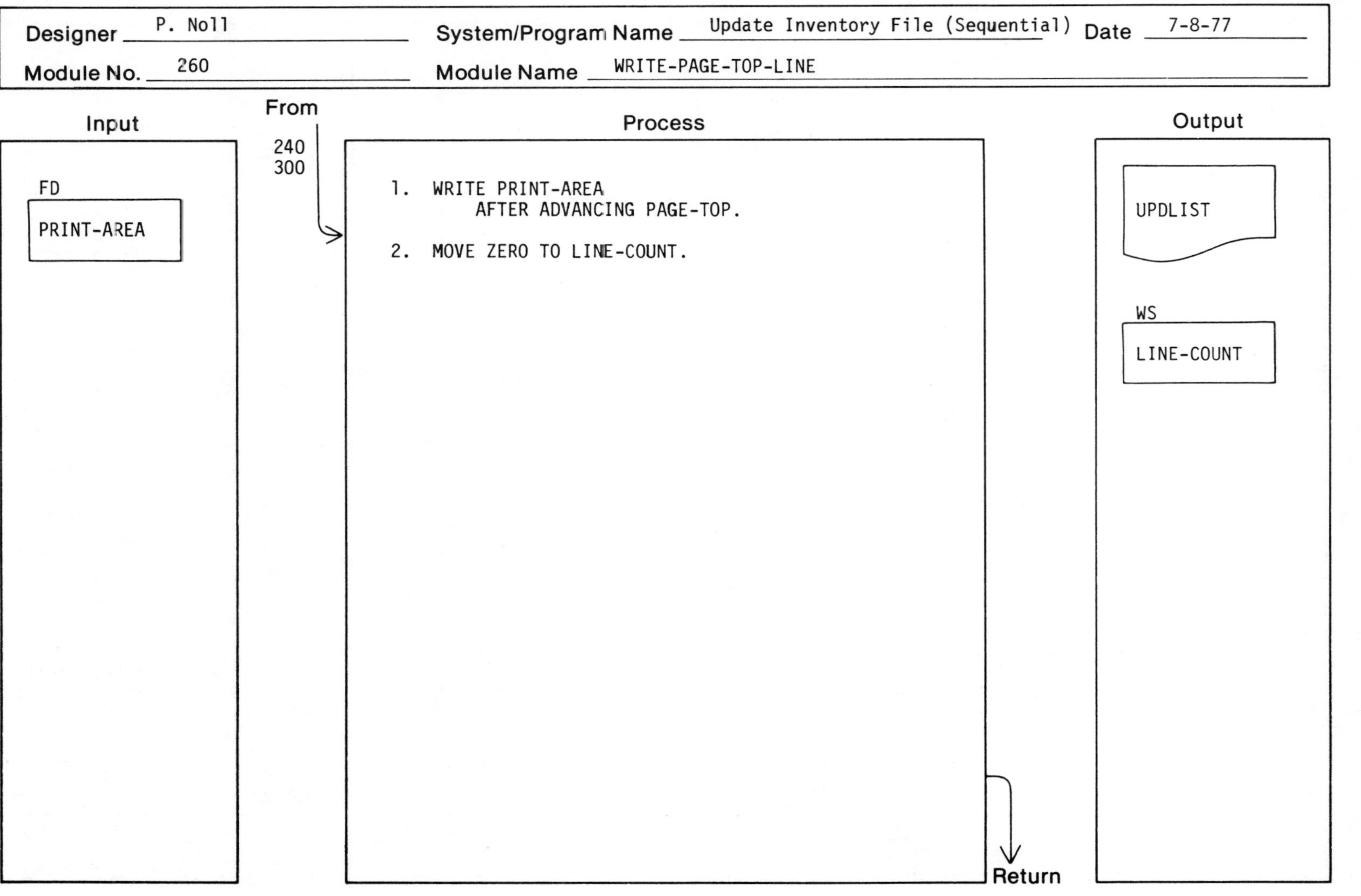

Designer P. Noll
System/Program Name Update Inventory File (Sequential)
Date 7-8-77
Module No. 260
Module Name WRITE-PAGE-TOP-LINE
Input
FD
PRINT-AREA
From
240
300
Process
1. WRITE PRINT-AREA
AFTER ADVANCING PAGE-TOP.
2. MOVE ZERO TO LINE-COUNT.
Return
Output
UPDLIST
WS
LINE-COUNT

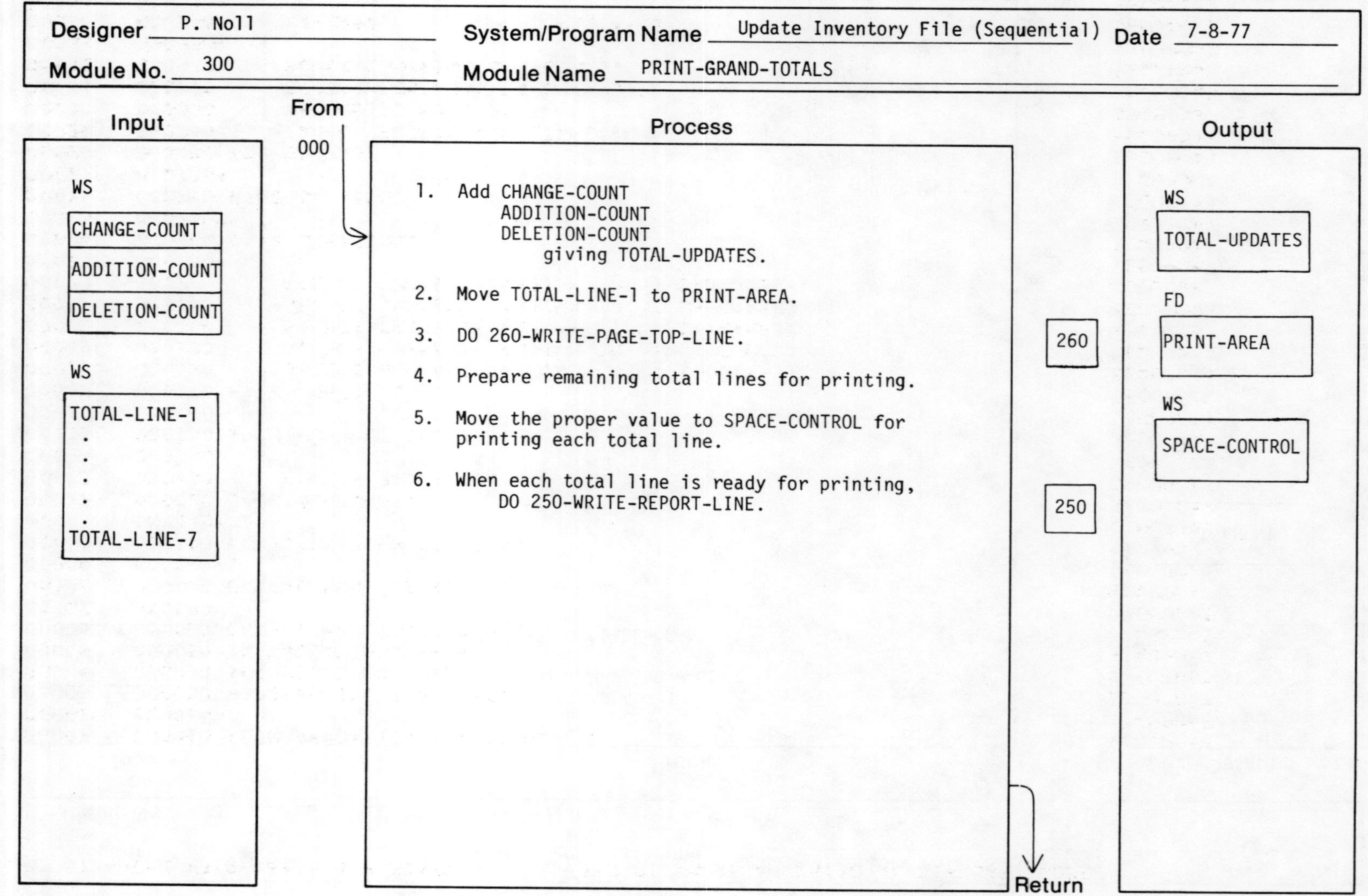

Designer P. Noll | System/Program Name Update Inventory File (Sequential) | Date 7-8-77

Module No. 300 | Module Name PRINT-GRAND-TOTALS

Input

WS
- CHANGE-COUNT
- ADDITION-COUNT
- DELETION-COUNT

WS
- TOTAL-LINE-1
- .
- .
- .
- TOTAL-LINE-7

From 000

Process

1. Add CHANGE-COUNT
      ADDITION-COUNT
      DELETION-COUNT
         giving TOTAL-UPDATES.
2. Move TOTAL-LINE-1 to PRINT-AREA.
3. DO 260-WRITE-PAGE-TOP-LINE. (260)
4. Prepare remaining total lines for printing.
5. Move the proper value to SPACE-CONTROL for printing each total line.
6. When each total line is ready for printing, DO 250-WRITE-REPORT-LINE. (250)

Return

Output

WS
- TOTAL-UPDATES

FD
- PRINT-AREA

WS
- SPACE-CONTROL

```
PP 5734-CB1 V3 RELEASE 3.2 30APR74       IBM OS AMERICAN NATIONAL STANDARD COBOL

   1

000010 IDENTIFICATION DIVISION.                                      SEQUPDAT
000020*                                                              SEQUPDAT
000030 PROGRAM-ID. SEQUPDAT.                                         SEQUPDAT
000040 AUTHOR. DOUG LOWE.                                            SEQUPDAT
000050 INSTALLATION. MM&A.                                           SEQUPDAT
000060 DATE-COMPILED. OCT 20,1977.                                   SEQUPDAT
000070*                                                              SEQUPDAT
000080 ENVIRONMENT DIVISION.                                         SEQUPDAT
000090*                                                              SEQUPDAT
000100 CONFIGURATION SECTION.                                        SEQUPDAT
000110*                                                              SEQUPDAT
000120 SPECIAL-NAMES.                                                SEQUPDAT
000130     C01 IS PAGE-TOP.                                          SEQUPDAT
000140*                                                              SEQUPDAT
000150 INPUT-OUTPUT SECTION.                                         SEQUPDAT
000160*                                                              SEQUPDAT
000170 FILE-CONTROL.                                                 SEQUPDAT
000180     SELECT OLDMAST  ASSIGN TO UT-S-OLDMAST.                   SEQUPDAT
000190     SELECT NEWMAST  ASSIGN TO UT-S-NEWMAST.                   SEQUPDAT
000200     SELECT TRANFILE ASSIGN TO UT-S-TRANFILE.                  SEQUPDAT
000210     SELECT ERRFILE  ASSIGN TO UT-S-ERRFILE.                   SEQUPDAT
000220     SELECT UPDLIST  ASSIGN TO UT-S-UPDLIST.                   SEQUPDAT
000230*                                                              SEQUPDAT
000240 DATA DIVISION.                                                SEQUPDAT
000250*                                                              SEQUPDAT
000260 FILE SECTION.                                                 SEQUPDAT
000270*                                                              SEQUPDAT
000280 FD  OLDMAST                                                   SEQUPDAT
000290     LABEL RECORDS ARE STANDARD                                SEQUPDAT
000300     RECORDING MODE IS F                                       SEQUPDAT
000310     RECORD CONTAINS 38 CHARACTERS                             SEQUPDAT
000320     BLOCK CONTAINS 0 RECORDS.                                 SEQUPDAT
000330*                                                              SEQUPDAT
000340 01  MA-AREA                PIC X(38).                         SEQUPDAT
000350*                                                              SEQUPDAT
```

```
2

000360 FD  NEWMAST                                                      SEQUPDAT
000370     LABEL RECORDS ARE STANDARD                                   SEQUPDAT
000380     RECORDING MODE IS F                                          SEQUPDAT
000390     RECORD CONTAINS 38 CHARACTERS                                SEQUPDAT
000400     BLOCK CONTAINS 0 RECORDS.                                    SEQUPDAT
000410*                                                                 SEQUPDAT
000420 01  NM-RECORD.                                                   SEQUPDAT
000430*                                                                 SEQUPDAT
000440     05  NM-ITEM-NUMBER        PIC X(5).                          SEQUPDAT
000450     05  NM-ITEM-DESCR         PIC X(20).                         SEQUPDAT
000460     05  NM-UNIT-COST          PIC 999V99.                        SEQUPDAT
000470     05  NM-UNIT-PRICE         PIC 999V99.                        SEQUPDAT
000480     05  NM-ON-HAND            PIC 9(3).                          SEQUPDAT
000490*                                                                 SEQUPDAT
000500 FD  TRANFILE                                                     SEQUPDAT
000510     LABEL RECORDS ARE STANDARD                                   SEQUPDAT
000520     RECORDING MODE IS F                                          SEQUPDAT
000530     RECORD CONTAINS 40 CHARACTERS                                SEQUPDAT
000540     BLOCK CONTAINS 0 RECORDS.                                    SEQUPDAT
000550*                                                                 SEQUPDAT
000560 01  TR-AREA               PIC X(40).                             SEQUPDAT
000570*                                                                 SEQUPDAT
000580 FD  ERRFILE                                                      SEQUPDAT
000590     LABEL RECORDS ARE STANDARD                                   SEQUPDAT
000600     RECORDING MODE IS F                                          SEQUPDAT
000610     RECORD CONTAINS 40 CHARACTERS                                SEQUPDAT
000620     BLOCK CONTAINS 0 RECORDS.                                    SEQUPDAT
000630*                                                                 SEQUPDAT
000640 01  ER-RECORD             PIC X(40).                             SEQUPDAT
000650*                                                                 SEQUPDAT
000660 FD  UPDLIST                                                      SEQUPDAT
000670     LABEL RECORDS ARE STANDARD                                   SEQUPDAT
000680     RECORDING MODE IS F                                          SEQUPDAT
000690     RECORD CONTAINS 133 CHARACTERS                               SEQUPDAT
000700     BLOCK CONTAINS 0 RECORDS.                                    SEQUPDAT
000710*                                                                 SEQUPDAT
000720 01  PRINT-AREA            PIC X(133).                            SEQUPDAT
000730*                                                                 SEQUPDAT
```

```
000740 WORKING-STORAGE SECTION.                                                SEQUPDAT
000750*                                                                        SEQUPDAT
000760 01  SWITCHES.                                                           SEQUPDAT
000770*                                                                        SEQUPDAT
000780     05  ALL-RECORDS-PROCESSED-SW     PIC X     VALUE 'N'.               SEQUPDAT
000790         88  ALL-RECORDS-PROCESSED               VALUE 'Y'.               SEQUPDAT
000800     05  NEED-TRANSACTION-SW          PIC X     VALUE 'Y'.               SEQUPDAT
000810         88  NEED-TRANSACTION                    VALUE 'Y'.               SEQUPDAT
000820     05  NEED-MASTER-SW               PIC X     VALUE 'Y'.               SEQUPDAT
000830         88  NEED-MASTER                         VALUE 'Y'.               SEQUPDAT
000840     05  WRITE-MASTER-SW              PIC X     VALUE 'N'.               SEQUPDAT
000850         88  WRITE-MASTER                        VALUE 'Y'.               SEQUPDAT
000860     05  PRINT-UPDATE-SW              PIC X     VALUE 'N'.               SEQUPDAT
000870         88  PRINT-UPDATE                        VALUE 'Y'.               SEQUPDAT
000880*                                                                        SEQUPDAT
000890 01  PRINT-FIELDS                COMP      SYNC.                         SEQUPDAT
000900*                                                                        SEQUPDAT
000910     05  LINE-COUNT              PIC S999  VALUE +999.                   SEQUPDAT
000920     05  LINES-ON-PAGE           PIC S999  VALUE +57.                    SEQUPDAT
000930     05  SPACE-CONTROL           PIC S9.                                 SEQUPDAT
000940     05  PAGE-NUMBER             PIC S999  VALUE ZERO.                   SEQUPDAT
000950*                                                                        SEQUPDAT
000960 01  COUNTS                           COMP-3.                            SEQUPDAT
000970*                                                                        SEQUPDAT
000980     05  CHANGE-COUNT                 PIC S9(5)  VALUE ZERO.             SEQUPDAT
000990     05  ADDITION-COUNT               PIC S9(5)  VALUE ZERO.             SEQUPDAT
001000     05  DELETION-COUNT               PIC S9(5)  VALUE ZERO.             SEQUPDAT
001010     05  TOTAL-UPDATES                PIC S9(5)  VALUE ZERO.             SEQUPDAT
001020     05  ERROR-COUNT                  PIC S9(5)  VALUE ZERO.             SEQUPDAT
001030     05  TOTAL-TRANS-PROCESSED        PIC S9(7)  VALUE ZERO.             SEQUPDAT
001040*                                                                        SEQUPDAT
001050 01  ACTION-MESSAGES.                                                    SEQUPDAT
001060*                                                                        SEQUPDAT
001070     05  CHANGE-MESSAGE          PIC X(10)  VALUE 'CHANGED   '.          SEQUPDAT
001080     05  ADD-MESSAGE             PIC X(10)  VALUE 'ADDED     '.          SEQUPDAT
001090     05  DELETE-MESSAGE          PIC X(10)  VALUE 'DELETED   '.          SEQUPDAT
001100*                                                                        SEQUPDAT
001110 01  MA-RECORD.                                                          SEQUPDAT
```

4

```
001120*                                                                     SEQUPDAT
001130         05  MA-ITEM-NUMBER        PIC X(5).                          SEQUPDAT
001140         05  MA-ITEM-DESCR         PIC X(20).                         SEQUPDAT
001150         05  MA-UNIT-COST          PIC 999V99.                        SEQUPDAT
001160         05  MA-UNIT-PRICE         PIC 999V99.                        SEQUPDAT
001170         05  MA-ON-HAND            PIC 9(3).                          SEQUPDAT
001180*                                                                     SEQUPDAT
001190 01  TR-RECORD.                                                       SEQUPDAT
001200*                                                                     SEQUPDAT
001210     05  TR-ACTION-CODE                  PIC X.                       SEQUPDAT
001220         88  CHANGE                                 VALUE 'C'.        SEQUPDAT
001230         88  ADDITION                               VALUE 'A'.        SEQUPDAT
001240         88  DELETION                               VALUE 'D'.        SEQUPDAT
001250*                                                                     SEQUPDAT
001260     05  TR-INV-RECORD.                                               SEQUPDAT
001270         10  TR-ITEM-NUMBER              PIC X(5).                    SEQUPDAT
001280         10  TR-ITEM-DESCR               PIC X(20).                   SEQUPDAT
001290         10  TR-UNIT-COST.                                            SEQUPDAT
001300             15  TR-UNIT-COST-NUM        PIC 999V99.                  SEQUPDAT
001310         10  TR-UNIT-PRICE.                                           SEQUPDAT
001320             15  TR-UNIT-PRICE-NUM       PIC 999V99.                  SEQUPDAT
001330         10  TR-ON-HAND.                                              SEQUPDAT
001340             15  TR-ON-HAND-NUM          PIC 999.                     SEQUPDAT
001350*                                                                     SEQUPDAT
001360     05  FILLER                          PIC X.                       SEQUPDAT
001370*                                                                     SEQUPDAT
001380 01  HDG-LINE-1.                                                      SEQUPDAT
001390*                                                                     SEQUPDAT
001400     05  HDG1-CC          PIC X.                                      SEQUPDAT
001410     05  HDG1-DATE        PIC X(8).                                   SEQUPDAT
001420     05  FILLER           PIC X(22)   VALUE SPACE.                    SEQUPDAT
001430     05  FILLER           PIC X(20)   VALUE 'UPDATE LISTING      '.SEQUPDAT
001440     05  FILLER           PIC X(20)   VALUE '                 PAG'.SEQUPDAT
001450     05  FILLER           PIC XX      VALUE 'E '.                     SEQUPDAT
001460     05  HDG1-PAGE-NO     PIC ZZ9.                                    SEQUPDAT
001470     05  FILLER           PIC X(57)   VALUE SPACE.                    SEQUPDAT
001480*                                                                     SEQUPDAT
001490 01  HDG-LINE-2.                                                      SEQUPDAT
```

```
001500*                                                                     SEQUPDAT
001510     05  HDG2-CC            PIC X.                                    SEQUPDAT
001520     05  FILLER             PIC X(20)   VALUE 'ITEM NO.   ITEM DESC'.SEQUPDAT
001530     05  FILLER             PIC X(20)   VALUE 'RIPTION       UNIT C'.SEQUPDAT
001540     05  FILLER             PIC X(20)   VALUE 'OST   UNIT PRICE   O'.SEQUPDAT
001550     05  FILLER             PIC X(20)   VALUE 'N HAND   ACTION      '.SEQUPDAT
001560     05  FILLER             PIC X(52)   VALUE SPACE.                  SEQUPDAT
001570*                                                                     SEQUPDAT
001580 01  NEXT-UPDATE-LINE.                                                SEQUPDAT
001590*                                                                     SEQUPDAT
001600     05  NUL-CC                 PIC X.                                SEQUPDAT
001610     05  FILLER                 PIC X       VALUE SPACE.              SEQUPDAT
001620     05  NUL-ITEM-NUMBER        PIC 9(5).                             SEQUPDAT
001630     05  FILLER                 PIC X(5)    VALUE SPACE.              SEQUPDAT
001640     05  NUL-ITEM-DESCR         PIC X(20).                            SEQUPDAT
001650     05  FILLER                 PIC X(4)    VALUE SPACE.              SEQUPDAT
001660     05  NUL-UNIT-COST          PIC ZZ9.99.                           SEQUPDAT
001670     05  FILLER                 PIC X(7)    VALUE SPACE.              SEQUPDAT
001680     05  NUL-UNIT-PRICE         PIC ZZ9.99.                           SEQUPDAT
001690     05  FILLER                 PIC X(7)    VALUE SPACE.              SEQUPDAT
001700     05  NUL-ON-HAND            PIC ZZ9.                              SEQUPDAT
001710     05  FILLER                 PIC X(5)    VALUE SPACE.              SEQUPDAT
001720     05  NUL-ACTION             PIC X(10).                            SEQUPDAT
001730     05  FILLER                 PIC X(53)   VALUE SPACE.              SEQUPDAT
001740*                                                                     SEQUPDAT
001750 01  TOTAL-LINE-1.                                                    SEQUPDAT
001760*                                                                     SEQUPDAT
001770     05  TOT1-CC            PIC X.                                    SEQUPDAT
001780     05  FILLER             PIC X(20)   VALUE 'SUMMARY FOR UPDATE R'.SEQUPDAT
001790     05  FILLER             PIC X(6)    VALUE 'UN OF '.               SEQUPDAT
001800     05  TOT1-DATE          PIC X(8).                                 SEQUPDAT
001810     05  FILLER             PIC X(98)   VALUE SPACE.                  SEQUPDAT
001820*                                                                     SEQUPDAT
001830 01  TOTAL-LINE-2.                                                    SEQUPDAT
001840*                                                                     SEQUPDAT
001850     05  TOT2-CC            PIC X.                                    SEQUPDAT
001860     05  FILLER             PIC X(20)   VALUE 'CHANGES            '.SEQUPDAT
001870     05  FILLER             PIC X(5)    VALUE SPACE.                  SEQUPDAT
```

6

```
001880        05  TOT2-CHANGES    PIC ZZ,ZZ9.                                SEQUPDAT
001890        05  FILLER          PIC X(101)  VALUE SPACE.                   SEQUPDAT
001900*                                                                      SEQUPDAT
001910 01   TOTAL-LINE-3.                                                    SEQUPDAT
001920*                                                                      SEQUPDAT
001930        05  TOT3-CC         PIC X.                                     SEQUPDAT
001940        05  FILLER          PIC X(20)   VALUE 'ADDITIONS           '.SEQUPDAT
001950        05  FILLER          PIC X(5)    VALUE SPACE.                   SEQUPDAT
001960        05  TOT3-ADDITIONS  PIC ZZ,ZZ9.                                SEQUPDAT
001970        05  FILLER          PIC X(101)  VALUE SPACE.                   SEQUPDAT
001980*                                                                      SEQUPDAT
001990 01   TOTAL-LINE-4.                                                    SEQUPDAT
002000*                                                                      SEQUPDAT
002010        05  TOT4-CC         PIC X.                                     SEQUPDAT
002020        05  FILLER          PIC X(20)   VALUE 'DELETIONS           '.SEQUPDAT
002030        05  FILLER          PIC X(5)    VALUE SPACE.                   SEQUPDAT
002040        05  TOT4-DELETIONS  PIC ZZ,ZZ9.                                SEQUPDAT
002050        05  FILLER          PIC X(101)  VALUE SPACE.                   SEQUPDAT
002060*                                                                      SEQUPDAT
002070 01   TOTAL-LINE-5.                                                    SEQUPDAT
002080*                                                                      SEQUPDAT
002090        05  TOT5-CC         PIC X.                                     SEQUPDAT
002100        05  FILLER          PIC X(20)   VALUE 'TOTAL UPDATES       '.SEQUPDAT
002110        05  FILLER          PIC X(5)    VALUE SPACE.                   SEQUPDAT
002120        05  TOT5-UPDATES    PIC ZZ,ZZ9.                                SEQUPDAT
002130        05  FILLER          PIC XX      VALUE ' *'.                    SEQUPDAT
002140        05  FILLER          PIC X(99)   VALUE SPACE.                   SEQUPDAT
002150*                                                                      SEQUPDAT
002160 01   TOTAL-LINE-6.                                                    SEQUPDAT
002170*                                                                      SEQUPDAT
002180        05  TOT6-CC         PIC X.                                     SEQUPDAT
002190        05  FILLER          PIC X(20)   VALUE 'ERRORS              '.SEQUPDAT
002200        05  FILLER          PIC X(5)    VALUE SPACE.                   SEQUPDAT
002210        05  TOT6-ERRORS     PIC ZZ,ZZ9.                                SEQUPDAT
002220        05  FILLER          PIC X(101)  VALUE SPACE.                   SEQUPDAT
002230*                                                                      SEQUPDAT
002240 01   TOTAL-LINE-7.                                                    SEQUPDAT
002250*                                                                      SEQUPDAT
```

```
002260     05  TOT7-CC          PIC X.                                      SEQUPDAT
002270     05  FILLER           PIC X(20)   VALUE 'TRANSACTIONS PROCESS'.SEQUPDAT
002280     05  FILLER           PIC XX      VALUE 'ED'.                     SEQUPDAT
002290     05  TOT7-TOTAL       PIC Z,ZZZ,ZZ9.                              SEQUPDAT
002300     05  FILLER           PIC X(4)    VALUE ' * *'.                   SEQUPDAT
002310     05  FILLER           PIC X(97)   VALUE SPACE.                    SEQUPDAT
002320*                                                                     SEQUPDAT
002330 PROCEDURE DIVISION.                                                  SEQUPDAT
002340*                                                                     SEQUPDAT
002350 000-UPDATE-INVENTORY-FILE.                                           SEQUPDAT
002360*                                                                     SEQUPDAT
002370     OPEN INPUT  OLDMAST                                              SEQUPDAT
002380                 TRANFILE                                             SEQUPDAT
002390          OUTPUT NEWMAST                                              SEQUPDAT
002400                 ERRFILE                                              SEQUPDAT
002410                 UPDLIST.                                             SEQUPDAT
002420     MOVE CURRENT-DATE TO HDG1-DATE.                                  SEQUPDAT
002430     MOVE HDG1-DATE    TO TOT1-DATE.                                  SEQUPDAT
002440     PERFORM 100-UPDATE-INVENTORY-MASTER                              SEQUPDAT
002450         UNTIL ALL-RECORDS-PROCESSED.                                 SEQUPDAT
002460     PERFORM 300-PRINT-GRAND-TOTALS.                                  SEQUPDAT
002470     CLOSE OLDMAST                                                    SEQUPDAT
002480           TRANFILE                                                   SEQUPDAT
002490           NEWMAST                                                    SEQUPDAT
002500           ERRFILE                                                    SEQUPDAT
002510           UPDLIST.                                                   SEQUPDAT
002520     STOP RUN.                                                        SEQUPDAT
002530*                                                                     SEQUPDAT
002540 100-UPDATE-INVENTORY-MASTER.                                         SEQUPDAT
002550*                                                                     SEQUPDAT
002560     IF NEED-TRANSACTION                                              SEQUPDAT
002570         PERFORM 110-GET-INVENTORY-TRANSACTION                        SEQUPDAT
002580         MOVE 'N' TO NEED-TRANSACTION-SW.                             SEQUPDAT
002590     IF NEED-MASTER                                                   SEQUPDAT
002600         PERFORM 120-GET-INVENTORY-MASTER                             SEQUPDAT
002610         MOVE 'N' TO NEED-MASTER-SW.                                  SEQUPDAT
002620     PERFORM 130-MATCH-MASTER-TRAN.                                   SEQUPDAT
002630     IF WRITE-MASTER                                                  SEQUPDAT
```

8

```
                PERFORM 140-WRITE-NEW-MASTER                          SEQUPDAT
                MOVE 'N' TO WRITE-MASTER-SW.                          SEQUPDAT
            IF PRINT-UPDATE                                           SEQUPDAT
                PERFORM 150-PRINT-UPDATE-LINE                         SEQUPDAT
                MOVE 'N' TO PRINT-UPDATE-SW.                          SEQUPDAT
      *                                                               SEQUPDAT
       110-GET-INVENTORY-TRANSACTION.                                 SEQUPDAT
      *                                                               SEQUPDAT
            READ TRANFILE INTO TR-RECORD                              SEQUPDAT
                AT END                                                SEQUPDAT
                    MOVE HIGH-VALUES TO TR-ITEM-NUMBER.               SEQUPDAT
            IF TR-ITEM-NUMBER NOT = HIGH-VALUES                       SEQUPDAT
                ADD 1 TO TOTAL-TRANS-PROCESSED.                       SEQUPDAT
      *                                                               SEQUPDAT
       120-GET-INVENTORY-MASTER.                                      SEQUPDAT
      *                                                               SEQUPDAT
            READ OLDMAST INTO MA-RECORD                               SEQUPDAT
                AT END                                                SEQUPDAT
                    MOVE HIGH-VALUES TO MA-ITEM-NUMBER.               SEQUPDAT
      *                                                               SEQUPDAT
       130-MATCH-MASTER-TRAN.                                         SEQUPDAT
      *                                                               SEQUPDAT
            IF MA-ITEM-NUMBER GREATER THAN TR-ITEM-NUMBER             SEQUPDAT
                PERFORM 160-PROCESS-HI-MASTER                         SEQUPDAT
            ELSE IF MA-ITEM-NUMBER LESS THAN TR-ITEM-NUMBER           SEQUPDAT
                PERFORM 200-PROCESS-LO-MASTER                         SEQUPDAT
            ELSE                                                      SEQUPDAT
                PERFORM 210-PROCESS-MAST-TRAN-EQUAL.                  SEQUPDAT
      *                                                               SEQUPDAT
       140-WRITE-NEW-MASTER.                                          SEQUPDAT
      *                                                               SEQUPDAT
            WRITE NM-RECORD.                                          SEQUPDAT
      *                                                               SEQUPDAT
       150-PRINT-UPDATE-LINE.                                         SEQUPDAT
      *                                                               SEQUPDAT
            IF LINE-COUNT GREATER THAN LINES-ON-PAGE                  SEQUPDAT
                PERFORM 240-PRINT-HEADING-LINES.                      SEQUPDAT
            MOVE NEXT-UPDATE-LINE TO PRINT-AREA.                      SEQUPDAT
```

```
003020      PERFORM 250-WRITE-REPORT-LINE.                              SEQUPDAT
003030      MOVE 1 TO SPACE-CONTROL.                                    SEQUPDAT
003040*                                                                 SEQUPDAT
003050 160-PROCESS-HI-MASTER.                                           SEQUPDAT
003060*                                                                 SEQUPDAT
003070      IF ADDITION                                                 SEQUPDAT
003080          PERFORM 170-ADD-INVENTORY-MASTER                        SEQUPDAT
003090      ELSE                                                        SEQUPDAT
003100          PERFORM 180-PUT-ERROR-RECORD.                           SEQUPDAT
003110*                                                                 SEQUPDAT
003120 170-ADD-INVENTORY-MASTER.                                        SEQUPDAT
003130*                                                                 SEQUPDAT
003140      MOVE TR-INV-RECORD TO NM-RECORD.                            SEQUPDAT
003150      MOVE 'Y' TO WRITE-MASTER-SW.                                SEQUPDAT
003160      MOVE TR-ITEM-NUMBER      TO NUL-ITEM-NUMBER.                SEQUPDAT
003170      MOVE TR-ITEM-DESCR       TO NUL-ITEM-DESCR.                 SEQUPDAT
003180      MOVE TR-UNIT-COST-NUM    TO NUL-UNIT-COST.                  SEQUPDAT
003190      MOVE TR-UNIT-PRICE-NUM   TO NUL-UNIT-PRICE.                 SEQUPDAT
003200      MOVE TR-ON-HAND-NUM      TO NUL-ON-HAND.                    SEQUPDAT
003210      MOVE ADD-MESSAGE         TO NUL-ACTION.                     SEQUPDAT
003220      MOVE 'Y' TO PRINT-UPDATE-SW.                                SEQUPDAT
003230      MOVE 'Y' TO NEED-TRANSACTION-SW.                            SEQUPDAT
003240      ADD 1 TO ADDITION-COUNT.                                    SEQUPDAT
003250*                                                                 SEQUPDAT
003260 180-PUT-ERROR-RECORD.                                            SEQUPDAT
003270*                                                                 SEQUPDAT
003280      MOVE TR-RECORD TO ER-RECORD.                                SEQUPDAT
003290      PERFORM 190-WRITE-ERROR-RECORD.                             SEQUPDAT
003300      MOVE 'Y' TO NEED-TRANSACTION-SW.                            SEQUPDAT
003310      ADD 1 TO ERROR-COUNT.                                       SEQUPDAT
003320*                                                                 SEQUPDAT
003330 190-WRITE-ERROR-RECORD.                                          SEQUPDAT
003340*                                                                 SEQUPDAT
003350      WRITE ER-RECORD.                                            SEQUPDAT
003360*                                                                 SEQUPDAT
003370 200-PROCESS-LO-MASTER.                                           SEQUPDAT
003380*                                                                 SEQUPDAT
003390      MOVE MA-RECORD TO NM-RECORD.                                SEQUPDAT
```

```
003400     MOVE 'Y' TO WRITE-MASTER-SW.                                 SEQUPDAT
003410     MOVE 'Y' TO NEED-MASTER-SW.                                  SEQUPDAT
003420*                                                                 SEQUPDAT
003430 210-PROCESS-MAST-TRAN-EQUAL.                                     SEQUPDAT
003440*                                                                 SEQUPDAT
003450     IF MA-ITEM-NUMBER = HIGH-VALUES                              SEQUPDAT
003460         MOVE 'Y' TO ALL-RECORDS-PROCESSED-SW                     SEQUPDAT
003470     ELSE                                                         SEQUPDAT
003480         IF DELETION                                              SEQUPDAT
003490             PERFORM 220-DELETE-INVENTORY-MASTER                  SEQUPDAT
003500         ELSE                                                     SEQUPDAT
003510             IF CHANGE                                            SEQUPDAT
003520                 PERFORM 230-CHANGE-INVENTORY-MASTER              SEQUPDAT
003530             ELSE                                                 SEQUPDAT
003540                 PERFORM 180-PUT-ERROR-RECORD.                    SEQUPDAT
003550*                                                                 SEQUPDAT
003560 220-DELETE-INVENTORY-MASTER.                                     SEQUPDAT
003570*                                                                 SEQUPDAT
003580     MOVE MA-ITEM-NUMBER TO NUL-ITEM-NUMBER.                      SEQUPDAT
003590     MOVE MA-ITEM-DESCR  TO NUL-ITEM-DESCR.                       SEQUPDAT
003600     MOVE MA-UNIT-COST   TO NUL-UNIT-COST.                        SEQUPDAT
003610     MOVE MA-UNIT-PRICE  TO NUL-UNIT-PRICE.                       SEQUPDAT
003620     MOVE MA-ON-HAND     TO NUL-ON-HAND.                          SEQUPDAT
003630     MOVE DELETE-MESSAGE TO NUL-ACTION.                           SEQUPDAT
003640     MOVE 'Y' TO PRINT-UPDATE-SW.                                 SEQUPDAT
003650     MOVE 'Y' TO NEED-MASTER-SW.                                  SEQUPDAT
003660     MOVE 'Y' TO NEED-TRANSACTION-SW.                             SEQUPDAT
003670     ADD 1 TO DELETION-COUNT.                                     SEQUPDAT
003680*                                                                 SEQUPDAT
003690 230-CHANGE-INVENTORY-MASTER.                                     SEQUPDAT
003700*                                                                 SEQUPDAT
003710     IF TR-ITEM-DESCR NOT = SPACE                                 SEQUPDAT
003720         MOVE TR-ITEM-DESCR TO MA-ITEM-DESCR.                     SEQUPDAT
003730     IF TR-UNIT-COST NOT = SPACE                                  SEQUPDAT
003740         MOVE TR-UNIT-COST  TO MA-UNIT-COST.                      SEQUPDAT
003750     IF TR-UNIT-PRICE NOT = SPACE                                 SEQUPDAT
003760         MOVE TR-UNIT-PRICE TO MA-UNIT-PRICE.                     SEQUPDAT
003770     IF TR-ON-HAND NOT = SPACE                                    SEQUPDAT
```

```
003780             MOVE TR-ON-HAND       TO MA-ON-HAND.                        SEQUPDAT
003790         MOVE MA-ITEM-NUMBER       TO NUL-ITEM-NUMBER.                   SEQUPDAT
003800         MOVE MA-ITEM-DESCR        TO NUL-ITEM-DESCR.                    SEQUPDAT
003810         MOVE MA-UNIT-COST         TO NUL-UNIT-COST.                     SEQUPDAT
003820         MOVE MA-UNIT-PRICE        TO NUL-UNIT-PRICE.                    SEQUPDAT
003830         MOVE MA-ON-HAND           TO NUL-ON-HAND.                       SEQUPDAT
003840         MOVE CHANGE-MESSAGE       TO NUL-ACTION.                        SEQUPDAT
003850         MOVE 'Y' TO PRINT-UPDATE-SW.                                    SEQUPDAT
003860         MOVE 'Y' TO NEED-TRANSACTION-SW.                                SEQUPDAT
003870         ADD 1 TO CHANGE-COUNT.                                          SEQUPDAT
003880*                                                                        SEQUPDAT
003890 240-PRINT-HEADING-LINES.                                                SEQUPDAT
003900*                                                                        SEQUPDAT
003910         ADD 1 TO PAGE-NUMBER.                                           SEQUPDAT
003920         MOVE PAGE-NUMBER TO HDG1-PAGE-NO.                               SEQUPDAT
003930         MOVE HDG-LINE-1  TO PRINT-AREA.                                 SEQUPDAT
003940         PERFORM 260-WRITE-PAGE-TOP-LINE.                                SEQUPDAT
003950         MOVE HDG-LINE-2 TO PRINT-AREA.                                  SEQUPDAT
003960         MOVE 2 TO SPACE-CONTROL.                                        SEQUPDAT
003970         PERFORM 250-WRITE-REPORT-LINE.                                  SEQUPDAT
003980*                                                                        SEQUPDAT
003990 250-WRITE-REPORT-LINE.                                                  SEQUPDAT
004000*                                                                        SEQUPDAT
004010         WRITE PRINT-AREA                                                SEQUPDAT
004020             AFTER ADVANCING SPACE-CONTROL LINES.                        SEQUPDAT
004030         ADD SPACE-CONTROL TO LINE-COUNT.                                SEQUPDAT
004040*                                                                        SEQUPDAT
004050 260-WRITE-PAGE-TOP-LINE.                                                SEQUPDAT
004060*                                                                        SEQUPDAT
004070         WRITE PRINT-AREA                                                SEQUPDAT
004080             AFTER ADVANCING PAGE-TOP.                                   SEQUPDAT
004090         MOVE ZERO TO LINE-COUNT.                                        SEQUPDAT
004100*                                                                        SEQUPDAT
004110 300-PRINT-GRAND-TOTALS.                                                 SEQUPDAT
004120*                                                                        SEQUPDAT
004130         ADD CHANGE-COUNT                                                SEQUPDAT
004140             ADDITION-COUNT                                              SEQUPDAT
004150             DELETION-COUNT GIVING TOTAL-UPDATES.                        SEQUPDAT
```

12

```
004160    MOVE TOTAL-LINE-1 TO PRINT-AREA.                        SEQUPDAT
004170    PERFORM 260-WRITE-PAGE-TOP-LINE.                        SEQUPDAT
004180    MOVE CHANGE-COUNT TO TOT2-CHANGES.                      SEQUPDAT
004190    MOVE TOTAL-LINE-2 TO PRINT-AREA.                        SEQUPDAT
004200    MOVE 2 TO SPACE-CONTROL.                                SEQUPDAT
004210    PERFORM 250-WRITE-REPORT-LINE.                          SEQUPDAT
004220    MOVE ADDITION-COUNT TO TOT3-ADDITIONS.                  SEQUPDAT
004230    MOVE TOTAL-LINE-3 TO PRINT-AREA.                        SEQUPDAT
004240    MOVE 1 TO SPACE-CONTROL.                                SEQUPDAT
004250    PERFORM 250-WRITE-REPORT-LINE.                          SEQUPDAT
004260    MOVE DELETION-COUNT TO TOT4-DELETIONS.                  SEQUPDAT
004270    MOVE TOTAL-LINE-4 TO PRINT-AREA.                        SEQUPDAT
004280    PERFORM 250-WRITE-REPORT-LINE.                          SEQUPDAT
004290    MOVE TOTAL-UPDATES TO TOT5-UPDATES.                     SEQUPDAT
004300    MOVE TOTAL-LINE-5 TO PRINT-AREA.                        SEQUPDAT
004310    PERFORM 250-WRITE-REPORT-LINE.                          SEQUPDAT
004320    MOVE ERROR-COUNT TO TOT6-ERRORS.                        SEQUPDAT
004330    MOVE TOTAL-LINE-6 TO PRINT-AREA.                        SEQUPDAT
004340    MOVE 2 TO SPACE-CONTROL.                                SEQUPDAT
004350    PERFORM 250-WRITE-REPORT-LINE.                          SEQUPDAT
004360    MOVE TOTAL-TRANS-PROCESSED TO TOT7-TOTAL.               SEQUPDAT
004370    MOVE TOTAL-LINE-7 TO PRINT-AREA.                        SEQUPDAT
004380    MOVE 2 TO SPACE-CONTROL.                                SEQUPDAT
004390    PERFORM 250-WRITE-REPORT-LINE.                          SEQUPDAT
```

```
                                      CROSS-REFERENCE DICTIONARY

DATA NAMES                         DEFN      REFERENCE

ACTION-MESSAGES                    000105
ADD-MESSAGE                        000108    000321
ADDITION-COUNT                     000099    000324   000413   000422
ALL-RECORDS-PROCESSED-SW           000078    000346
CHANGE-COUNT                       000098    000387   000413   000418
CHANGE-MESSAGE                     000107    000384
COUNTS                             000096
DELETE-MESSAGE                     000109    000363
DELETION-COUNT                     000100    000367   000413   000426
ER-RECORD                          000064    000328   000335
ERRFILE                            000021    000237   000247   000335
ERROR-COUNT                        000102    000331   000432
HDG-LINE-1                         000138    000393
HDG-LINE-2                         000149    000395
HDG1-CC                            000140
HDG1-DATE                          000141    000242   000243
HDG1-PAGE-NO                       000146    000392
HDG2-CC                            000151
LINE-COUNT                         000091    000299   000403   000409
LINES-ON-PAGE                      000092    000299
MA-AREA                            000034    000280
MA-ITEM-DESCR                      000114    000359   000372   000380
MA-ITEM-NUMBER                     000113    000282   000286   000288   000345   000358   000379
MA-ON-HAND                         000117    000362   000378   000383
MA-RECORD                          000111    000280   000339
MA-UNIT-COST                       000115    000360   000374   000381
MA-UNIT-PRICE                      000116    000361   000376   000382
NEED-MASTER-SW                     000082    000261   000341   000365
NEED-TRANSACTION-SW                000080    000258   000323   000330   000366   000386
NEWMAST                            000019    000237   000247   000295
NEXT-UPDATE-LINE                   000158    000301
NM-ITEM-DESCR                      000045
```

```
22

NM-ITEM-NUMBER                000044
NM-ON-HAND                    000048
NM-RECORD                     000042  000295  000314  000339
NM-UNIT-COST                  000046
NM-UNIT-PRICE                 000047
NUL-ACTION                    000172  000321  000363  000384
NUL-CC                        000160
NUL-ITEM-DESCR                000164  000317  000359  000380
NUL-ITEM-NUMBER               000162  000316  000358  000379
NUL-ON-HAND                   000170  000320  000362  000383
NUL-UNIT-COST                 000166  000318  000360  000381
NUL-UNIT-PRICE                000168  000319  000361  000382
OLDMAST                       000018  000237  000247  000280
PAGE-NUMBER                   000094  000391  000392
PRINT-AREA                    000072  000301  000393  000395  000401  000407  000416  000419  000423  000427  000430
                                      000433  000437
PRINT-FIELDS                  000089
PRINT-UPDATE-SW               000086  000268  000322  000364  000385
SPACE-CONTROL                 000093  000303  000396  000401  000403  000420  000424  000434  000438
SWITCHES                      000076
TOTAL-LINE-1                  000175  000416
TOTAL-LINE-2                  000183  000419
TOTAL-LINE-3                  000191  000423
TOTAL-LINE-4                  000199  000427
TOTAL-LINE-5                  000207  000430
TOTAL-LINE-6                  000216  000433
TOTAL-LINE-7                  000224  000437
TOTAL-TRANS-PROCESSED         000103  000276  000436
TOTAL-UPDATES                 000101  000413  000429
TOT1-CC                       000177
TOT1-DATE                     000180  000243
TOT2-CC                       000185
TOT2-CHANGES                  000188  000418
TOT3-ADDITIONS                000196  000422
TOT3-CC                       000193
TOT4-CC                       000201
TOT4-DELETIONS                000204  000426
TOT5-CC                       000209
```

```
TOT5-UPDATES          000212  000429
TOT6-CC               000218
TOT6-ERRORS           000221  000432
TOT7-CC               000226
TOT7-TOTAL            000229  000436
TR-ACTION-CODE        000121
TR-AREA               000056  000272
TR-INV-RECORD         000126  000314
TR-ITEM-DESCR         000128  000317  000371  000372
TR-ITEM-NUMBER        000127  000274  000275  000286  000288  000316
TR-ON-HAND            000133  000377  000378
TR-ON-HAND-NUM        000134  000320
TR-RECORD             000119  000272  000323
TR-UNIT-COST          000129  000373  000374
TR-UNIT-COST-NUM      000130  000318
TR-UNIT-PRICE         000131  000375  000376
TR-UNIT-PRICE-NUM     000132  000319
TRANFILE              000020  000237  000247  000272
UPDLIST               000022  000237  000247  000401  000407
WRITE-MASTER-SW       000084  000265  000315  000340
```

```
24

PROCEDURE NAMES                  DEFN     REFERENCE

000-UPDATE-INVENTORY-FILE        000235
100-UPDATE-INVENTORY-MASTER      000254   000244
110-GET-INVENTORY-TRANSACTION    000270   000257
120-GET-INVENTORY-MASTER         000278   000260
130-MATCH-MASTER-TRAN            000284   000262
140-WRITE-NEW-MASTER             000293   000264
150-PRINT-UPDATE-LINE            000297   000267
160-PROCESS-HI-MASTER            000305   000287
170-ADD-INVENTORY-MASTER         000312   000308
180-PUT-ERROR-RECORD             000326   000310   000354
190-WRITE-ERROR-RECORD           000333   000329
200-PROCESS-LO-MASTER            000337   000289
210-PROCESS-MAST-TRAN-EQUAL      000343   000291
220-DELETE-INVENTORY-MASTER      000356   000349
230-CHANGE-INVENTORY-MASTER      000369   000352
240-PRINT-HEADING-LINES          000389   000300
250-WRITE-REPORT-LINE            000399   000302   000397   000421   000425   000428   000431   000435   000439
260-WRITE-PAGE-TOP-LINE          000405   000394   000417
300-PRINT-GRAND-TOTALS           000411   000246
```

The Random-Update Program

System flowchart:

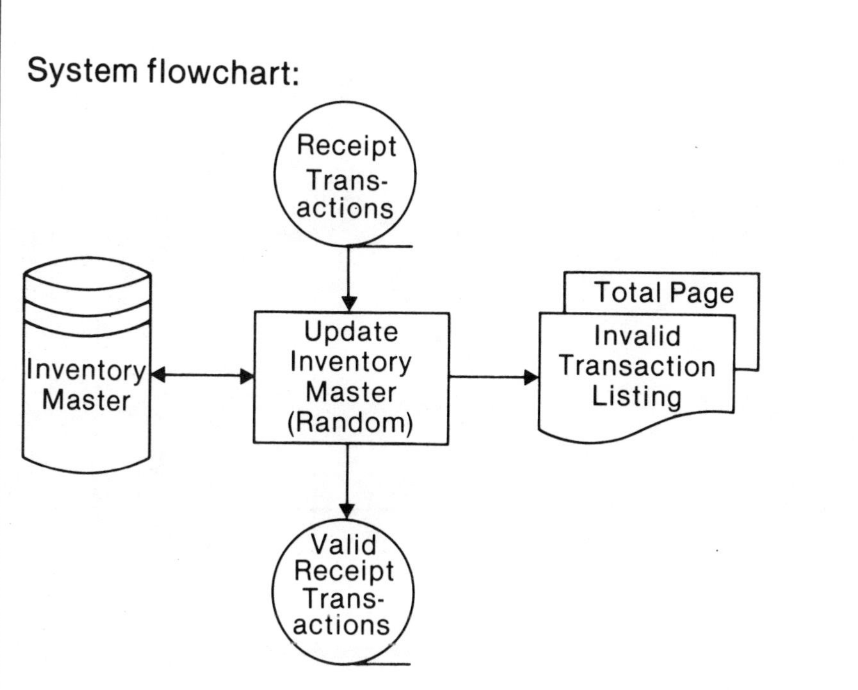

Narrative:

1. The master file has indexed sequential organization. It is a large file with low receipt activity.
2. The input file of receipt transactions is in random order.
3. The receipts must be edited and only valid receipts should be used to update the master records. The rules for editing the individual fields will be supplied later. The error code on the invalid listing will indicate only the first field that is invalid: FIELD 1, FIELD 2, etc.
4. After this update run, the valid receipt transactions are needed in item number sequence.
5. The totals for the update run must be printed on a separate page.

Record layouts:

Inventory Master Records

Field Name	Delete Code	Item No.	Item Description	On-hand Balance
Characteristics	X	X(5)	X(20)	9(3)
Position	1	2-6	7-26	27-29

Receipt Transaction Records

Field Name	Item No.	Vendor No.	Receipt Date	Receipt Quantity
Characteristics	X(5)	X(3)	9(6)	9(3)
Position	1–5	6–8	9–14	15–17

Output format:

Record	Line	Print layout
HDG-LINE-1	1	INVALID TRANSACTIONS IN UPDATE RUN OF 99-99-99 PAGE 999
	2	
HDG-LINE-2	3	ITEM NO. VENDOR NO DATE QUANTITY ERROR CODE
	4	
NEXT-REPORT-LINE	5	XXXXX XXX 99-99-99 999 FIELD 1
	6	
	7	XXXXX XXX 99-99-99 999 FIELD 2
	8	
	9	XXXXX XXX 99-99-99 999 FIELD 3
	10	
	11	XXXXX XXX 99-99-99 999 FIELD 4
	12	
	13	XXXXX XXX 99-99-99 999 NOT FOUND
	14	
	15	
Total page: TOTAL-LINE-1	16	SUMMARY FOR UPDATE RUN OF 99-99-99
	17	
TOTAL-LINE-2	18	99,999 TRANSACTIONS READ
TOTAL-LINE-3	19	99,999 VALID TRANSACTIONS
TOTAL-LINE-4	20	99,999 INVALID TRANSACTIONS
	21	

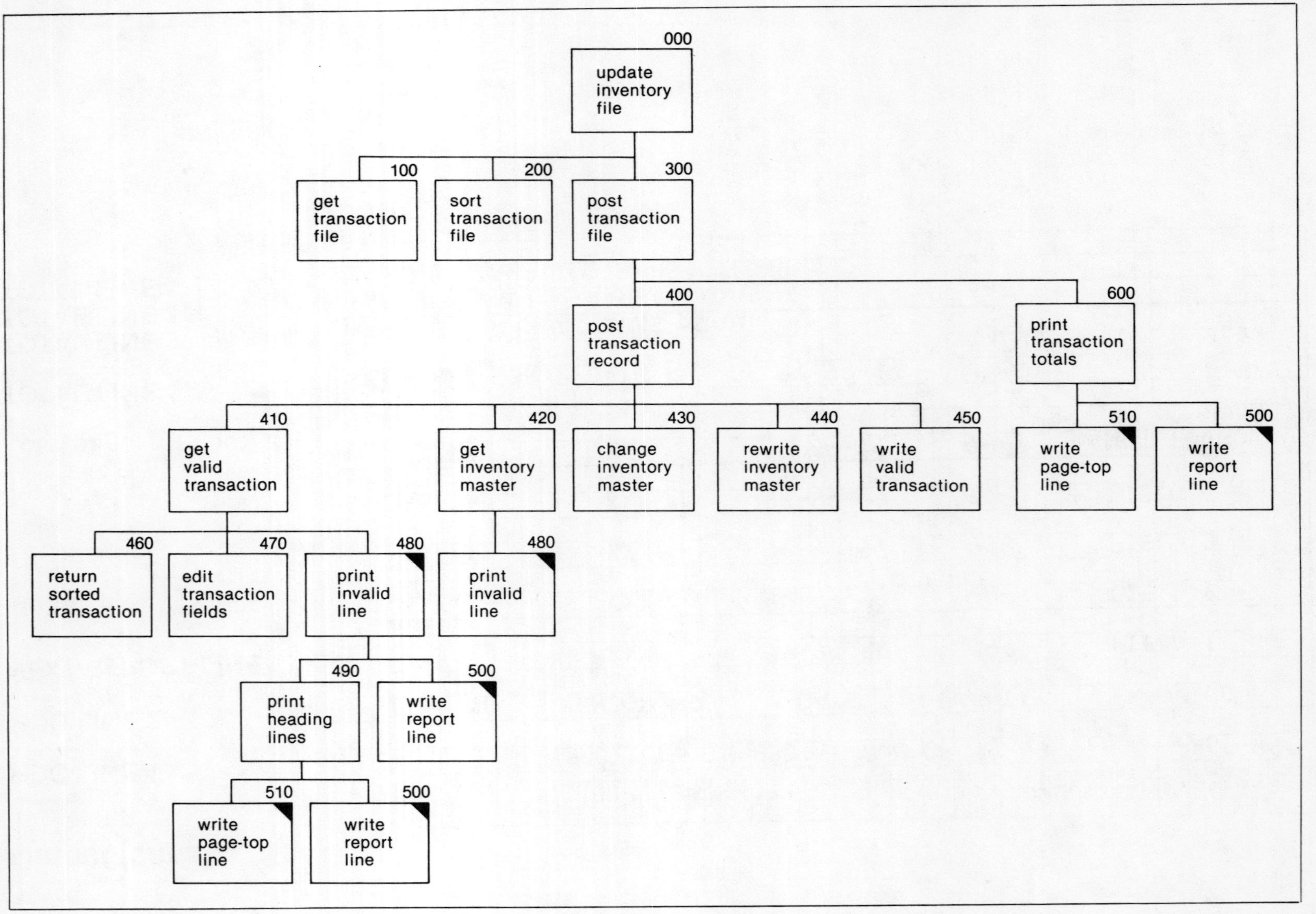

000 update inventory file
100 get transaction file
200 sort transaction file
300 post transaction file
400 post transaction record
600 print transaction totals
410 get valid transaction
420 get inventory master
430 change inventory master
440 rewrite inventory master
450 write valid transaction
510 write page-top line
500 write report line
460 return sorted transaction
470 edit transaction fields
480 print invalid line
480 print invalid line
490 print heading lines
500 write report line
510 write page-top line
500 write report line

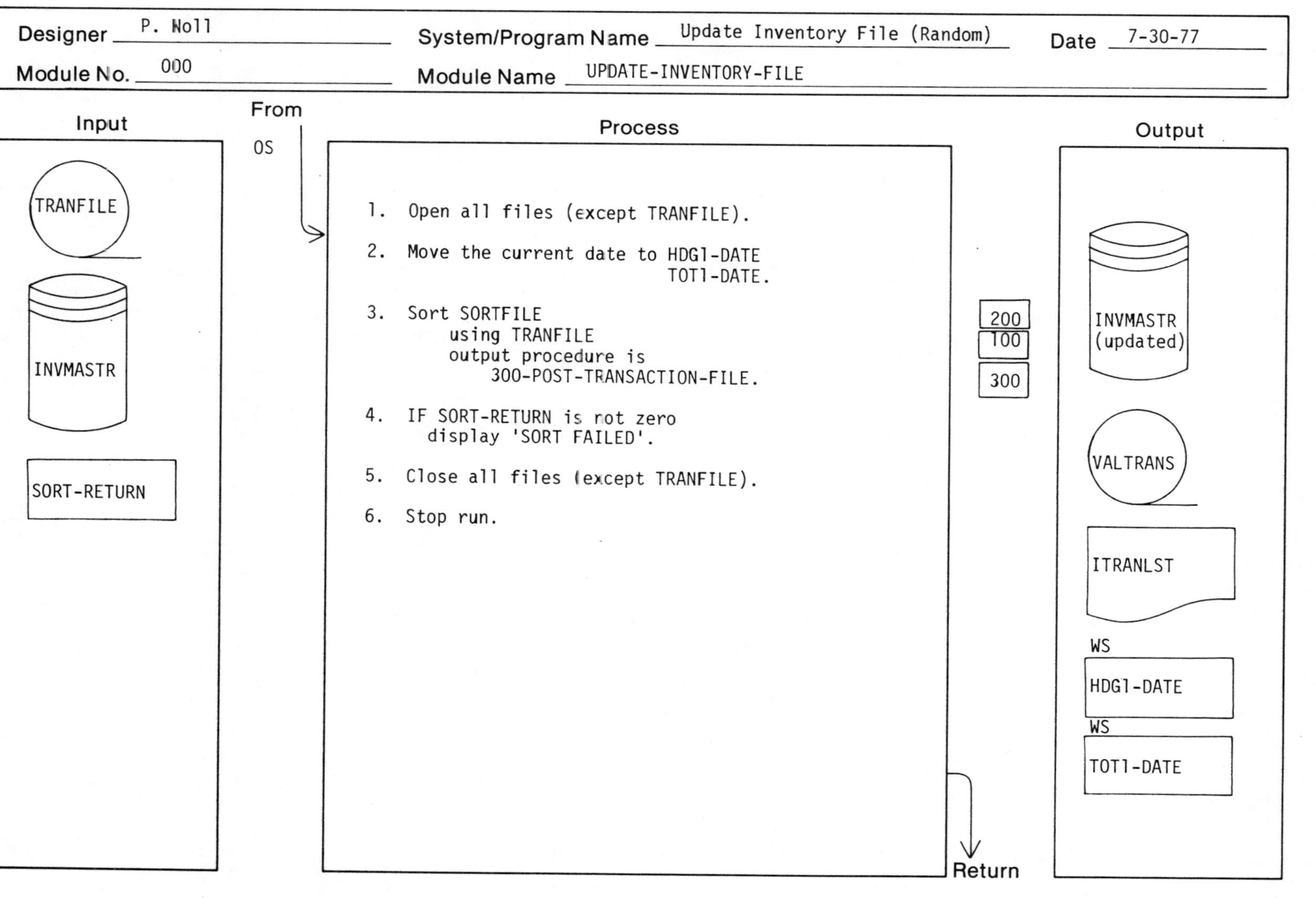
Designer P. Noll
System/Program Name Update Inventory File (Random)
Date 7-30-77
Module No. 000
Module Name UPDATE-INVENTORY-FILE
Input
TRANFILE
INVMASTR
SORT-RETURN
From
OS
Process
1. Open all files (except TRANFILE).
2. Move the current date to HDG1-DATE
TOT1-DATE.
3. Sort SORTFILE
using TRANFILE
output procedure is
300-POST-TRANSACTION-FILE.
4. IF SORT-RETURN is not zero
display 'SORT FAILED'.
5. Close all files (except TRANFILE).
6. Stop run.
200
100
300
Return
Output
INVMASTR
(updated)
VALTRANS
ITRANLST
WS
HDG1-DATE
WS
TOT1-DATE

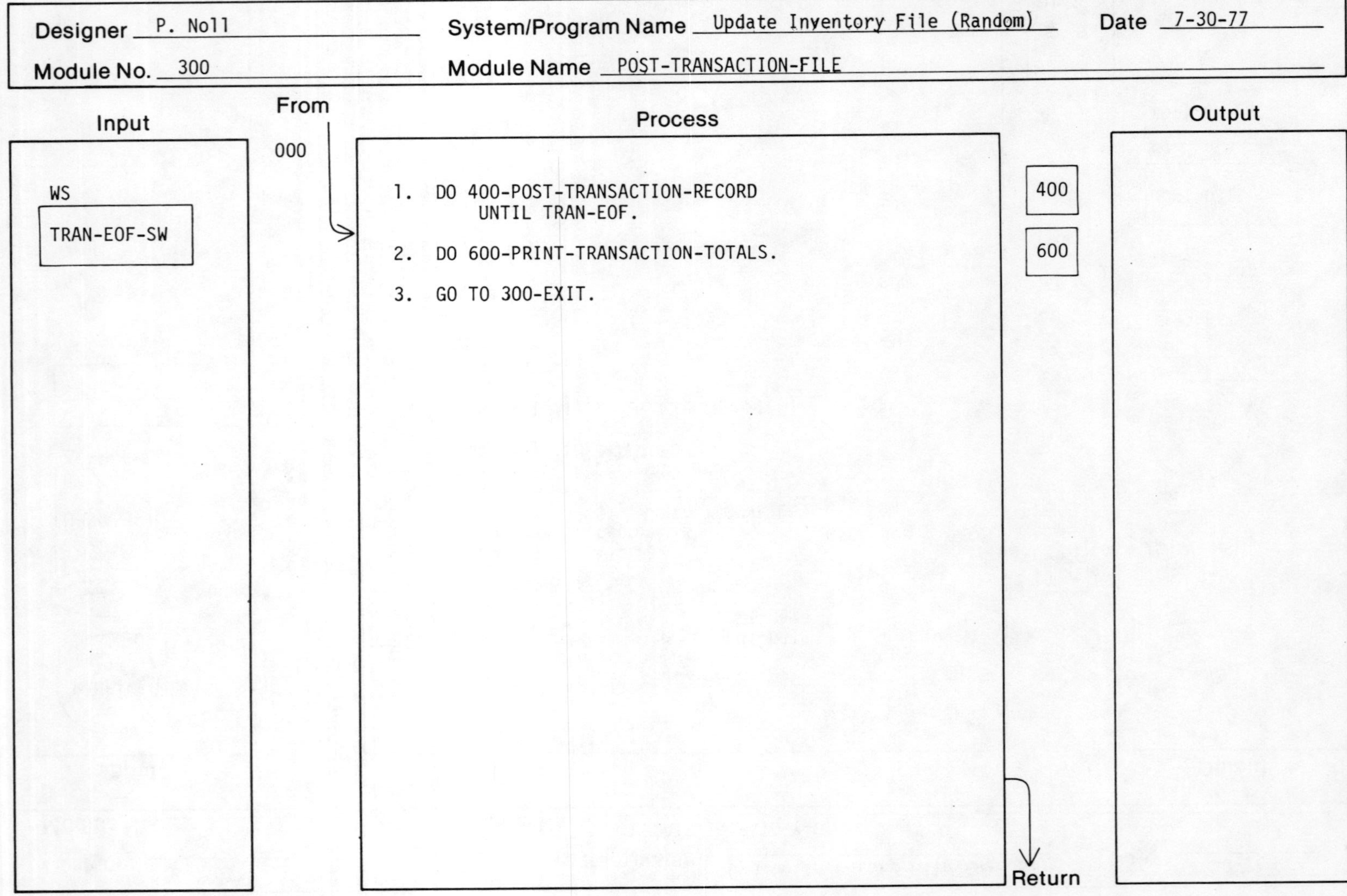
Designer P. Noll
System/Program Name Update Inventory File (Random)
Date 7-30-77
Module No. 300
Module Name POST-TRANSACTION-FILE
Input
WS
TRAN-EOF-SW
From
000
Process
1. DO 400-POST-TRANSACTION-RECORD
UNTIL TRAN-EOF.
2. DO 600-PRINT-TRANSACTION-TOTALS.
3. GO TO 300-EXIT.
400
600
Return
Output

Designer: P. Noll
System/Program Name: Update Inventory File (Random)
Date: 7-30-77
Module No.: 400
Module Name: POST-TRANSACTION-RECORD

Input

WS: TRAN-EOF-SW

WS: VALID-TRAN-SW

WS: MASTER-FOUND-SW

From 300

Process

```
1.  DO 410-GET-VALID-TRANSACTION                 410
        UNTIL TRAN-EOF or VALID-TRAN.

2.  IF not TRAN-EOF
      DO 420-GET-INVENTORY-MASTER                420
      IF MASTER-FOUND
        DO 430-CHANGE-INVENTORY-MASTER           430
        DO 440-REWRITE-INVENTORY-MASTER          440
        DO 450-WRITE-VALID-TRANSACTION.          450

3.  Move 'N' to VALID-TRAN-SW.
```

Return

Output

WS: VALID-TRAN-SW

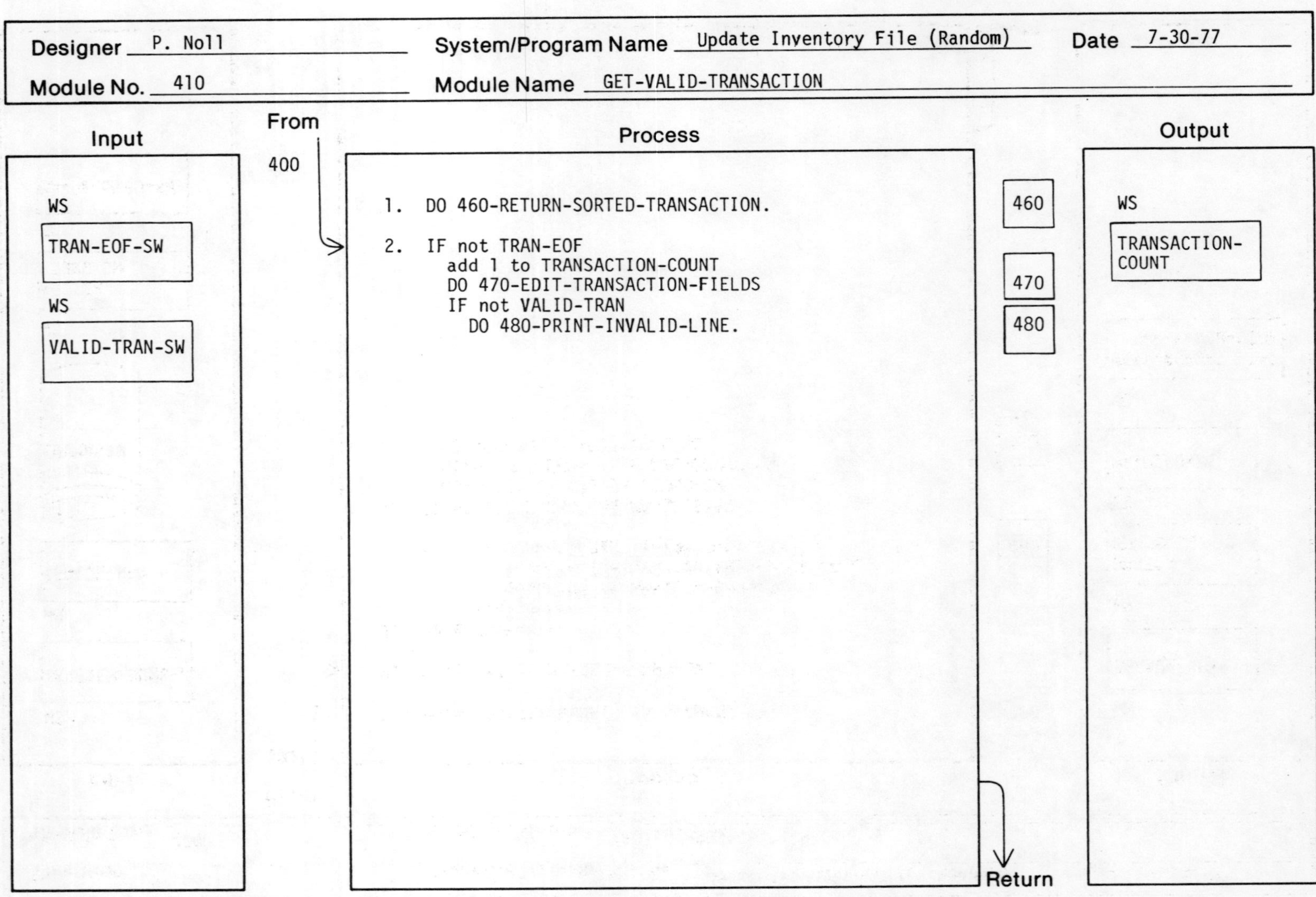

Designer P. Noll System/Program Name Update Inventory File (Random) Date 7-30-77

Module No. 410 Module Name GET-VALID-TRANSACTION

Input	Process	Output
WS TRAN-EOF-SW WS VALID-TRAN-SW	From 400	WS TRANSACTION-COUNT

```
1.  DO 460-RETURN-SORTED-TRANSACTION.                 460

2.  IF not TRAN-EOF
      add 1 to TRANSACTION-COUNT
      DO 470-EDIT-TRANSACTION-FIELDS                  470
      IF not VALID-TRAN
        DO 480-PRINT-INVALID-LINE.                    480
```

Return

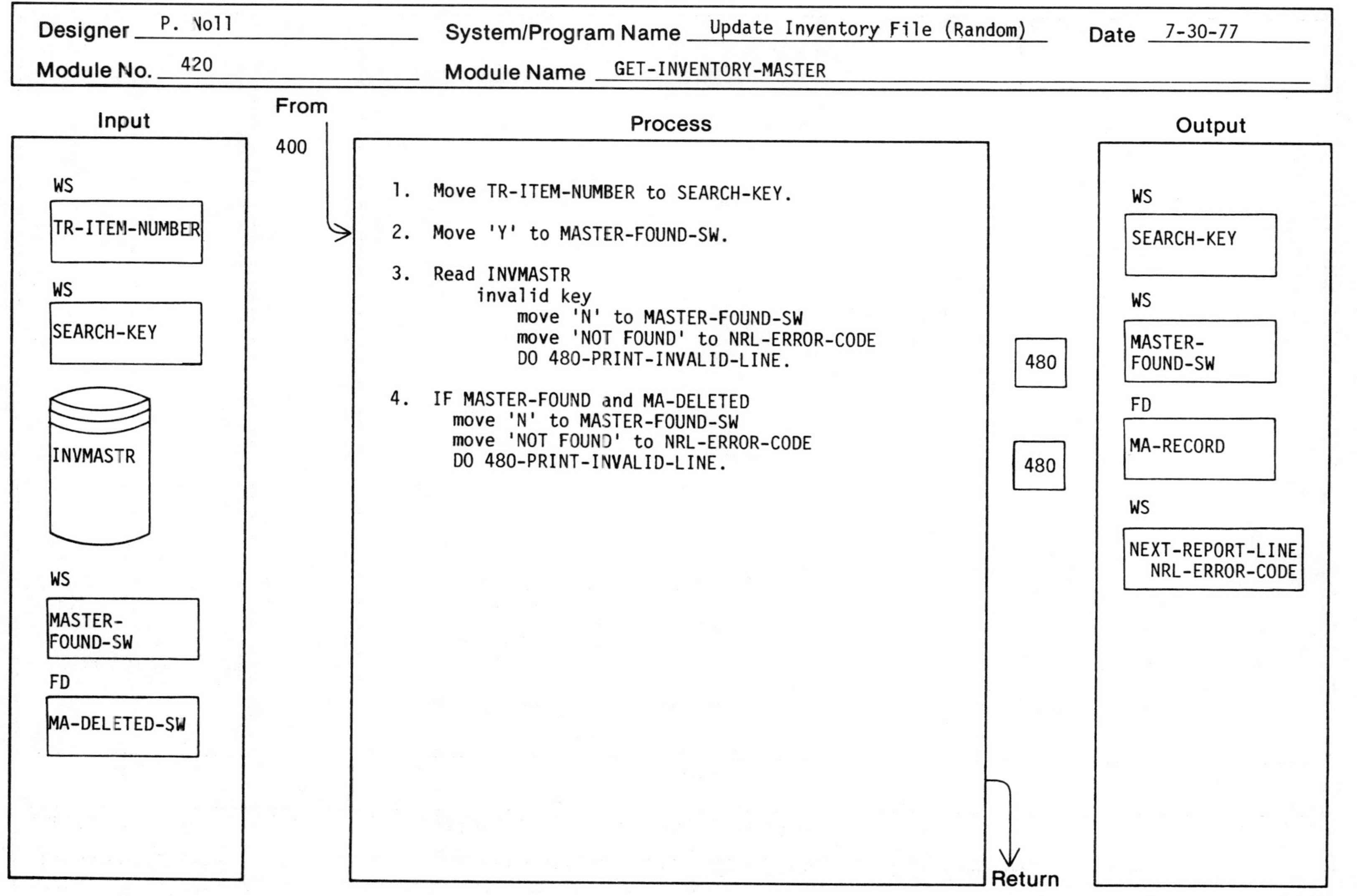
Designer P. Noll
System/Program Name Update Inventory File (Random)
Date 7-30-77
Module No. 420
Module Name GET-INVENTORY-MASTER
Input
WS
TR-ITEM-NUMBER
WS
SEARCH-KEY
INVMASTR
WS
MASTER-FOUND-SW
FD
MA-DELETED-SW
From
400
Process
1. Move TR-ITEM-NUMBER to SEARCH-KEY.
2. Move 'Y' to MASTER-FOUND-SW.
3. Read INVMASTR
invalid key
move 'N' to MASTER-FOUND-SW
move 'NOT FOUND' to NRL-ERROR-CODE
DO 480-PRINT-INVALID-LINE.
4. IF MASTER-FOUND and MA-DELETED
move 'N' to MASTER-FOUND-SW
move 'NOT FOUND' to NRL-ERROR-CODE
DO 480-PRINT-INVALID-LINE.
480
480
Return
Output
WS
SEARCH-KEY
WS
MASTER-FOUND-SW
FD
MA-RECORD
WS
NEXT-REPORT-LINE
NRL-ERROR-CODE

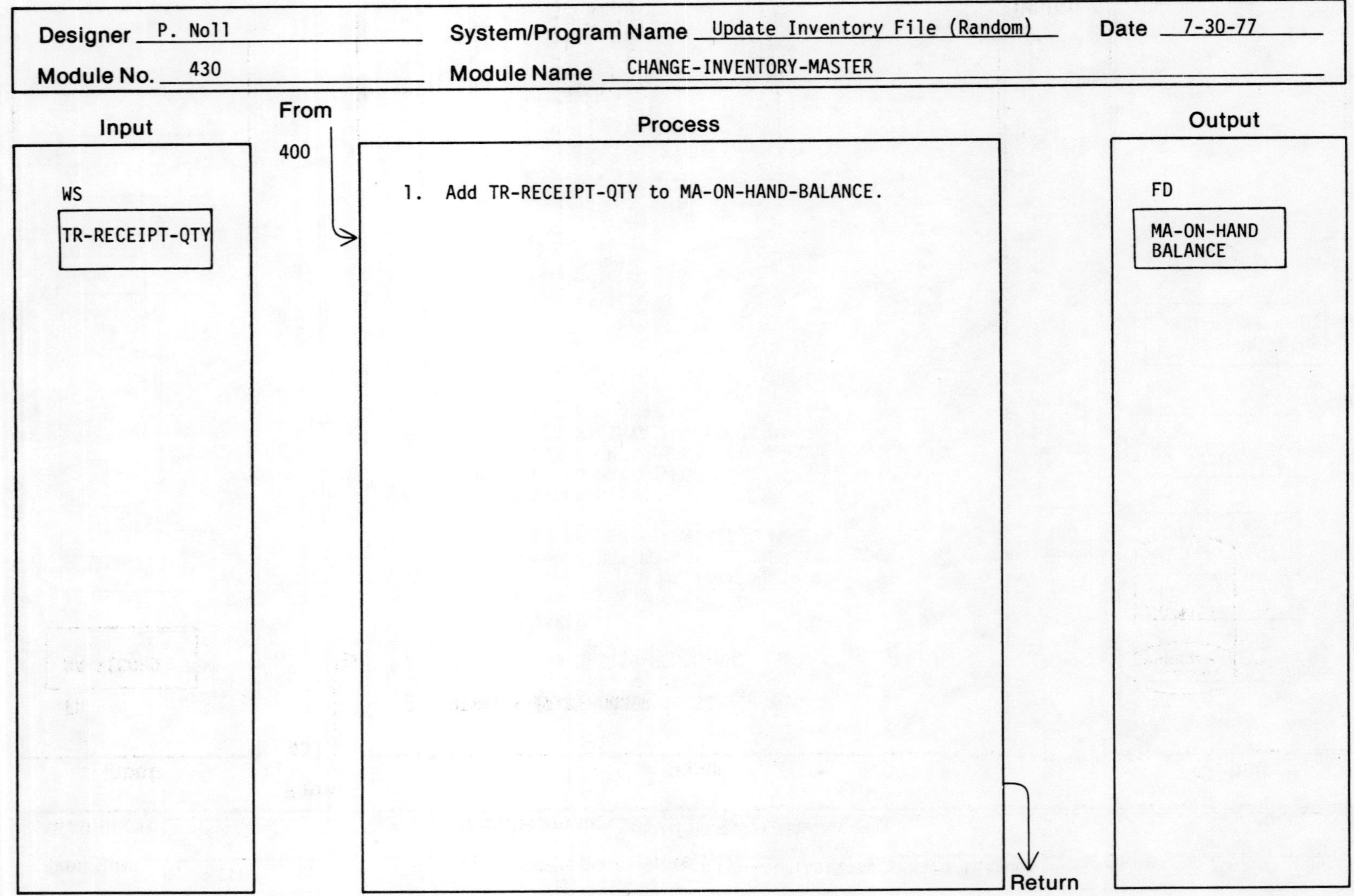
Designer P. Noll
System/Program Name Update Inventory File (Random)
Date 7-30-77
Module No. 430
Module Name CHANGE-INVENTORY-MASTER
Input
WS
TR-RECEIPT-QTY
From
400
Process
1. Add TR-RECEIPT-QTY to MA-ON-HAND-BALANCE.
Return
Output
FD
MA-ON-HAND
BALANCE

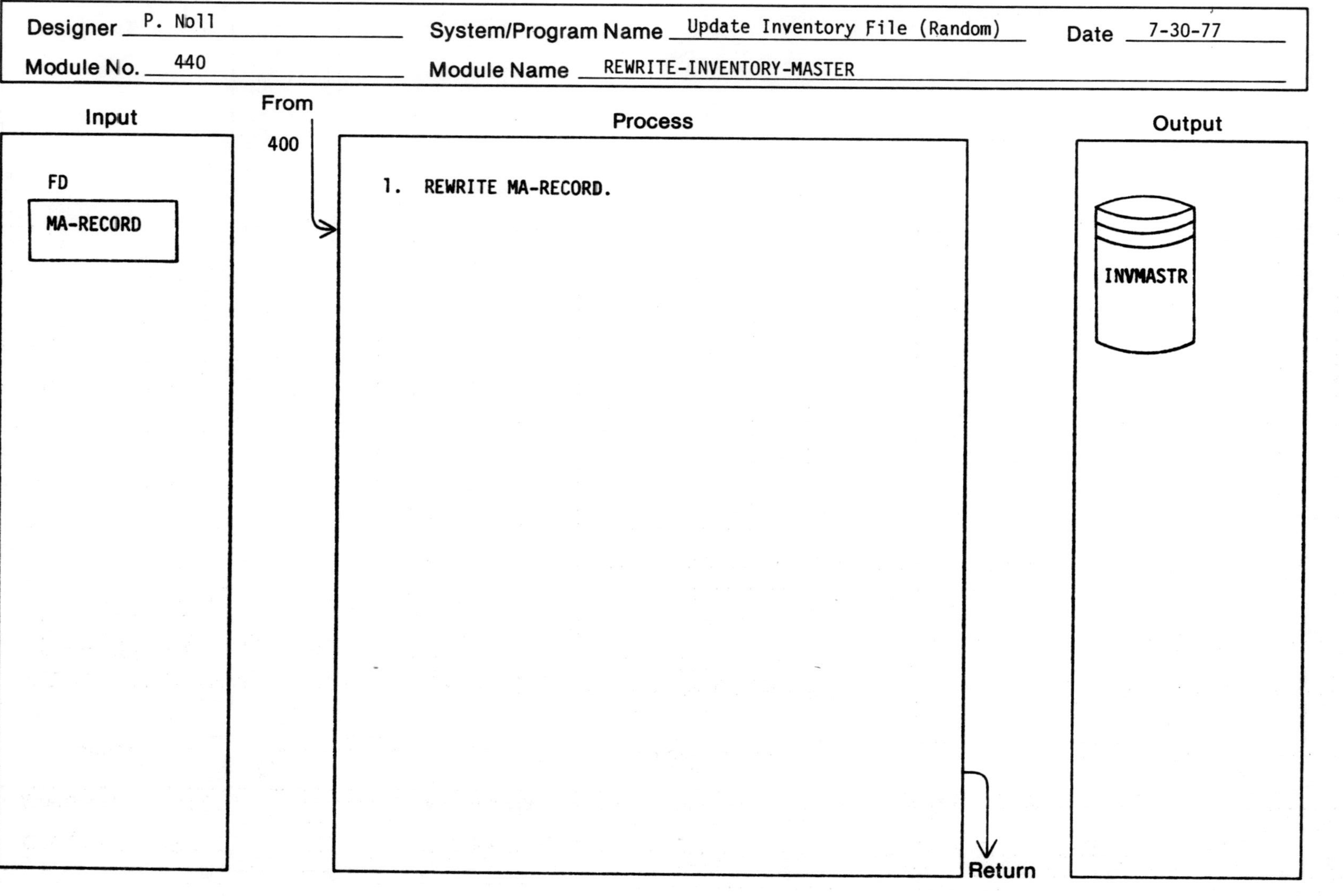

Designer P. Noll
System/Program Name Update Inventory File (Random)
Date 7-30-77
Module No. 440
Module Name REWRITE-INVENTORY-MASTER
Input
From
400
Process
Output
FD
MA-RECORD
1. REWRITE MA-RECORD.
INVMASTR
Return

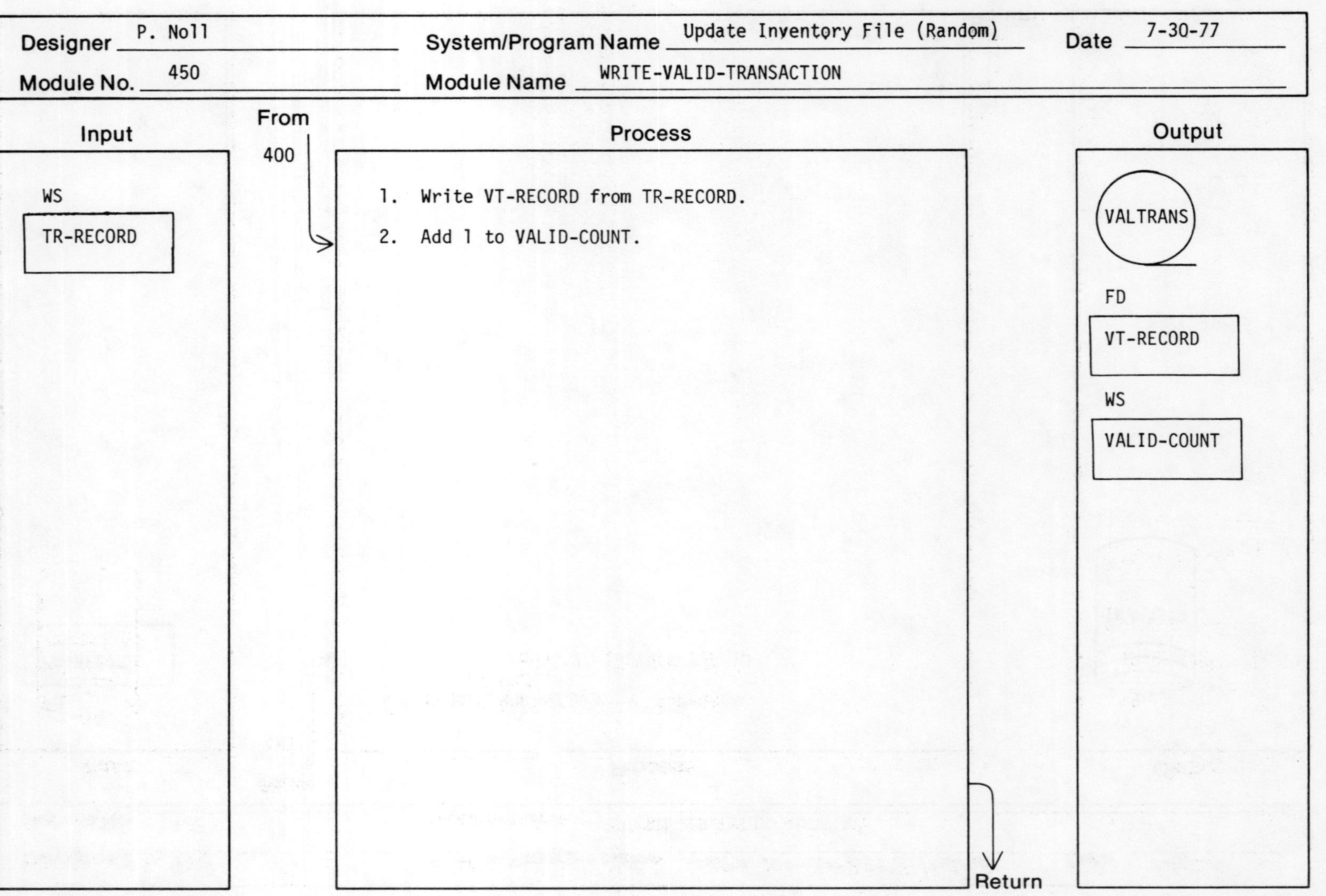
Designer P. Noll
System/Program Name Update Inventory File (Random)
Date 7-30-77
Module No. 450
Module Name WRITE-VALID-TRANSACTION
Input
WS
TR-RECORD
From
400
Process
1. Write VT-RECORD from TR-RECORD.
2. Add 1 to VALID-COUNT.
Return
Output
VALTRANS
FD
VT-RECORD
WS
VALID-COUNT

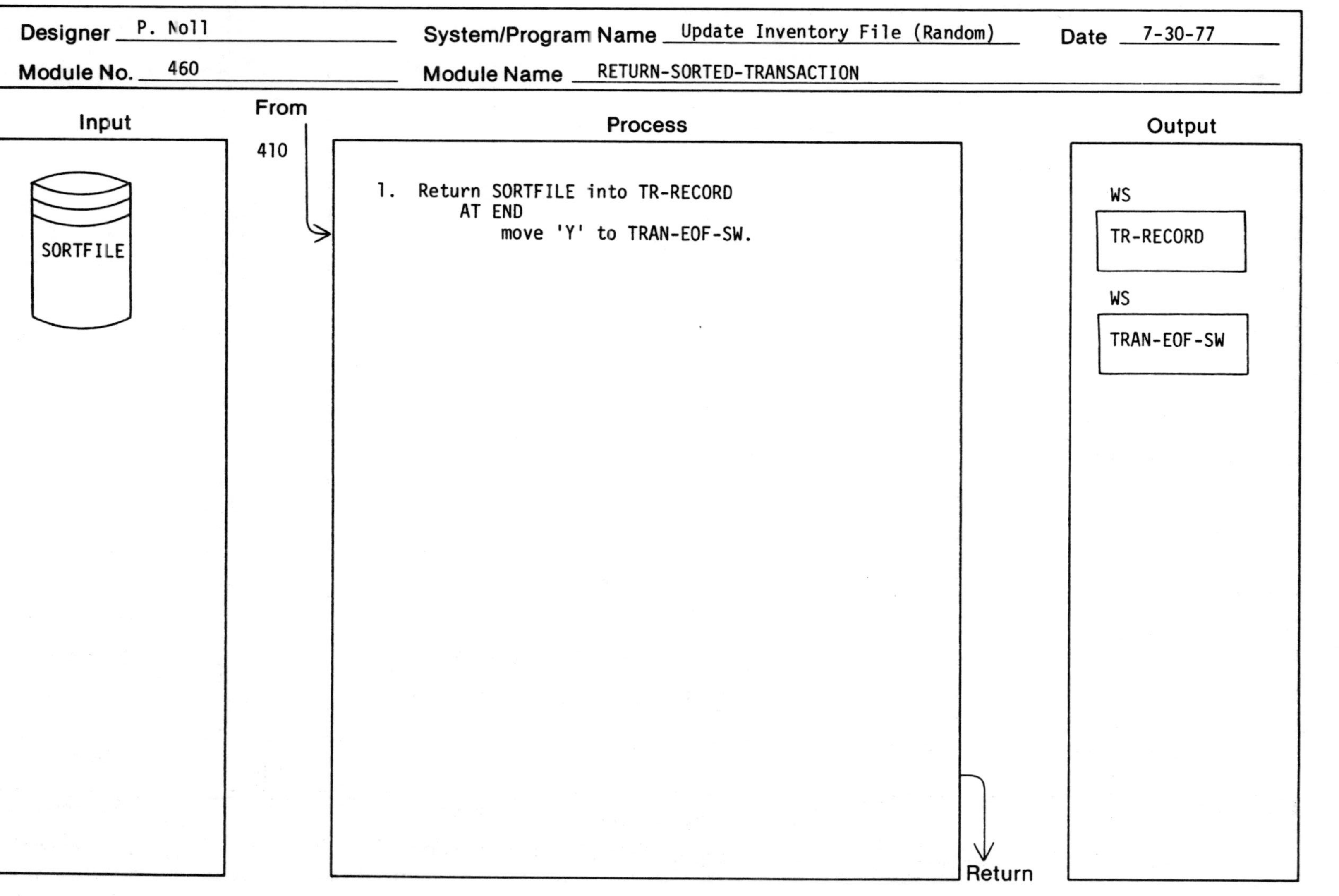
Designer P. Noll
System/Program Name Update Inventory File (Random)
Date 7-30-77
Module No. 460
Module Name RETURN-SORTED-TRANSACTION
Input
SORTFILE
From
410
Process
1. Return SORTFILE into TR-RECORD
AT END
move 'Y' to TRAN-EOF-SW.
Return
Output
WS
TR-RECORD
WS
TRAN-EOF-SW

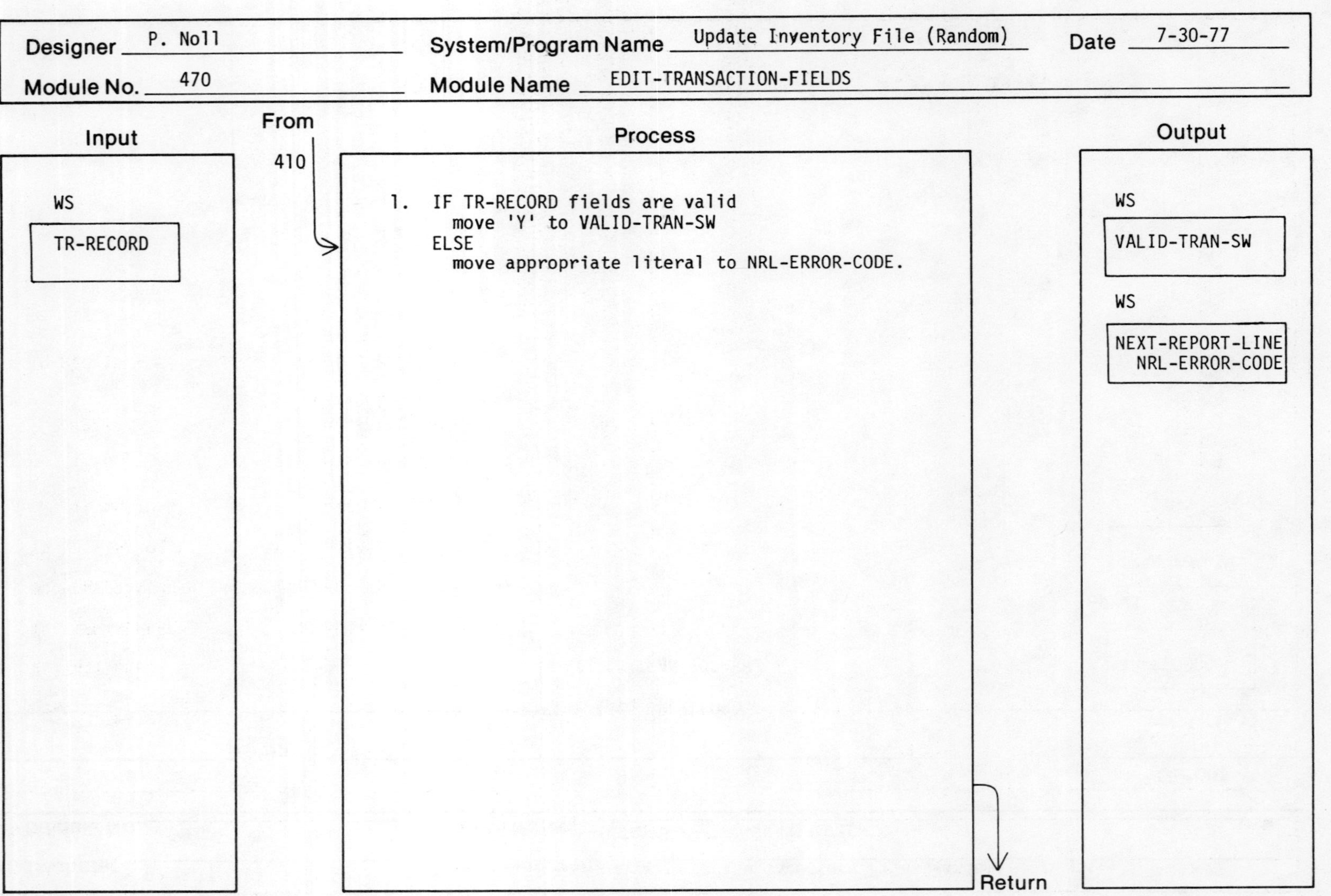
Designer P. Noll
System/Program Name Update Inventory File (Random)
Date 7-30-77
Module No. 470
Module Name EDIT-TRANSACTION-FIELDS
Input
WS
TR-RECORD
From
410
Process
1. IF TR-RECORD fields are valid
move 'Y' to VALID-TRAN-SW
ELSE
move appropriate literal to NRL-ERROR-CODE.
Return
Output
WS
VALID-TRAN-SW
WS
NEXT-REPORT-LINE
NRL-ERROR-CODE

Designer P. Noll | System/Program Name Update Inventory File (Random) | Date 8-19-77

Module No. 470 | Module Name EDIT-TRANSACTION-FIELDS

Notes		Ref.
Validity is:		
TR-ITEM-NUMBER	Numeric and positive	
TR-VENDOR-NUMBER	Numeric and positive	
TR-RECEIPT-DATE	Numeric and:	
TR-MONTH	less than 13	
TR-DAY	less than 32	
TR-YEAR	current year or current year - 1	
TR-RECEIPT-QTY	Numeric and positive	

Notes	Ref.

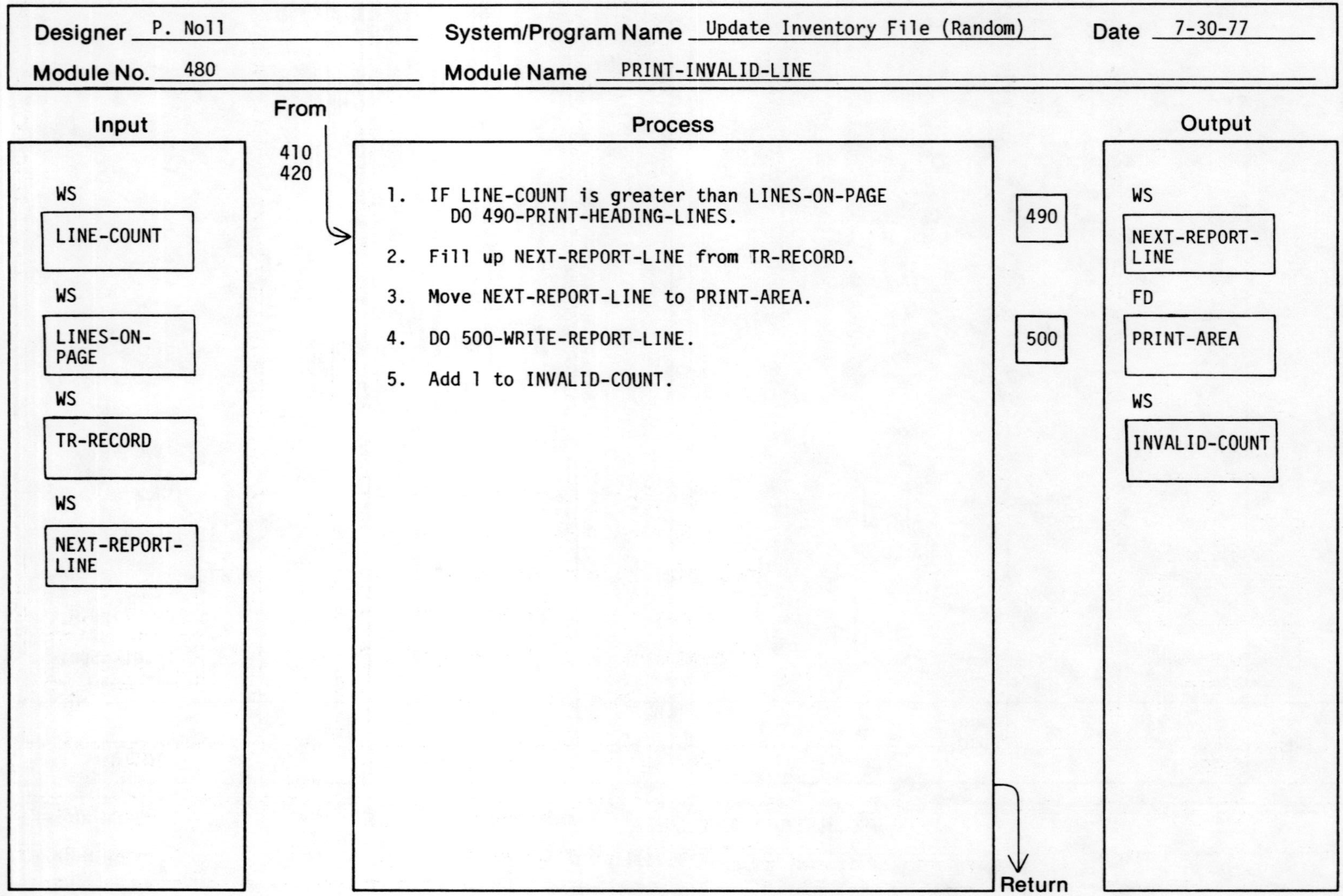
Designer P. Noll
System/Program Name Update Inventory File (Random)
Date 7-30-77
Module No. 480
Module Name PRINT-INVALID-LINE
Input
WS
LINE-COUNT
WS
LINES-ON-PAGE
WS
TR-RECORD
WS
NEXT-REPORT-LINE
From
410
420
Process
1. IF LINE-COUNT is greater than LINES-ON-PAGE DO 490-PRINT-HEADING-LINES.
2. Fill up NEXT-REPORT-LINE from TR-RECORD.
3. Move NEXT-REPORT-LINE to PRINT-AREA.
4. DO 500-WRITE-REPORT-LINE.
5. Add 1 to INVALID-COUNT.
490
500
Return
Output
WS
NEXT-REPORT-LINE
FD
PRINT-AREA
WS
INVALID-COUNT

Designer	P. Noll	System/Program Name	Update Inventory File (Random)	Date	7-30-77
Module No.	490	Module Name	PRINT-HEADING-LINES		

Input

WS

- HDG-LINE-1
- HDG-LINE-2

From 480

Process

1. Add 1 to HDG1-PAGE-NO.
2. Move HDG-LINE-1 to PRINT-AREA.
3. DO 510-WRITE-PAGE-TOP-LINE. [510]
4. Move HDG-LINE-2 to PRINT-AREA.
5. Move 2 to SPACE-CONTROL.
6. DO 500-WRITE-REPORT-LINE. [500]

Return

Output

WS

- HDG1-PAGE-NO

FD

- PRINT-AREA

WS

- SPACE-CONTROL

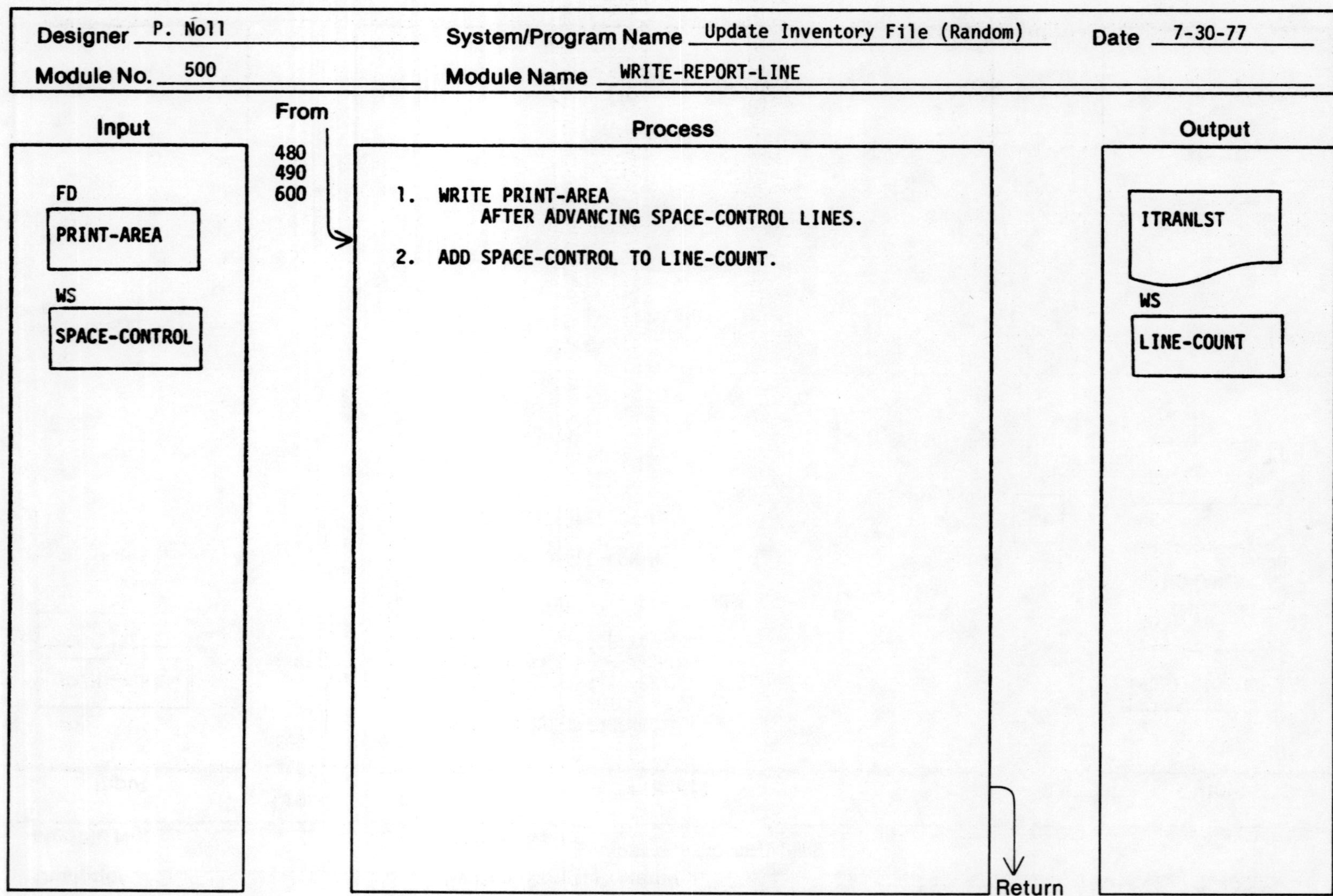

Designer P. Noll
System/Program Name Update Inventory File (Random)
Date 7-30-77
Module No. 500
Module Name WRITE-REPORT-LINE
Input
FD
PRINT-AREA
WS
SPACE-CONTROL
From
480
490
600
Process
1. WRITE PRINT-AREA
AFTER ADVANCING SPACE-CONTROL LINES.
2. ADD SPACE-CONTROL TO LINE-COUNT.
Return
Output
ITRANLST
WS
LINE-COUNT

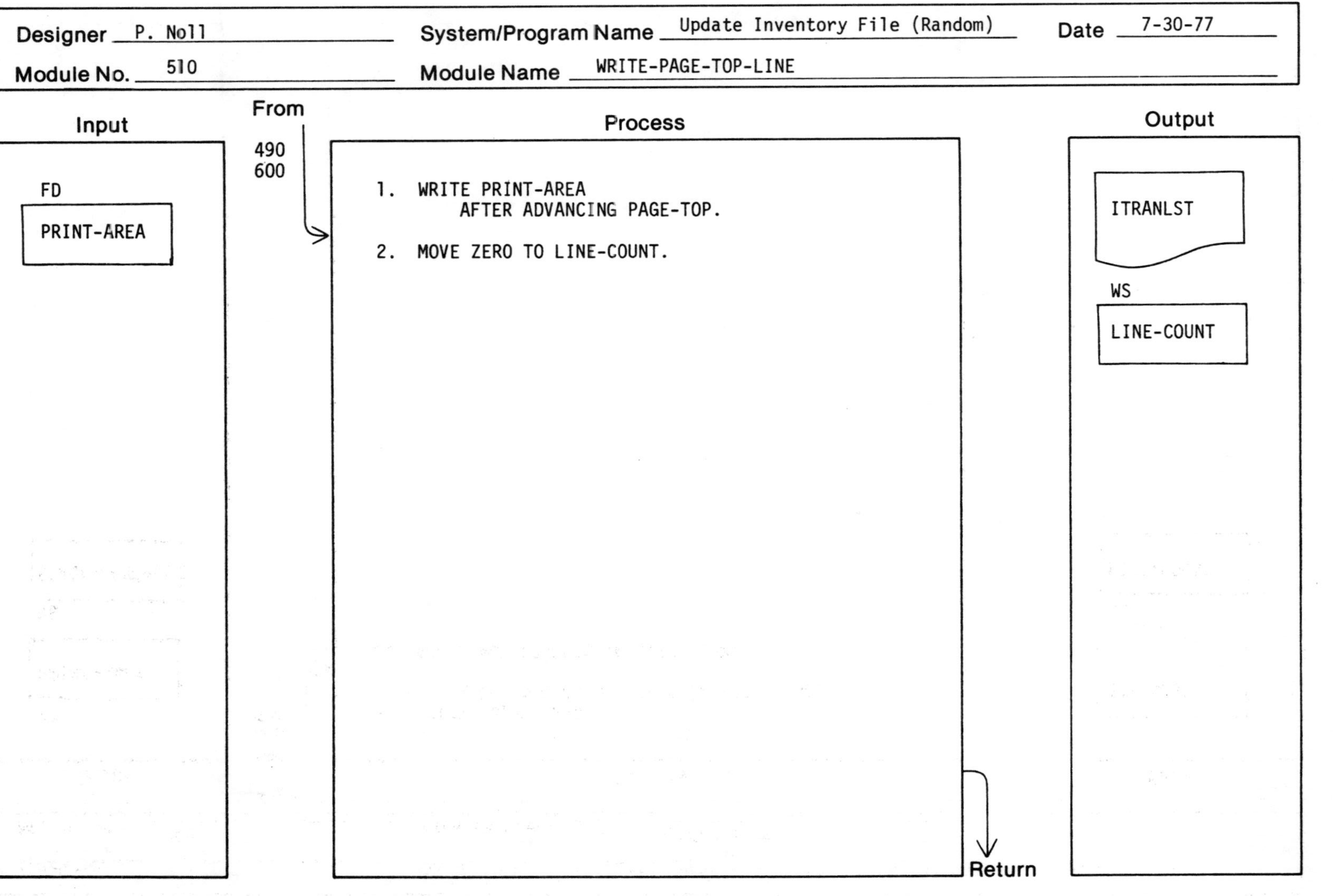
Designer P. Noll
System/Program Name Update Inventory File (Random)
Date 7-30-77
Module No. 510
Module Name WRITE-PAGE-TOP-LINE
Input
FD
PRINT-AREA
From
490
600
Process
1. WRITE PRINT-AREA
AFTER ADVANCING PAGE-TOP.
2. MOVE ZERO TO LINE-COUNT.
Return
Output
ITRANLST
WS
LINE-COUNT

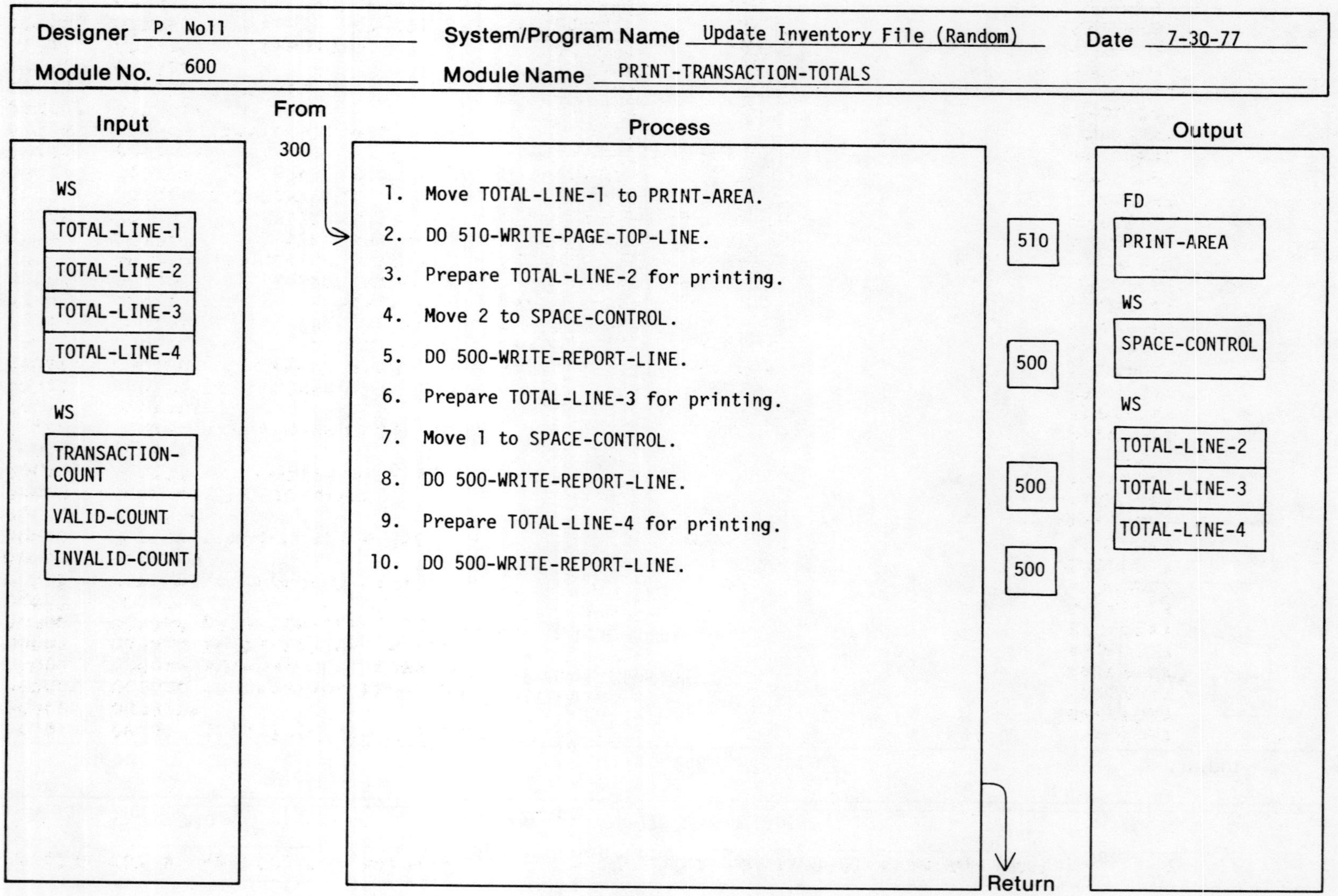
Designer P. Noll
System/Program Name Update Inventory File (Random)
Date 7-30-77
Module No. 600
Module Name PRINT-TRANSACTION-TOTALS
Input
WS
TOTAL-LINE-1
TOTAL-LINE-2
TOTAL-LINE-3
TOTAL-LINE-4
WS
TRANSACTION-COUNT
VALID-COUNT
INVALID-COUNT
From 300
Process
1. Move TOTAL-LINE-1 to PRINT-AREA.
2. DO 510-WRITE-PAGE-TOP-LINE.
3. Prepare TOTAL-LINE-2 for printing.
4. Move 2 to SPACE-CONTROL.
5. DO 500-WRITE-REPORT-LINE.
6. Prepare TOTAL-LINE-3 for printing.
7. Move 1 to SPACE-CONTROL.
8. DO 500-WRITE-REPORT-LINE.
9. Prepare TOTAL-LINE-4 for printing.
10. DO 500-WRITE-REPORT-LINE.
510
500
500
500
Return
Output
FD
PRINT-AREA
WS
SPACE-CONTROL
WS
TOTAL-LINE-2
TOTAL-LINE-3
TOTAL-LINE-4

```
000010 IDENTIFICATION DIVISION.                                        RNDUPDAT
000020*                                                                RNDUPDAT
000030 PROGRAM-ID. KNDUPDAT.                                           RNDUPDAT
000040 AUTHOR. DOUG LOWE.                                              RNDUPDAT
000050 INSTALLATION. MM&A.                                             RNDUPDAT
000060 DATE-COMPILED. OCT 20,1977.                                     RNDUPDAT
000070*                                                                RNDUPDAT
000080 ENVIRONMENT DIVISION.                                           RNDUPDAT
000090*                                                                RNDUPDAT
000100 CONFIGURATION SECTION.                                          RNDUPDAT
000110*                                                                RNDUPDAT
000120 SPECIAL-NAMES.                                                  RNDUPDAT
000130     C01 IS PAGE-TOP.                                            RNDUPDAT
000140*                                                                RNDUPDAT
000150 INPUT-OUTPUT SECTION.                                           RNDUPDAT
000160*                                                                RNDUPDAT
000170 FILE-CONTROL.                                                   RNDUPDAT
000180     SELECT INVMASTR ASSIGN TO DA-I-INVMASTR                     RNDUPDAT
000190         ACCESS MODE IS RANDOM                                   RNDUPDAT
000200         RECORD KEY IS MA-ITEM-NUMBER                            RNDUPDAT
000210         NOMINAL KEY IS SEARCH-KEY.                              RNDUPDAT
000220     SELECT TRANFILE ASSIGN TO UT-S-SORTIN.                      RNDUPDAT
000230     SELECT VALTRANS ASSIGN TO UT-S-VALTRANS.                    RNDUPDAT
000240     SELECT ITRANLST ASSIGN TO UT-S-ITRANLST.                    RNDUPDAT
000250     SELECT SORTFILE ASSIGN TO UT-S-SORTWK01.                    RNDUPDAT
000260 I-O-CONTROL.                                                    RNDUPDAT
000270     APPLY CORE-INDEX ON INVMASTR.                               RNDUPDAT
000280*                                                                RNDUPDAT
000290 DATA DIVISION.                                                  RNDUPDAT
000300*                                                                RNDUPDAT
000310 FILE SECTION.                                                   RNDUPDAT
000320*                                                                RNDUPDAT
000330 FD  INVMASTR                                                    RNDUPDAT
000340     LABEL RECORDS ARE STANDARD                                  RNDUPDAT
000350     RECORDING MODE IS F                                         RNDUPDAT
```

```
2

000360         RECORD CONTAINS 30 CHARACTERS                                          RNDUPDAT
000370         BLOCK CONTAINS 18 RECORDS.                                             RNDUPDAT
000380*                                                                               RNDUPDAT
000390 01      MA-RECORD.                                                             RNDUPDAT
000400*                                                                               RNDUPDAT
000410         05  MA-DELETED-SW        PIC X.                                        RNDUPDAT
000420             88  MA-DELETED                    VALUE HIGH-VALUES.               RNDUPDAT
000430         05  MA-ITEM-NUMBER       PIC X(5).                                     RNDUPDAT
000440         05  MA-ITEM-DESCR        PIC X(20).                                    RNDUPDAT
000450         05  MA-ON-HAND-BALANCE   PIC 9(3).                                     RNDUPDAT
000460         05  FILLER               PIC X.                                        RNDUPDAT
000470*                                                                               RNDUPDAT
000480 FD      TRANFILE                                                               RNDUPDAT
000490         LABEL RECORDS ARE STANDARD                                             RNDUPDAT
000500         RECORDING MODE IS F                                                    RNDUPDAT
000510         RECORD CONTAINS 18 CHARACTERS                                          RNDUPDAT
000520         BLOCK CONTAINS 0 RECORDS.                                              RNDUPDAT
000530*                                                                               RNDUPDAT
000540 01      TR-AREA              PIC X(18).                                        RNDUPDAT
000550*                                                                               RNDUPDAT
000560 FD      VALTRANS                                                               RNDUPDAT
000570         LABEL RECORDS ARE STANDARD                                             RNDUPDAT
000580         RECORDING MODE IS F                                                    RNDUPDAT
000590         RECORD CONTAINS 18 CHARACTERS                                          RNDUPDAT
000600         BLOCK CONTAINS 0 RECORDS.                                              RNDUPDAT
000610*                                                                               RNDUPDAT
000620 01      VT-RECORD            PIC X(18).                                        RNDUPDAT
000630*                                                                               RNDUPDAT
000640 FD      ITRANLST                                                               RNDUPDAT
000650         LABEL RECORDS ARE STANDARD                                             RNDUPDAT
000660         RECORDING MODE IS F                                                    RNDUPDAT
000670         RECORD CONTAINS 133 CHARACTERS                                         RNDUPDAT
000680         BLOCK CONTAINS 0 RECORDS.                                              RNDUPDAT
000690*                                                                               RNDUPDAT
000700 01      PRINT-AREA           PIC X(133).                                       RNDUPDAT
000710*                                                                               RNDUPDAT
000720 SD      SORTFILE                                                               RNDUPDAT
000730         RECORDING MODE IS F                                                    RNDUPDAT
```

```
000740     RECORD CONTAINS 18 CHARACTERS.                              RNDUPDAT
000750*                                                                RNDUPDAT
000760 01  SF-RECORD.                                                  RNDUPDAT
000770*                                                                RNDUPDAT
000780     05  SF-ITEM-NUMBER    PIC X(5).                             RNDUPDAT
000790     05  FILLER            PIC X(13).                            RNDUPDAT
000800*                                                                RNDUPDAT
000810 WORKING-STORAGE SECTION.                                        RNDUPDAT
000820*                                                                RNDUPDAT
000830 01  SWITCHES.                                                   RNDUPDAT
000840*                                                                RNDUPDAT
000850     05  TRAN-EOF-SW          PIC X         VALUE 'N'.           RNDUPDAT
000860         88  TRAN-EOF                       VALUE 'Y'.           RNDUPDAT
000870     05  VALID-TRAN-SW        PIC X.                             RNDUPDAT
000880         88  VALID-TRAN                     VALUE 'Y'.           RNDUPDAT
000890     05  MASTER-FOUND-SW      PIC X.                             RNDUPDAT
000900         88  MASTER-FOUND                   VALUE 'Y'.           RNDUPDAT
000910*                                                                RNDUPDAT
000920 01  PRINT-FIELDS             COMP          SYNC.                RNDUPDAT
000930*                                                                RNDUPDAT
000940     05  LINE-COUNT           PIC S999      VALUE +999.          RNDUPDAT
000950     05  LINES-ON-PAGE        PIC S999      VALUE +57.           RNDUPDAT
000960     05  SPACE-CONTROL        PIC S9.                            RNDUPDAT
000970     05  PAGE-NUMBER          PIC S999      VALUE ZERO.          RNDUPDAT
000980*                                                                RNDUPDAT
000990 01  COUNT-FIELDS             COMP-3.                            RNDUPDAT
001000*                                                                RNDUPDAT
001010     05  TRANSACTION-COUNT    PIC S9(5)     VALUE ZERO.          RNDUPDAT
001020     05  VALID-COUNT          PIC S9(5)     VALUE ZERO.          RNDUPDAT
001030     05  INVALID-COUNT        PIC S9(5)     VALUE ZERO.          RNDUPDAT
001040*                                                                RNDUPDAT
001050 01  SEARCH-KEY               PIC X(5).                          RNDUPDAT
001060*                                                                RNDUPDAT
001070 01  ERROR-CODES.                                                RNDUPDAT
001080*                                                                RNDUPDAT
001090     05  FIELD-1              PIC X(15)     VALUE 'FIELD-1     '. RNDUPDAT
001100     05  FIELD-2              PIC X(15)     VALUE 'FIELD-2     '. RNDUPDAT
001110     05  FIELD-3              PIC X(15)     VALUE 'FIELD-3     '. RNDUPDAT
```

```
4

001120        05  FIELD-4                  PIC X(15)   VALUE 'FIELD-4        '.  RNDUPDAT
001130        05  NOT-FOUND                PIC X(15)   VALUE 'NOT FOUND      '.  RNDUPDAT
001140*                                                                          RNDUPDAT
001150 01  DATE-FIELDS.                                                          RNDUPDAT
001160*                                                                          RNDUPDAT
001170        05  TODAYS-DATE.                                                   RNDUPDAT
001180            10  FILLER                   PIC X(6).                         RNDUPDAT
001190            10  TODAYS-YEAR              PIC XX.                           RNDUPDAT
001200        05  CURRENT-YEAR                 PIC 99.                           RNDUPDAT
001210        05  CURRENT-YEAR-MINUS-1         PIC 99.                           RNDUPDAT
001220*                                                                          RNDUPDAT
001230 01  TR-RECORD.                                                            RNDUPDAT
001240*                                                                          RNDUPDAT
001250        05  TR-ITEM-NUMBER               PIC X(5).                         RNDUPDAT
001260        05  TR-VENDOR-NUMBER             PIC X(3).                         RNDUPDAT
001270        05  TR-RECEIPT-DATE.                                               RNDUPDAT
001280            10  TR-MONTH                 PIC XX.                           RNDUPDAT
001290                88  GOOD-TR-MONTH            VALUE '01' THRU '12'.         RNDUPDAT
001300            10  TR-DAY                   PIC XX.                           RNDUPDAT
001310                88  GOOD-TR-DAY              VALUE '01' THRU '31'.         RNDUPDAT
001320            10  TR-YEAR                  PIC XX.                           RNDUPDAT
001330        05  TR-RECEIPT-QTY-ALFA.                                           RNDUPDAT
001340            10  TR-RECEIPT-QTY           PIC 999.                          RNDUPDAT
001350        05  FILLER                       PIC X.                            RNDUPDAT
001360*                                                                          RNDUPDAT
001370 01  HDG-LINE-1.                                                           RNDUPDAT
001380*                                                                          RNDUPDAT
001390        05  HDG1-CC           PIC X.                                       RNDUPDAT
001400        05  FILLER            PIC X(20)   VALUE 'INVALID TRANSACTIONS'.RNDUPDAT
001410        05  FILLER            PIC X(18)   VALUE ' IN UPDATE RUN OF '.      RNDUPDAT
001420        05  HDG1-DATE         PIC X(8).                                    RNDUPDAT
001430        05  FILLER            PIC X(10)   VALUE '     PAGE '.              RNDUPDAT
001440        05  HDG1-PAGE-NO      PIC ZZ9.                                     RNDUPDAT
001450        05  FILLER            PIC X(73)   VALUE SPACES.                    RNDUPDAT
001460*                                                                          RNDUPDAT
001470 01  HDG-LINE-2.                                                           RNDUPDAT
001480*                                                                          RNDUPDAT
001490        05  HDG2-CC           PIC X.                                       RNDUPDAT
```

```
001500     05  FILLER              PIC X(20)    VALUE ' ITEM NO.   VENDOR N'.RNDUPDAT
001510     05  FILLER              PIC X(20)    VALUE 'O.      DATE     QUAN'.RNDUPDAT
001520     05  FILLER              PIC X(20)    VALUE 'TITY    ERROR CODE   '.RNDUPDAT
001530     05  FILLER              PIC X(72)    VALUE SPACES.                 RNDUPDAT
001540*                                                                       RNDUPDAT
001550 01  NEXT-REPORT-LINE.                                                  RNDUPDAT
001560*                                                                       RNDUPDAT
001570     05  NRL-CC                   PIC X.                                RNDUPDAT
001580     05  FILLER                   PIC XX      VALUE SPACE.              RNDUPDAT
001590     05  NRL-ITEM-NUMBER          PIC X(5).                             RNDUPDAT
001600     05  FILLER                   PIC X(8)    VALUE SPACE.              RNDUPDAT
001610     05  NRL-VENDOR-NUMBER        PIC X(3).                             RNDUPDAT
001620     05  FILLER                   PIC X(7)    VALUE SPACE.              RNDUPDAT
001630     05  NRL-DATE.                                                      RNDUPDAT
001640         10  NRL-MONTH            PIC Z9.                               RNDUPDAT
001650         10  FILLER               PIC X       VALUE '-'.                RNDUPDAT
001660         10  NRL-DAY              PIC XX.                               RNDUPDAT
001670         10  FILLER               PIC X       VALUE '-'.                RNDUPDAT
001680         10  NRL-YEAR             PIC XX.                               RNDUPDAT
001690     05  FILLER                   PIC X(5)    VALUE SPACE.              RNDUPDAT
001700     05  NRL-RECEIPT-QTY          PIC X(3).                             RNDUPDAT
001710     05  FILLER                   PIC X(6)    VALUE SPACE.              RNDUPDAT
001720     05  NRL-ERROR-CODE           PIC X(15).                            RNDUPDAT
001730     05  FILLER                   PIC X(70)   VALUE SPACE.              RNDUPDAT
001740*                                                                       RNDUPDAT
001750 01  TOTAL-LINE-1.                                                      RNDUPDAT
001760*                                                                       RNDUPDAT
001770     05  TOT1-CC             PIC X.                                     RNDUPDAT
001780     05  FILLER              PIC X(20)    VALUE 'SUMMARY FOR UPDATE R'.RNDUPDAT
001790     05  FILLER              PIC X(6)     VALUE 'UN OF '.               RNDUPDAT
001800     05  TOT1-DATE           PIC X(8).                                  RNDUPDAT
001810     05  FILLER              PIC X(98)    VALUE SPACES.                 RNDUPDAT
001820                                                                        RNDUPDAT
001830*                                                                       RNDUPDAT
001840 01  TOTAL-LINE-2.                                                      RNDUPDAT
001850*                                                                       RNDUPDAT
001860     05  TOT2-CC             PIC X.                                     RNDUPDAT
001870     05  TOT2-TRAN-CNT       PIC ZZ,ZZ9.                                RNDUPDAT
```

6

```
001880     05  FILLER          PIC X(20)   VALUE ' TRANSACTIONS READ  '.RNDUPDAT
001890     05  FILLER          PIC X(106)  VALUE SPACES.                RNDUPDAT
001900*                                                                 RNDUPDAT
001910 01  TOTAL-LINE-3.                                                RNDUPDAT
001920*                                                                 RNDUPDAT
001930     05  TOT3-CC         PIC X.                                   RNDUPDAT
001940     05  TOT3-VAL-CNT    PIC ZZ,ZZ9.                              RNDUPDAT
001950     05  FILLER          PIC X(20)   VALUE ' VALID TRANSACTIONS '.RNDUPDAT
001960     05  FILLER          PIC X(106)  VALUE SPACES.                RNDUPDAT
001970*                                                                 RNDUPDAT
001980 01  TOTAL-LINE-4.                                                RNDUPDAT
001990*                                                                 RNDUPDAT
002000     05  TOT4-CC         PIC X.                                   RNDUPDAT
002010     05  TOT4-INV-CNT    PIC ZZ,ZZ9.                              RNDUPDAT
002020     05  FILLER          PIC X(20)   VALUE ' INVALID TRANSACTION'.RNDUPDAT
002030     05  FILLER          PIC X(20)   VALUE 'S                   '.RNDUPDAT
002040     05  FILLER          PIC X(86)   VALUE SPACES.                RNDUPDAT
002050*                                                                 RNDUPDAT
002060 PROCEDURE DIVISION.                                              RNDUPDAT
002070*                                                                 RNDUPDAT
002080 000-UPDATE-INVENTORY-FILE   SECTION.                             RNDUPDAT
002090*                                                                 RNDUPDAT
002100     OPEN OUTPUT VALTRANS                                         RNDUPDAT
002110                 ITRANLST                                         RNDUPDAT
002120          I-O    INVMASTR.                                        RNDUPDAT
002130     MOVE CURRENT-DATE TO TODAYS-DATE.                            RNDUPDAT
002140     MOVE TODAYS-DATE  TO HDG1-DATE                               RNDUPDAT
002150                          TOT1-DATE.                              RNDUPDAT
002160     MOVE TODAYS-YEAR  TO CURRENT-YEAR                            RNDUPDAT
002170     SUBTRACT 1 FROM CURRENT-YEAR GIVING CURRENT-YEAR-MINUS-1.    RNDUPDAT
002180     SORT SORTFILE                                                RNDUPDAT
002190         ON ASCENDING KEY SF-ITEM-NUMBER                          RNDUPDAT
002200         USING TRANFILE                                           RNDUPDAT
002210         OUTPUT PROCEDURE IS 300-POST-TRANSACTION-FILE.           RNDUPDAT
002220     IF SORT-RETURN IS NOT ZERO                                   RNDUPDAT
002230         DISPLAY 'SORT FAILED'.                                   RNDUPDAT
002240     CLOSE VALTRANS                                               RNDUPDAT
002250           ITRANLST                                               RNDUPDAT
```

```
002260                 INVMASTR.                                       RNDUPDAT
002270         STOP RUN.                                               RNDUPDAT
002280*                                                                RNDUPDAT
002290 300-POST-TRANSACTION-FILE    SECTION.                           RNDUPDAT
002300*                                                                RNDUPDAT
002310         PERFORM 400-POST-TRANSACTION-RECORD                     RNDUPDAT
002320             UNTIL TRAN-EOF.                                     RNDUPDAT
002330         PERFORM 600-PRINT-TRANSACTION-TOTALS.                   RNDUPDAT
002340         GO TO 300-EXIT.                                         RNDUPDAT
002350*                                                                RNDUPDAT
002360 400-POST-TRANSACTION-RECORD.                                    RNDUPDAT
002370*                                                                RNDUPDAT
002380         PERFORM 410-GET-VALID-TRANSACTION                       RNDUPDAT
002390             UNTIL TRAN-EOF OR VALID-TRAN.                       RNDUPDAT
002400         IF NOT TRAN-EOF                                         RNDUPDAT
002410             PERFORM 420-GET-INVENTORY-MASTER                    RNDUPDAT
002420             IF MASTER-FOUND                                     RNDUPDAT
002430                 PERFORM 430-CHANGE-INVENTORY-MASTER             RNDUPDAT
002440                 PERFORM 440-REWRITE-INVENTORY-MASTER            RNDUPDAT
002450                 PERFORM 450-WRITE-VALID-TRANSACTION.            RNDUPDAT
002460         MOVE 'N' TO VALID-TRAN-SW.                              RNDUPDAT
002470*                                                                RNDUPDAT
002480 410-GET-VALID-TRANSACTION.                                      RNDUPDAT
002490*                                                                RNDUPDAT
002500         PERFORM 460-RETURN-SORTED-TRANSACTION.                  RNDUPDAT
002510         IF NOT TRAN-EOF                                         RNDUPDAT
002520             ADD 1 TO TRANSACTION-COUNT                          RNDUPDAT
002530             PERFORM 470-EDIT-TRANSACTION-FIELDS                 RNDUPDAT
002540             IF NOT VALID-TRAN                                   RNDUPDAT
002550                 PERFORM 480-PRINT-INVALID-LINE.                 RNDUPDAT
002560*                                                                RNDUPDAT
002570 420-GET-INVENTORY-MASTER.                                       RNDUPDAT
002580*                                                                RNDUPDAT
002590         MOVE TR-ITEM-NUMBER TO SEARCH-KEY.                      RNDUPDAT
002600         MOVE 'Y' TO MASTER-FOUND-SW.                            RNDUPDAT
002610         READ INVMASTR                                           RNDUPDAT
002620             INVALID KEY                                         RNDUPDAT
002630                 MOVE 'N' TO MASTER-FOUND-SW                     RNDUPDAT
```

```
002640              MOVE NOT-FOUND TO NRL-ERROR-CODE                            RNDUPDAT
002650              PERFORM 480-PRINT-INVALID-LINE.                             RNDUPDAT
002660      IF MASTER-FOUND AND MA-DELETED                                      RNDUPDAT
002670          MOVE 'N' TO MASTER-FOUND-SW                                     RNDUPDAT
002680          MOVE NOT-FOUND TO NRL-ERROR-CODE                                RNDUPDAT
002690          PERFORM 480-PRINT-INVALID-LINE.                                 RNDUPDAT
002700*                                                                         RNDUPDAT
002710 430-CHANGE-INVENTORY-MASTER.                                             RNDUPDAT
002720*                                                                         RNDUPDAT
002730      ADD TR-RECEIPT-QTY TO MA-ON-HAND-BALANCE.                           RNDUPDAT
002740*                                                                         RNDUPDAT
002750 440-REWRITE-INVENTORY-MASTER.                                            RNDUPDAT
002760*                                                                         RNDUPDAT
002770      REWRITE MA-RECORD.                                                  RNDUPDAT
002780*                                                                         RNDUPDAT
002790 450-WRITE-VALID-TRANSACTION.                                             RNDUPDAT
002800*                                                                         RNDUPDAT
002810      WRITE VT-RECORD FROM TR-RECORD.                                     RNDUPDAT
002820      ADD 1 TO VALID-COUNT.                                               RNDUPDAT
002830*                                                                         RNDUPDAT
002840 460-RETURN-SORTED-TRANSACTION.                                           RNDUPDAT
002850*                                                                         RNDUPDAT
002860      RETURN SORTFILE INTO TR-RECORD                                      RNDUPDAT
002870          AT END                                                          RNDUPDAT
002880              MOVE 'Y' TO TRAN-EOF-SW.                                    RNDUPDAT
002890*                                                                         RNDUPDAT
002900 470-EDIT-TRANSACTION-FIELDS.                                             RNDUPDAT
002910*                                                                         RNDUPDAT
002920      IF        TR-ITEM-NUMBER NOT NUMERIC                                RNDUPDAT
002930             OR TR-ITEM-NUMBER NOT GREATER THAN ZERO                      RNDUPDAT
002940          MOVE FIELD-1 TO NRL-ERROR-CODE                                  RNDUPDAT
002950      ELSE                                                                RNDUPDAT
002960          IF        TR-VENDOR-NUMBER NOT NUMERIC                          RNDUPDAT
002970                 OR TR-VENDOR-NUMBER NOT GREATER THAN ZERO                RNDUPDAT
002980              MOVE FIELD-2 TO NRL-ERROR-CODE                              RNDUPDAT
002990          ELSE                                                            RNDUPDAT
003000              IF        TR-RECEIPT-DATE NOT NUMERIC                       RNDUPDAT
003010                     OR NOT GOOD-TR-MONTH                                 RNDUPDAT
```

```
003020                      OR NOT GOOD-TR-DAY                              RNDUPDAT
003030                      OR TR-YEAR NOT = (CURRENT-YEAR                  RNDUPDAT
003040                                    AND CURRENT-YEAR-MINUS-1)         RNDUPDAT
003050                   MOVE FIELD-3 TO NRL-ERROR-CODE                     RNDUPDAT
003060               ELSE                                                   RNDUPDAT
003070                   IF         TR-RECEIPT-QTY-ALFA NOT NUMERIC         RNDUPDAT
003080                          OR TR-RECEIPT-QTY-ALFA NOT GREATER ZERO     RNDUPDAT
003090                       MOVE FIELD-4 TO NRL-ERROR-CODE                 RNDUPDAT
003100                   ELSE                                               RNDUPDAT
003110                       MOVE 'Y' TO VALID-TRAN-SW.                     RNDUPDAT
003120*                                                                     RNDUPDAT
003130 480-PRINT-INVALID-LINE.                                              RNDUPDAT
003140*                                                                     RNDUPDAT
003150     IF LINE-COUNT GREATER THAN LINES-ON-PAGE                         RNDUPDAT
003160         PERFORM 490-PRINT-HEADING-LINES.                             RNDUPDAT
003170     MOVE TR-ITEM-NUMBER   TO NRL-ITEM-NUMBER.                        RNDUPDAT
003180     MOVE TR-VENDOR-NUMBER TO NRL-VENDOR-NUMBER.                      RNDUPDAT
003190     MOVE TR-MONTH         TO NRL-MONTH.                              RNDUPDAT
003200     MOVE TR-DAY           TO NRL-DAY.                                RNDUPDAT
003210     MOVE TR-YEAR          TO NRL-YEAR.                               RNDUPDAT
003220     MOVE TR-RECEIPT-QTY   TO NRL-RECEIPT-QTY.                        RNDUPDAT
003230     MOVE NEXT-REPORT-LINE TO PRINT-AREA.                             RNDUPDAT
003240     PERFORM 500-WRITE-REPORT-LINE.                                   RNDUPDAT
003250     ADD 1 TO INVALID-COUNT.                                          RNDUPDAT
003260*                                                                     RNDUPDAT
003270 490-PRINT-HEADING-LINES.                                             RNDUPDAT
003280*                                                                     RNDUPDAT
003290     ADD 1 TO PAGE-NUMBER.                                            RNDUPDAT
003300     MOVE PAGE-NUMBER TO HDG1-PAGE-NO.                                RNDUPDAT
003310     MOVE HDG-LINE-1 TO PRINT-AREA.                                   RNDUPDAT
003320     PERFORM 510-WRITE-PAGE-TOP-LINE.                                 RNDUPDAT
003330     MOVE HDG-LINE-2 TO PRINT-AREA.                                   RNDUPDAT
003340     MOVE 2 TO SPACE-CONTROL.                                         RNDUPDAT
003350     PERFORM 500-WRITE-REPORT-LINE.                                   RNDUPDAT
003360*                                                                     RNDUPDAT
003370 500-WRITE-REPORT-LINE.                                               RNDUPDAT
003380*                                                                     RNDUPDAT
003390     WRITE PRINT-AREA                                                 RNDUPDAT
```

10

```
00340   003400          AFTER ADVANCING SPACE-CONTROL LINES.               RNDUPDAT
00341   003410      ADD SPACE-CONTROL TO LINE-COUNT.                       RNDUPDAT
00342   003420*                                                            RNDUPDAT
00343   003430 510-WRITE-PAGE-TOP-LINE.                                    RNDUPDAT
00344   003440*                                                            RNDUPDAT
00345   003450      WRITE PRINT-AREA                                       RNDUPDAT
00346   003460          AFTER ADVANCING PAGE-TOP.                          RNDUPDAT
00347   003470      MOVE ZERO TO LINE-COUNT.                               RNDUPDAT
00348   003480*                                                            RNDUPDAT
00349   003490 600-PRINT-TRANSACTION-TOTALS.                               RNDUPDAT
00350   003500*                                                            RNDUPDAT
00351   003510      MOVE TOTAL-LINE-1 TO PRINT-AREA.                       RNDUPDAT
00352   003520      PERFORM 510-WRITE-PAGE-TOP-LINE.                       RNDUPDAT
00353   003530      MOVE TRANSACTION-COUNT TO TOT2-TRAN-CNT.               RNDUPDAT
00354   003540      MOVE TOTAL-LINE-2 TO PRINT-AREA.                       RNDUPDAT
00355   003550      MOVE 2 TO SPACE-CONTROL.                               RNDUPDAT
00356   003560      PERFORM 500-WRITE-REPORT-LINE.                         RNDUPDAT
00357   003570      MOVE VALID-COUNT TO TOT3-VAL-CNT.                      RNDUPDAT
00358   003580      MOVE TOTAL-LINE-3 TO PRINT-AREA.                       RNDUPDAT
00359   003590      MOVE 1 TO SPACE-CONTROL.                               RNDUPDAT
00360   003600      PERFORM 500-WRITE-REPORT-LINE.                         RNDUPDAT
00361   003610      MOVE INVALID-COUNT TO TOT4-INV-CNT.                    RNDUPDAT
00362   003620      MOVE TOTAL-LINE-4 TO PRINT-AREA.                       RNDUPDAT
00363   003630      PERFORM 500-WRITE-REPORT-LINE.                         RNDUPDAT
00364   003640*                                                            RNDUPDAT
00365   003650 300-EXIT.                                                   RNDUPDAT
00366   003660*                                                            RNDUPDAT
00367   003670      EXIT.                                                  RNDUPDAT
```

```
                          CROSS-REFERENCE DICTIONARY

DATA NAMES                DEFN    REFERENCE

COUNT-FIELDS              000099
CURRENT-YEAR              000120  000216  000217  000300
CURRENT-YEAR-MINUS-1      000121  000217  000300
DATE-FIELDS               000115
ERROR-CODES               000107
FIELD-1                   000109  000294
FIELD-2                   000110  000298
FIELD-3                   000111  000305
FIELD-4                   000112  000309
HDG-LINE-1                000137  000331
HDG-LINE-2                000147  000333
HDG1-CC                   000139
HDG1-DATE                 000142  000214
HDG1-PAGE-NO              000144  000330
HDG2-CC                   000149
INVALID-COUNT             000103  000325  000361
INVMASTR                  000018  000210  000224  000261  000277
ITRANLST                  000024  000210  000224  000339  000345
LINE-COUNT                000094  000315  000341  000347
LINES-ON-PAGE             000095  000315
MA-DELETED-SW             000041
MA-ITEM-DESCR             000044
MA-ITEM-NUMBER            000043
MA-ON-HAND-BALANCE        000045  000273
MA-RECORD                 000039  000277
MASTER-FOUND-SW           000089  000260  000263  000267
NEXT-REPORT-LINE          000155  000323
NOT-FOUND                 000113  000264  000268
NRL-CC                    000157
NRL-DATE                  000163
NRL-DAY                   000166  000320
NRL-ERROR-CODE            000172  000264  000268  000294  000298  000305  000309
```

```
20

NRL-ITEM-NUMBER          000159  000317
NRL-MONTH                000164  000319
NRL-RECEIPT-QTY          000170  000322
NRL-VENDOR-NUMBER        000161  000318
NRL-YEAR                 000168  000321
PAGE-NUMBER              000097  000329  000330
PRINT-AREA               000070  000323  000331  000333  000339  000345  000351  000354  000358  000362
PRINT-FIELDS             000092
SEARCH-KEY               000105  000259
SF-ITEM-NUMBER           000078  000218
SF-RECORD                000076  000218  000286
SORTFILE                 000072  000218  000286
SPACE-CONTROL            000096  000334  000339  000341  000355  000359
SWITCHES                 000083
TODAYS-DATE              000117  000213  000214
TODAYS-YEAR              000119  000216
TOTAL-LINE-1             000175  000351
TOTAL-LINE-2             000184  000354
TOTAL-LINE-3             000191  000358
TOTAL-LINE-4             000198  000362
TOT1-CC                  000177
TOT1-DATE                000180  000214
TOT2-CC                  000186
TOT2-TRAN-CNT            000187  000353
TOT3-CC                  000193
TOT3-VAL-CNT             000194  000357
TOT4-CC                  000200
TOT4-INV-CNT             000201  000361
TR-AREA                  000054  000218
TR-DAY                   000130  000320
TR-ITEM-NUMBER           000125  000259  000292  000317
TR-MONTH                 000128  000319
TR-RECEIPT-DATE          000127  000300
TR-RECEIPT-QTY           000134  000273  000322
TR-RECEIPT-QTY-ALFA      000133  000307
TR-RECORD                000123  000281  000286
TR-VENDOR-NUMBER         000126  000296  000318
TR-YEAR                  000132  000300  000321
```

```
 21

TRAN-EOF-SW                       000085   000288
TRANFILE                          000022   000218
TRANSACTION-COUNT                 000101   000252   000353
VALID-COUNT                       000102   000282   000357
VALID-TRAN-SW                     000087   000246   000311
VALTRANS                          000023   000210   000224   000281
VT-RECORD                         000062   000281


 22

PROCEDURE NAMES                   DEFN     REFERENCE

000-UPDATE-INVENTORY-FILE         000208
300-EXIT                          000365   000234
300-POST-TRANSACTION-FILE         000229   000218
400-POST-TRANSACTION-RECORD       000236   000231
410-GET-VALID-TRANSACTION         000248   000238
420-GET-INVENTORY-MASTER          000257   000241
430-CHANGE-INVENTORY-MASTER       000271   000243
440-REWRITE-INVENTORY-MASTER      000275   000244
450-WRITE-VALID-TRANSACTION       000279   000245
460-RETURN-SORTED-TRANSACTION     000284   000250
470-EDIT-TRANSACTION-FIELDS       000290   000253
480-PRINT-INVALID-LINE            000313   000255   000265   000269
490-PRINT-HEADING-LINES           000327   000316
500-WRITE-REPORT-LINE             000337   000324   000335   000356   000360   000363
510-WRITE-PAGE-TOP-LINE           000343   000332   000352
600-PRINT-TRANSACTION-TOTALS      000349   000233
```

Comment Form

Your opinions count

If you have comments, criticisms, or suggestions, I'm eager to get them. Your opinions today will affect our products of tomorrow. If you have questions, you can expect an answer within one week from the time we receive them. And if you discover any errors in this book, typographical or otherwise, please point them out so we can make corrections when the book is reprinted.

Thanks for your help.

Mike Murach
Fresno, California

fold | fold

Book title: The Structured Programming Cookbook (COBOL)

Dear Mike: ______________________________

____

____

____

____

____

____

____

____

fold | fold

____

____

____

____

Name and Title ______________________________

Company (if any) ______________________________

Address ______________________________

City, State, & Zip ______________________________

Fold where indicated and staple.
No postage necessary if mailed in the United States.

fold

fold

First Class
Permit No. 3063
Fresno, Calif.

BUSINESS REPLY MAIL

No Postage Stamp Necessary if Mailed in the United States

Mike Murach & Associates, Inc.

4905 North West Avenue, Suite 102

Fresno, California 93705

fold

fold